Sexing War/Policing Gender

Historically, there has been reluctance, from mainstream IR scholars as well as feminists, to seriously engage with women's agency in warfare. Instead, scholarship has tended to focus on women's activism for peace or to ignore women's agency altogether.

This book rectifies this omission by exploring the cultural understanding of actors, agents and structures of war and how can we make sense of attitudes towards women, agency and war today. By using a poststructuralist feminist perspective and by analysing empirical cases from a Western 'war on terror' cultural context, Åhäll argues that all types of stories are informed by ideas about motherhood and maternal reproduction as the foundation of sexual difference. This does not only mean that women are judged/read/valued based on the shape of their, maternalised, bodies, rather than what they actually do, but, it means that ideas about motherhood, not motherhood itself, function to police contemporary gender norms and contemporary understandings of agency in war. Overall, this book argues that maternalist war stories function to reiterate traditional heteronormative gender roles. This is how a 'body politics' of war is not only policing gender norms but actually writing 'sex' itself. The body politics of war told through maternalist war stories is a process in which the sexing of war means the policing of gender borders, with motherhood acting as the border agent.

This work will be of interest to students and scholars in areas such as gender, political violence and international relations.

Linda Åhäll is Lecturer in International Relations at Keele University, UK.

Popular Culture and World Politics

Edited by Matt Davies, Newcastle University, Kyle Grayson, Newcastle University, Simon Philpott, Newcastle University, Christina Rowley, University of Bristol, & Jutta Weldes, University of Bristol

The Popular Culture World Politics (PCWP) book series is the forum for leading interdisciplinary research that explores the profound and diverse interconnections between popular culture and world politics. It aims to bring further innovation, rigor, and recognition to this emerging sub-field of international relations.

To these ends, the PCWP series is interested in various themes, from the juxtaposition of cultural artefacts that are increasingly global in scope and regional, local and domestic forms of production, distribution and consumption; to the confrontations between cultural life and global political, social, and economic forces; to the new or emergent forms of politics that result from the rescaling or internationalization of popular culture.

Similarly, the series provides a venue for work that explores the effects of new technologies and new media on established practices of representation and the making of political meaning. It encourages engagement with popular culture as a means for contesting powerful narratives of particular events and political settlements as well as explorations of the ways that popular culture informs mainstream political discourse. The series promotes investigation into how popular culture contributes to changing perceptions of time, space, scale, identity, and participation while establishing the outer limits of what is popularly understood as 'political' or 'cultural'.

In addition to film, television, literature, and art, the series actively encourages research into diverse artefacts including sound, music, food cultures, gaming, design, architecture, programming, leisure, sport, fandom and celebrity. The series is fiercely pluralist in its approaches to the study of popular culture and world politics and is interested in the past, present, and future cultural dimensions of hegemony, resistance and power.

Gender, Violence and Popular Culture
Telling stories
Laura J. Shepherd

Aesthetic Modernism and Masculinity in Fascist Italy
John Champagne

Sexing War/Policing Gender

Motherhood, myth and women's political violence

Linda Åhäll

Routledge
Taylor & Francis Group

LONDON AND NEW YORK

First published 2015 by Routledge

2 Park Square, Milton Park, Abingdon, Oxfordshire OX14 4RN
711 Third Avenue, New York, NY 10017

Routledge is an imprint of the Taylor & Francis Group, an informa business

First issued in paperback 2017

British Library Cataloguing in Publication Data
A catalogue record for this book is available from the British Library

Library of Congress Cataloging in Publication Data
Åhäll, Linda, 1979-
   Sexing war/policing gender : motherhood, myth and women's political
violence / Linda Ahall.
      pages cm. – (Popular culture and world politics)
   Includes bibliographical references and index.
   1. Sex role–Political aspects. 2. Women and war. 3. Political violence. 4.
Feminism. 5. Feminist theory. I. Title.
   HQ1075.A355 2015
   305.4201–dc23
                     2014034255

ISBN: 978-0-415-72044-1 (hbk)
ISBN: 978-0-8153-7772-6 (pbk)

Typeset in Times New Roman
by Taylor & Francis Books

Contents

Table

Acknowledgements

As I write this brief statement in an office at Malmö University in Sweden, my current work-place but also the place where I started my academic studies all those years ago, it dawns on me: this book is the result of a journey, not just an intellectual journey but a personal one. It is somewhat strange to reflect upon where my interests, but also just chance, have taken me – to Aberystwyth, Birmingham, Warwick, Keele University, and, surprisingly, back to Malmö University (albeit temporarily). It has been a ride.

Along this journey, there are many friends and colleagues to thank for providing support and for all the fun times I have had in the UK. As this book is the result of my doctoral research though, I would like to start by thanking my supervisors at the University of Birmingham: the ridiculously impressive, talented and inspirational Laura Shepherd whose detailed feedback on my work simply was priceless, and Cerwyn Moore, Ces, whose support and care, especially during my post-PhD job-hunting days, I truly appreciate. Thank you both!

Although I might not have enjoyed it as much as I should have done at the time, I would also like to thank the Examiners of my doctoral thesis, Marysia Zalewski and Jill Steans, for providing excellent feedback on my work. Thank you!

I would also like to mention how much I benefited from the great postgraduate community in POLSIS at the University of Birmingham. Caroline Kenny, Ben Taylor, Zoe Phlaeger, Amin Samman, Laurence Cooley, Dave Norman, and later Jonna Nyman and Liam Stanley deserve particular thanks for lunching and listening to me when I just needed to think out loud to gather my thoughts, and of course for all those fun evenings out in Birmingham.

At the University of Warwick I would like to thank Joao Nunes, Toni Haastrup, Nick Vaughan-Williams, James Brassett, Chris Rossdale, Chris Clarke, Alex Sutton, Ben Richardson, Andy Hammond, Madeleine Fagan, Nicola Pratt, Maurice Stierl and Chris Moran but most of all, Simon Willmetts for introducing me to his music: ideal for creative writing but also for getting through the sometimes seemingly never-ending marking sessions.

Thank you Simon for being awesome. Sharing an office with you was a pleasure.

I would like to thank the School of Politics, International Relations, Philosophy and Environment at Keele University for support and for giving me a two-year research leave. Special thanks goes to Helen Parr, Liz Carter, Brian Doherty, Bulent Gokay, Barry Ryan, Sherilyn McGregor, Tim Doyle, Andy Dobson and also Chris Zebrowski. At Keele I also benefited immensely from the tight research community across academic disciplines and from hanging out with my friends in Humanities: Joe Stretch, Mariangela Palladino, Rachel Bright, Nick Seager, Kelcey Swain and Ben Anderson.

At Malmö University, I am incredibly grateful to Susan Jackson for giving me enough time and space to actually finish this book. Susan, thanks for being so understanding!

Last, I wish to thank Annick Wibben, Tom Gregory, Moran Mandelbaum and the editors of the series, in particular Kyle Grayson, for great feedback on the first draft of this book; the three anonymous external reviewers who were all very supportive of this book project; Peter Harris at Routledge for editorial support in putting this volume together; all the colleagues who have engaged with my work at various conferences throughout the years and helped me to fine-tune my ideas, in particular the feminist community in IR/Security Studies. I would like to end by expressing a huge thank you to my friends and family in Sweden, whom I now have the luxury of seeing much more frequently. It's great to be back!

Linda Åhäll
Malmö, Sweden, June 2014

Foreword

Kyle Grayson

Co-editor of the Popular Culture World Politics Series

The intersections of identity and violence have long influenced dynamics central to popular culture and world politics. Representations of violence as well as processes through which these representations become mythologies of 'hidden ideological abuse' are important (p. 1). How violence is understood and made meaningful involves a series of deeply political acts. As such, popular culture is an important site through which the politics of violence is produced, mobilised and circulated.

In this volume, Linda Åhäll analyses agency as a grammatical construct in order to explore the possibilities and limits that shape predominant understandings of violence. In focussing on cultural representations of women associated with violent acts, her aim is not to determine why they have engaged in violence but rather to demonstrate how these acts of violence, in the terminology of Jacques Ranciére, have been made sensible. It is here that the logics of security and gender meet, producing the myth of the 'sacrifical, nurturing mother' (p. 10). Åhäll then traces how this myth functions to discipline our understandings of violence and women who commit violent acts. As she argues, 'contemporary examples of female agency in political violence are still negotiated, communicated, and made sense of, through ideas of motherhood' (p. 15). The conclusion is both inescapable and important: motherhood is central to situating war and violence in world politics.

In deconstructing gender and violence, this volume offers an innovative treatment of Roland Barthes, emphasising a latent poststructuralism in his work. This is supplemented by a methodological approach that 'translates' the methods of discourse analysis into the visual and emotional realms of communication. In this way, Åhäll is able to present a convincing case that the myths of motherhood are also embodied and that the power of their myth function is strengthened by these forms of embodiment. We see this in her empirical treatment of specific case studies, including cinematic depictions of terrorists, televisual series featuring secret agents during the Second World War, and media coverage of individual women who have risen to prominence in the recent conflicts and skirmishes of global counter-insurgency. She demonstrates that the sexing of war requires a careful cultural policing of gender boundaries. In this process, it is the figure of the mother who acts as the 'border agent'.

In presenting a compelling case for the importance of motherhood to our understandings of political violence and war, this volume adds to work previously published in the Popular Culture and World Politics series. Shepherd (2012); Kaklamanidou (2013); and Champagne (2012) have also highlighted how world politics is gendered and conditioned by forms of embodied sensibility produced through culture. What then becomes evident, whether in ideological constructions like fascism or neoliberalism, or through practices of war and violence, is that bodies matter and that bodies always matter for both politics and culture. More broadly, Sexing War/Policing Gender makes an important contribution to security studies by refusing to treat gender as an add-on to existing frameworks that seek to explain war and peace. Instead, Åhäll applies a critical insight raised by feminist scholarship in security studies and international relations more broadly: gender is not a variable for political analysis but rather is constitutive of the political itself. In doing so, she challenges us not only to think about war and violence differently but also where the logics of war are (re)produced and how we can identify them.

Introduction

Securitising feminism or feminist security studies?[1]

> How do you feel Faye, seeing that back now?
>   What were your emotions on being separated from the rest of your colleagues?
>   Did you ever cry yourself to sleep?
>   (Questions put to Faye Turney during the ITV Tonight Special, 8 April 2007)

> The starting point of these reflections was usually a feeling of impatience at the sight of the 'naturalness' with which newspapers, art and common sense constantly dress up a reality which, even though it is the one we live in, is undoubtedly determined by history. In short, in the account given of our contemporary circumstances, I resented seeing Nature and History confused at every turn, and I wanted to track down, in the decorative display of what-goes-without-saying, the ideological abuse which, in my view, is hidden there.
>   (Roland Barthes 2000a: 11)

My interest for this study was initially sparked by the media coverage of the British naval officer Faye Turney when she, together with fifteen other marines and sailors, was held hostage in Iran for two weeks in 2007. Being a woman and a mother, Turney was singled out and treated very differently to the other naval officers, who were all male. The focus on Turney's gendered identity as a woman rather than as a soldier annoyed me. Something was clearly going on in these representations as femininity and masculinity was depicted and portrayed in particular, valued ways. My 'feminist curiosity' (Enloe 2004) had kicked in and I decided to frame my doctoral research project, which this book is based on, around it in an attempt at tracing the politics of the female body; to track down the 'hidden ideological abuse', as Barthes says in the preface to *Mythologies* (written between 1954 and 1956), involved in the way in which the female body is represented, negotiated, understood and ultimately valued in the particular context of agency in political violence. This book explores cultural understanding of actors, agents and structures of war. How can we make sense of attitudes towards women, agency and war today?

This book shows that an increased visibility of female perpetrators of political violence on the one hand makes visible the destabilisation of gender itself as such actors expose the boundary of what certain bodies should or should not do. In my research, I have found three different types of stories told in representations of female agency in political violence, all of which include a tension between life-giving and life-taking. My argument is that all types of stories are informed by *ideas* about motherhood and maternal reproduction as the foundation of sexual difference. This does not only mean that women are judged/read/valued based on the shape of their, maternalised, bodies, rather than what they actually do, but, it means that *ideas about motherhood*, not motherhood itself, function to police contemporary gender norms and contemporary understandings of agency in war. Overall, this book argues that maternalist war stories function to reiterate traditional heteronormative gender roles. This is how a 'body politics' of war is not only policing gender norms but actually writing 'sex' itself. The body politics of war told through maternalist war stories is a process in which the sexing of war means the policing of gender borders, with motherhood acting as the border agent.

Convinced that our understandings of global political events are not limited to news reports and policy documents it made sense to also include representations of female agency in political violence as communicated through popular culture. As Cynthia Weber explains: '*All cultural sites are powerful arenas in which political struggles take place. Culture is not opposed to politics. Culture is political, and politics is cultural*' (Weber 2005: 188, emphasis in original). The decision to 'go cultural' (Weldes 1999) meant, however, that much of the existing literature on methodology in International Relations (IR) and security studies at the time when I started this research project was limited. It also means that the project in many ways is a project of tensions, or at least assumed tensions: the marginalised use of empirical cases from popular culture to study IR is one and the compatibility of Roland Barthes' thinking with poststructuralist theorising is another. This book aims to show how these tensions are but imaginary; or at least, that these tensions are a source for exciting and fruitful discussions. In this introductory chapter, therefore, I start by addressing yet another tension, between feminism and security studies.

Securitising feminism?

Historically, women have and continue to play active parts in warfare, whether that is as politicians making decisions to use political violence, or by actually taking up arms themselves. Indeed, as historian Joanna Bourke points out: 'female bellicosity and the feminine warring imagination have a long and distinguished past' (Bourke 1999: 311–2).[2] In the last decade, we have seen an increase in female suicide bombers; women depicted as participating in acts of torture at Abu Ghraib prison; we have seen more female characters in leading roles in television programmes and films about heroism, intelligence, counter-terrorism etc. such as *Homeland*, *The Americans* and *Zero Dark Thirty*. Moreover, with recent changes in the way in which wars are fought, including a blurring of *where* war takes place ('the frontlines'), of *who* 'the enemy' is and what s/he looks like and *how* combat/killing works ('press of a button'), individual soldiers' core physical strength has arguably become less important. With these developments, exclusion policies keeping women out of certain positions within the armed forces has become more difficult to justify and we have subsequently seen more and more positions in armed forces open up to women. For example, in 2010 so called Female Engagement Teams started operating in frontline operations in Iraq and later also in Afghanistan; in 2011 Australia removed their ban on women in combat roles; in December 2012 the UK announced that they were to allow women on submarines; in January 2013 the United States announced they were to remove their ban on women in combat roles. And, during the writing of this book the UK has made an interesting U-turn with regards to their combat exclusion policy – from, in 2013, insisting on waiting until 2018 when they are legally obliged to review the ban – to, in 2014, announcing that they will undertake an immediate review. The blurring of the 'where, who and how' of warfare has also led to an increasing occurrence, visibility and securitisation of female 'terrorists'. That increased visibility of women as actors in warfare more broadly has led to that feminist and non-feminist scholars alike now paying more attention to such actors. Yet, the topic of women's agency in political violence remains controversial.

Since the 1980s (at least), feminist scholarship has challenged, influenced and constituted the academic discipline of IR, which for some seventy years of its history was thought to be 'gender-neutral'. Prominent scholars such as Cynthia Enloe, J. Ann Tickner, Spike Peterson, Carol Cohn, Marysia Zalewski, Cynthia Weber and Christine Sylvester have transformed not only the academic discipline of IR but also the debate regarding what counts as politics.[3] Feminist scholarship has done much to highlight how the ways in which wars are fought, justified and made sense of, has everything to do with gender, which means that ideas about 'security' are also inherently gendered. As Jennifer Lobasz and Laura Sjoberg note:

> Feminist work addressing security has pointed out gender's key role, *conceptually*, in understanding security; *empirically*, in seeing causes and predicting outcomes; *normatively*, in understanding what is good and bad about security practices; and *prescriptively*, in terms of looking to solve the world's most serious security problems.
>
> (Lobasz and Sjoberg 2011: 573, my emphasis)

Some of the most ground-breaking feminist critiques of 'security' and the way in which wars are gendered can be attributed to Cynthia Enloe's work on militarisation – the specific sort of transforming process by which something becomes controlled by, dependent on, or derives its value from the military as an institution or militaristic ideas and criteria (Enloe 2000a: 291). It concerns how ideas about states, nationalism and above all, militarism are gendered.

However, because of the links between masculinity, militarism and war, and the military as perhaps the most masculinised institution of all, feminist scholarship, and activism, have often been associated, and self-identified, with anti-war sentiments and pacifism and, as a result, been wary of any engagement with the academic discipline of Security/War/Strategic Studies. For example, reflecting on a 2008 conference on 'the War Question in Feminism' Christine Sylvester notes that to the majority of the conference participants 'there was no war question in feminism at all; there was only a continuing peace question to be both asserted and fleshed out' (Sylvester 2012: x). More recently, a Twitter conversation among feminist IR scholars about the so-called hashtag '#ReadFemSecSt' illustrates just how uncomfortable some feminist scholars are to be associated with the discipline of security studies. 'Worrying about how all feminist IR now gets represented as security studies' was one concern raised (see Wibben's Storify of #ReadFemSecSt at https://storify.com/ATRWibben/readfemsecst).

As a result of the tension between a feminist politics and the study of war, feminist scholarship on gender, agency and war has tended to either focus on questions of women's roles and equal opportunities in the military or women's agency in peace movements. And, with regards to women in armed forces the issue remains controversial. The danger, as Enloe argues in *Maneuvers* first published in 2000, is that narratives about women's integration in militaries as 'liberation' could just be another 'maneuver' actually camouflaging the militarisation of women's lives (Enloe 2000a: 45). This is because patriarchal governments have their own, non-feminist reasons for introducing women into their militaries or for expanding the numbers and roles of women as soldiers (ibid.: 279). By researching women's roles, experiences and ideas within militaries, researchers risk helping to legitimise both the military as a public institution and soldiering as an occupation (Enloe 2007: 82). Something that appears as a move towards increased 'gender equality' may in reality on the contrary function to securitise or militarise those [liberal] feminist voices calling for women's inclusion in armed forces. The adding of women to the military, Enloe argues, is not in itself a formula for transforming that military's patriarchal institutional culture or diluting its militarising influence on the society as a whole (ibid.: 76).

There are therefore tensions between feminist anti-militarist scholars who oppose women's military participation out of pacifist reasons and scholars who favour women's integration in the name of gender equality (see Stachowitsch 2012). The tension here can also be situated in discussions about whether it is possible to do gender research without feminism. In the foreword to *Gender, War, and Militarism: Feminist Perspectives* (2010) edited by Laura Sjoberg and Sandra Via, Cynthia Enloe notes how today we have become more used to 'gender': we collect gender data and 'mainstream' development programs and security institutions etc., but, these formal inclusions, Enloe warns, have 'not succeeded as yet to transform the consciousness of most people'. To Enloe, a feminist perspective is necessary to all gender research simply because it puts *politics* – and thereby *power* – at the core of the analysis in a way that a gender analysis does not (Enloe 2010: xi–xii). Treating gender as a variable is not enough for a research project to be feminist.

Today, despite initial hesitation, Feminist Security Studies (FSS) is a fast expanding and vibrant area of research. That is not to say that there is, nor should there be, a single, coherent, feminist perspective on security, as two forums for discussions on 'The State of Feminist Security Studies' show.

In the first forum, published in *Gender and Politics* (2011), Laura Sjoberg and Jennifer Lobasz; Ann Tickner; Carol Cohn; Valerie Hudson; Annick Wibben; and Lauren Wilcox offer their reflections on what Feminist Security Studies is/should be. In 2013, a response, edited by Laura Shepherd, with commentaries by Swati Parashar; Christine Sylvester; Soumita Basu; Bina D'Costa and Katrina Lee-Koo; Teresia Teaiwa and Claire Slatter; and Laura McLeod, was published in *International Studies Perspectives* (2013). The response conversation mainly centred on the narrow geographic and demographic focus of the first. As all pieces in the initial 'conversation' were written by US-based academics it was accused of endorsing an exclusionary 'camp politics' for its oversight of feminist works on security outside the United States (Parashar 2013). In both conversation pieces a feminist methodological commitment to *listening* (Wibben 2011b), to a methodology framed around the *political problem* rather than the academic field (Cohn 2011), and to methodology focusing on *experiences* of war (Sylvester 2013) were encouraged:

> US-based discussions of feminist security can make the mistake much of mainstream IR does: Both dwell comfortably in an abstracted world. But security has experiential aspects, as does war … and focusing on those experiences … can provide reality tests that lead to episodes of life-grounded theoretical insight.
>
> (Sylvester 2013: 444–5)

In the next section, I draw on these debates and disagreements to demonstrate how, to me, there is not necessarily a tension between studying security and embracing a feminist politics.

Feminist security studies

In the first 'conversation' there are disagreements on what 'Feminist Security Studies' (FSS) is. While Ann Tickner emphasises the value of the rich and methodologically varied research and Valerie Hudson argues that FSS should 'remain a large tent' ('Do not exclude, do not refuse to engage, do not define the boundaries of FSS and say who is "in" and who is "out"') (Hudson 2011: 589), Annick Wibben argues that feminist research, by default, encompasses some basic commitments that are not negotiable: 'feminism is a political project committed to emancipation/ empowerment and broader social justice'

(Wibben 2011b: 591). In the response conversation, Soumita Basu makes a similar claim: '[U]nless a research project takes account of its emancipatory potential, what is feminist about it?' (Basu 2013: 457).

To anchor my own contribution to these debates Carol Cohn's reflection on the ambiguity of the label itself is useful. Cohn notes that it makes a difference which of the three words one sees as most closely linked, 'feminist', 'security' or 'studies':

> If the two words most closely linked are "security" and "studies," then the preexisting field of security studies is the subject, and the question – both grammatical and epistemological – is in what way the adjective "feminist" modifies it.
>
> (Cohn 2011: 581)

Cohn questions whether Feminist Security Studies should have the capital letters, whether it should be thought of or aspire to be a field, and ends up calling for a problem-based methodology: 'In short, I cannot make progress on the problems I am most interested in ameliorating in global politics within the confines of security studies. Thus, I choose not to devote much energy to engaging with it' (ibid.: 584). To me, however, who have a background in a European tradition of *critical* security studies, it not only makes sense to participate and engage the discipline but I am convinced that feminist scholarship is essential to how critical security studies performs itself, which in turn offers an additional platform with which to influence 'traditional' state-based understandings of security studies. Thus, while I am sympathetic to Basu's critique of Cohn's distinction between feminist 'security studies' and 'feminist security' studies in that 'the confluence of feminism (broadly, a worldview) and security (a concept) has yielded a field of research that is more than the sum of its parts' (Basu 2013: 457), it is still within this academic context that I situate my own feminist security studies perspective. I self-identify as a feminist *critical* security studies scholar, aware of the limitations to my own geographical and demographic background, and convinced that 'security' has just as much, or even more, to do with 'insecurity'. It is within this mind-set that Laura Sjoberg's concluding remarks resonate with me:

> [T]he purpose of doing research in Feminist Security Studies is to raise problems, not to solve them; to draw attention to a field of inquiry, rather than survey it fully; to provoke discussion, rather than serve as a systematic treatise.
>
> (Sjoberg 2011: 602)

To reiterate some key points with regards to the European tradition of critical security studies to which my research makes a contribution: since the end of the Cold War we have seen a move away from the previously dominant, but rather narrow (neorealist), approach to security studies that considers states the most important actors – both as threats to security and as referent objects in need of security – and where the means to achieve 'security' predominantly involves military force and capabilities. This move has seen a broadening and deepening of the concept of 'security' itself. Today, what is referred to as critical security studies is a very broad strand of literature, perhaps only united in their rejection of traditional post-positivist state-centric approaches. In critical security studies, to varying degrees of course, other actors of security; other threats to security; other referent objects to secure; and other means to achieve security have been not only included but prioritised.[4] However, we also need to remember that the development of [critical] security studies in the post-Cold War period has not been the same everywhere. We only need to think of the geographically labelled different 'Schools' of security often mentioned – the Welsh (Aberystwyth); Copenhagen; and Paris Schools of security – as European; Canada's role in relation to 'human security'; or think about the exclusionary practices that have kept much of non-Western approaches to, and experiences of, security out of sight. As a result, and also following broader trends, debates and discussion about what 'IR' is, what one considers the mainstream, as in the most common approach to the study of the international/global, is not necessarily the same in different parts of the world. There are multiple IR audiences and academic borders and the reinforcement of 'insiders and outsiders' is policed in different ways.

In a recent textbook on critical approaches to security edited by Laura Shepherd, seven approaches, of which 'feminist' is one, are included under 'theories'. Despite their variety, the common denominator is that different critical approaches to security all acknowledge the 'implication of theory in the constitution of what we recognize as "everyday life" and the need to challenge and question these constitutive processes' (Shepherd 2012b: 4–5). In other words, critical security studies is an umbrella term but, as Shepherd notes, it is the *questioning* that makes critical approaches 'critical' and also makes sense of their variety (ibid.: 5). To reiterate, how we define 'security studies' depends on whose and which security studies we are talking about. Whether or not one sees feminism and security as compatible might have something to do with how the field, and aim, of 'security studies' is perceived.

Importantly, however, Wibben makes a simple but crucial point: even critical security scholars most often fail to ask feminist research questions which means that feminist security scholars, with their unique methodological choices offer different research agendas, findings, and policy recommendations (Wibben 2011b: 592). I also agree with Wibben that feminist security scholars need to 'take traditional conceptions of security seriously because they have serious implications, but they also need to challenge their relevance and reveal their limit(s)' (ibid.: 594). Echoing Wibben, but also Enloe and Basu, I also think it is important that feminist security studies moves beyond the adding of women or gender as this is not necessarily feminist. What makes feminist security studies feminist is ultimately that it asks feminist questions (Wibben 2011b: 591).

In addition, in the *Gender and Politics* conversations, Lauren Wilcox points out another important aspect as to why feminist research is needed in security studies: security studies is largely about violence and bodies, yet, 'the body' remains under-theorised. To Wilcox, feminist theory is at its most powerful when it calls into question accounts of the '"biological body," in whatever form they take, to analyze the relations of force, violence, and language that compose the deeply unnatural bodies of humans' (Wilcox 2011: 598). Wilcox argues, and I agree, that feminists are uniquely positioned to theorise the body-politics of war, violence and vulnerability, without necessarily reducing these concerns to something that specifically affects women or men as sexed bodies (ibid.: 596–8).

To sum up, while I recognise the hesitation and understand the risks with having a feminist agenda co-opted and in effect revamped in militaristic language, i.e. gender integration for non-feminist purposes, feminist security studies is needed to engage critically with practices of war. Feminist security studies is crucial to keep not just *adding* a feminist perspective to security studies but to actually *do* and *produce* the discipline of security studies from a critical perspective. In other words, feminist contributions have something important to add to the way in which the discipline of critical security studies performs itself. To ignore the extensive tradition of fantastic feminist scholarship that has problematised notions of security, state, sovereignty, border, politics would be regrettable, for any critically minded security studies scholar.

The topic: women's political violence

The literature on women and/or gender and militaries/armed forces now includes a focus on gender integration policies; gender mainstreaming security institutions and peacekeeping practices; how strategies of counterinsurgency are gendered; how the way in which states fight wars, the geopolitical, relies on and inform gendered and racialised experiences of soldiers' everyday experiences.[5] Furthermore, by looking at female perpetrators of political violence, this book, per definition, adds to an already existing contribution of scholarship, whether feminist or not, that has deconstructed the common gendered assumption of women as 'naturally' passive and peaceful. Some of these scholars have explained the 'phenomenon' of women terrorists through personal narratives, exploring what drives women to turn to violence etc., others focus on how the representation of terrorism is gendered, or attempts to problematise the way in which societies treat female aggression more broadly.[6]

For example, Laura Sjoberg and Caron Gentry argue that women who commit acts of violence in defiance of national or international law are not seen as criminals, warriors or terrorists, but as *women criminals, women warriors* or *women terrorists* (Sjoberg and Gentry 2007: 7). Women's violence is often discussed in terms of violent women's gender: *women* are not supposed to be violent (ibid.: 2). In her book *Women and War*, first published in 1985, political theorist Jean Bethke Elshtain argues that 'the woman fighter is, for us, an identity *in extremis*, not an expectation' (Elshtain 1995: 173). That the violence of female groups is a sign that signifies formlessness, dis-order, breakdown, mis-rule and often appears as an out-of-control mob, a crowd, a food riot, usually of lower-class composition:

> Not being politically constituted, women are not politically accountable. Male violence could be moralized as a structured activity – war – and thus be depersonalized and idealized. Female violence, however, brooked no good. It was overpersonalized and vindictive.
>
> (Elshtain 1995: 169)

Another common representation of women's violence is that women are either taking more pleasure in the bloodshed than male combatants (Bourke 1999: 312), or are more aggressive than male soldiers (Eager 2008). For example, stories of the brutality of rebel women became a popular theme during and after the war in Sierra Leone as female fighters were regarded by the civilian population as monsters, barbarians and frequently as more cold blooded than male rebels (Coulter 2008: 57, 59). Men who refused to fight were often ridiculed, jailed, or even killed for their cowardice or lack of manliness, whereas women who opposed female stereotypes in war often were regarded as deviant or unnatural. In this way, Coulter argues, the notion of a militarised masculinity has consequences for how female combatants are interpreted (ibid.: 63). Similarly, Miranda Alison explains that in Sri Lanka, female Tamil Tigers had a fearsome reputation, and it was often said that they were more violent and frightening than male members. Some suggest this is because female soldiers have to be tougher, more ruthless and macho and less sympathetic in order to compete for status and recognition in a traditional patriarchal context, while others suggest it may only be the representation of such violence that differs. Bourke points out that historically there is no evidence that female combatants actually are more liable to play dirty (Bourke 1999: 341) and Alison suggests that it is because women's involvement in violence remains more shocking and disturbing than men's involvement that women's violence is represented as more aggressive (Alison 2004: 457). This indicates an 'underlying discomfort with such a challenge to gendered expectations that may be widely cross-cultural' (ibid.: 462).

Both Sjoberg and Gentry (2007) and Eager (2008) argue that women who participate in violence that is not endorsed by state governments and is therefore committed outside exceptional circumstances are described as aberrant and 'less than a woman' and as less than humans (Sjoberg and Gentry 2007: 22; Eager 2008: 3). Sjoberg and Gentry argue that women engaged in proscribed violence are often portrayed either as 'mothers', women who are fulfilling their biological destinies; as 'monsters', women who are pathologically damaged and are therefore drawn to violence; or as 'whores', women whose violence is inspired by sexual dependence and depravity. Each narrative has gendered assumptions about what is appropriate female behaviour. The mother narrative describe women's violence as a need to belong, a need to nurture, and a way of taking care of and being loyal to men; it is motherhood gone awry (Sjoberg and Gentry 2007: 30–36). The monster narrative eliminates rational behaviour, ideological motivation and culpability from women engaged in political violence. Instead, here violent women are described as insane, in denial of their femininity, no longer women or human (ibid.: 36–41). The whore narrative blames women's violence on the evils of female sexuality at its most intense or its most vulnerable (ibid.: 41–49). Sjoberg and Gentry argue that because women who commit violence are most often perceived of as having acted outside of a prescribed gender role, their agency as perpetrators of violence represent inappropriate femininity. Furthermore, when women's violent practices are captured in fantasies that reify gender stereotypes and subordination, women's agency is denied (ibid.: 5).

While this book resonates with the work and arguments covered in this section, particularly Laura Sjoberg and Caron Gentry's, to which I am sympathetic, it has a slightly different aim. This study is underpinned by a post-structuralist understanding of key concepts of gender, discourse, agency and representation inspired by scholars such as Judith Butler (2006, 2011), Stuart Hall (1997a), Michael Shapiro (2009, 2013), Laura Shepherd (2006; 2012c), Roland Bleiker (2001; 2009), Cynthia Weber (2005) and Roxanne Doty (1993). As will become clear, the topic of female perpetrators of political violence has so far tended to focus on a *material* understanding of agency in political violence, what might be described as a form of 'ethnographic' approach to agency in the sense that it is focusing on the actions of individuals, and often specifically on the question *why* women choose to take violent action. My approach to analysing agency, in contrast, which I think of as 'grammatical', means that I analyse *representations* of agency in relation to subject-positions in order to expose the boundaries of possibility and, importantly, the policing of such boundaries. These representations of agency are *ideational*. In this way, I explore something different than merely determining which narratives of subjectivity are allowed and which are not. This book is not as much about demonstrating how and where women are choosing violence for their political struggles (for they are political), as about questioning deeper cultural sentiments and understandings for how we in a broader cultural community make sense of such violence and such choices. I investigate, in Belinda Morrissey's words, how 'discursive imaginaries, evinced through metanarratives, work to constrain the production of some narratives of subjectivity and to enable others' (Morrissey 2003: 56). I am tracing the myth of the sacrificial, nurturing mother in places where one is least likely to find it, in representations of agency in political violence, through two different 'logics' – of security and of gender. This book takes a step back and attempts to make sense of underlying commonalities of how these actors are understood; to theorise what this myth does, how it culturally structures the way we think, breathe and feel stories of war.

Mapping the text

In order to grasp the cultural intelligibility of women as agents of political violence, the cultural grammar with which such actors and actions are understood, I have chosen to look into three 'real' and three fictional empirical cases. I put 'real' within citation marks because in my reading of agency in political violence both 'real' and fictional cases are representations of events. They are both part of story-telling. Furthermore, as I am interested in the body-politics involved in relation to how these actors are represented through their *capacity* to give life versus *capacity* to take life, rather than the outcomes of their acts, I am not judging whether these actors' participation is [morally] right or wrong. As a result, the broader definition of agency in political violence means that there is no need to distinguish between agency in political violence in the form of what is often labelled 'terrorism' or through roles in the armed forces. What makes the empirical cases comparable is not their individual 'politics', aims or ambitions, in a sense the context surrounding the fact that they have chosen to take violent action, but the fact that they all communicate ideas about female bodies and agency in political violence, whether such violence is state-sanctioned or not.

More specifically, I have chosen six different cases that all communicate ideas about gender, agency and political violence within a Western 'war on terror' context. The empirical cases are limited spatially to a predominantly British, and to a lesser extent, US cultural context and temporally to the post-9/11 years of the George W. Bush administration, i.e. between 2001 and 2009. Then, within the particular time-frame I first selected three 'real' empirical cases: British Navy sailor Faye Turney; US Private Lynndie England who became the most well-known involved in the Abu Ghraib scandal; and US General Janis Karpinski, also involved in the Abu Ghraib scandal. These cases were chosen because they were some of the most publicised, discussed and debated stories involving female bodies in the war on terror in Western media. They also offered a great opportunity to explore *ideas about motherhood* as Turney was a mother, England was pregnant during her trials whereas Karpinski does not have children.

Also keen on exploring understandings of gender, agency and political violence as communicated in popular culture, the fictional cases were chosen either because they enabled a move beyond agency in political violence as linked to state armies – to female bodies and 'terrorism'– or because they seemingly offered a particular revaluing of the role played by female bodies in war. Both *Britz* (2007), a British television programme about a female suicide bomber, and *The Baader-Meinhof Complex* (2008), an Academy Award-nominated film about the German left-wing terrorist group the Red Army Faction (RAF) were chosen due to their emphasis on female perpetrators of political violence. To complement these cases, the British/French film *Female Agents* (2008) was chosen due to its explicit focus on women's heroism in war.

Importantly, my analysis in this book is not of the popular culture artefacts per se, but of particular scenes in which ideas about female bodies and agency in political violence take centre-stage. As a result, within each of these three fictional cases I am focusing on particular characters and often the way in which such characters are 'written' by being intimately linked with other characters. In the empirical chapters I focus on the following characters from the chosen cases: Nasima in *Britz*, Ulrike Meinhof/Gudrun Ensslin in *The Baader-Meinhof Complex* and four characters from the film *Female Agents*, namely Louise, Suzy, Gaelle and Jeanne. While these characters are the 'leading ladies' in the chosen stories, each story/event/case also includes additional characters in 'supporting roles'. Between Chapter 2 and 3, immediately before the analytical discussion, there is more information about each empirical case and also a 'casting list' of additional characters discussed in this book.

While these empirical cases might have been produced in different national cultures, they are all interpreted and mediated for an English-speaking culture or population; the stories written about these cases are all constructed and produced within a Western 'war on terror' culture. This means that even though two of the empirical cases are depicting events that took place long before the launch of the global 'war on terror', we still interpret and understand these representations with references to the 'war on terror'; all cases were 'made' by/for people inhabiting such a cultural terrain. For example, *The Baader-Meinhof Complex* is based on a book by Stefan Aust, initially published in the 1980s but re-launched in 2008 to correspond with the film. Interestingly, in the preface to the 2008 edition, Aust contextualises the RAF's activities in Germany with the terror attacks in the United States on 11 September, 2001 (Aust 2008). Similarly, in the extra material accompanying the DVD, Peter Kosminsky, the writer and Director of *Britz*, explains how he, after the London bombings on 7 July 2005, was inspired by stories in the media of networks of female terrorists as a potential new threat.

To sum up, the chosen cases by no means provide a sample of the world but they are a series of highly publicised representations of the political puzzle in question. Thus, due to their focus on women's role in heroism, terrorism or torture, as prisoners of war or their capabilities as military commanders, separate and combined these cases form part of discursive practices creating contemporary knowledge about gender, agency and political violence.

In what follows, I develop a case for how to make sense of the stories told about female bodies in relation to agency in political violence. My aim is to show how *ideas* about motherhood, not actual motherhood, are informing such stories; this book is about maternalist war stories, and how to make feminist sense of such stories. In the first chapter, I therefore start by discussing how motherhood and maternalism have been understood, theorised and valued as agency in war in IR. I discuss gendered peace stories through a 'maternal peace thinking'; gendered war stories by discussing maternalism's relation to militarism and militarisation, and also the 'twisted maternalism' (Gentry 2009) with which the agency of female perpetrators of political violence is usually explained. I end the chapter by signposting how this book offers a more in-depth engagement with how gender, agency and motherhood is understood in relation to war and political violence. *To this end, the ideas, representations, cultural values and power invested in such understandings are taking centre-stage, rather than how individual women act.* I am interested in the implications and, as suggested at the start of this introduction, the hidden abuse, involved in the representation of events involving female bodies at war. In the second chapter, I expand on the theoretical framework and methodological assumptions that facilitate such an analysis of gender, security and popular culture. I unpack assumed tensions between feminism and post-structuralist analysis; explain how I draw on Roland Barthes' thinking and how such a theorising is compatible with a poststructuralist analysis. I also discuss how I have 'translated' textual methods for discourse analysis to apply to a study where 'language' also includes visual and emotional communication. I conclude by summarising my approach as an analysis of the cultural grammar of body politics at war.

In Chapters 3, 4 and 5, I draw on my analysis of the chosen empirical material. I focus on a set of particular scenes, events and themes that I have found most relevant to explore the political puzzle in question. The focus is thereby on the chosen cases as *mapping-exercises* of the broader, underlying topic of female agency in political violence. The cultural grammar rather than the empirical cases per se guides the analysis, which means that the abstracted scenes and debates from the mass media representation, film or television series are necessarily a partial reading of these empirical cases.

Throughout this book the empirical chapters are structured along three different maternalist war stories, all of which constitute elements of what I call the Myth of Motherhood. While I expand on what such a myth *is* and *does* in the concluding chapter, the constituting elements can be summarised as follows: 1) How female bodies are seen as requiring special protection due to their assumed maternal capabilities (inversions of motherhood); 2) How agency of female bodies are enabled by maternal thinking (versions of motherhood); 3) The disciplining practices involved when female bodies are seen to threaten maternal gender norms (perversions of motherhood). These constitutive elements are then mapped onto specific subject positions analysed in Chapters 3, 4 and 5 respectively. Table 1.1 is an attempt at visualising the argument and structure of this book.

In Chapter 3, I focus on the way in which female bodies are written as Victimised Objects, and thereby denied agency in political violence. I build on feminist literature on the Myth of Protection to theorise three main narrative tropes informing such stories: the 'default position' of *passivity*; the 'motherhood performance' of '*womenandchildren*' and the 'disciplining move' through *emotionality*. I conclude the chapter by arguing that in this type of story motherhood is communicated as 'inversions of motherhood' and that such stories are not seen as threatening or challenging the Myth of Motherhood.

Chapter 4 focuses on how female bodies are written as Heroic Subjects with agency in political violence. I build on literature in cultural studies about

Table I.1 The Myth of Motherhood – sexing war/policing gender

Sexing war/policing gender	Chapter 3	Chapter 4	Chapter 5
Subject positioning/ agential potential	VICTIMISED OBJECTS	HEROIC SUBJECTS	MONSTROUS ABJECTS
Default position	*Passivity*	*Vacant Womb*	*Monstrous-Feminine*
Motherhood performance	*'Womenandchildren'*	*Protective mother*	*Deviant Womb*
Disciplining move	*Emotionality*	*Masculinised Subject*	*Femme Castratrice*
Border crossing (Threat to Myth?)	No	No	Yes
Type of maternalist story	Inversions of motherhood	Versions of motherhood	Perversions of motherhood

female heroines as 'action chicks' but also contributions to feminist IR on how female soldiers are constructed as 'Rambettes', heroines at war. Again, I identify three main themes informing such stories of female agency in violence: the 'default position' of the *Vacant Womb*, the 'motherhood performance' of the *Protective Mother* and the 'disciplining move' through the idea of the *Masculinised Subject*. In this chapter the type of story told is 'versions of motherhood' and similarly to the stories in Chapter 3 they are not seen as threatening to the Myth of Motherhood.

Chapter 5 focuses on what happens when female bodies are seen to 'act against their femininity', in other words, when there seems to be a tension between how gender and sex is culturally understood. Here, I draw on contributions to feminist film theory, feminist legal theory, sociology and IR that have built on Julia Kristeva's discussion of abjection. Here too, I discuss three narrative tropes that are informing stories of how female bodies are abjected, seen as monstrous abjects rather than subjects: the 'default position' of the *Monstrous-Feminine*; the 'motherhood performance' of the *Deviant Womb* and the 'disciplining move' through the notion of the *Femme Castratrice*. I also build on discussions on the politics of disgust and interpellation in order to argue that there is a distancing process involved in the writing of monstrous abjects. This means that the writing of monstrous abjects has more to do with 'us' than the monster itself. I conclude by arguing that in this type of story motherhood is communicated as perversion and that the subject positioning in this type of maternalist war story does threaten the Myth of Motherhood. The three different stories told in representations of female agency in political violence, I argue, all include a tension between life-giving and life-taking which means that they are all informed by ideas about motherhood and maternal reproduction as the foundation of sexual difference. Not only are all three types of stories told as maternalist war stories but they also in different ways illuminate borders at which normative gender behaviour is negotiated.

In the concluding chapter, I return to Roland Barthes' writings on myth and Judith Butler's theorisation of the cultural construction, materialisation, of gender and sex in order to theorise a Myth of Motherhood. The overall argument of the book is that maternalist war stories told about female agency in political violence are founded in a Myth of Motherhood. Here, I am using motherhood as a *value* that function to not only 'sex' war, but to police gender more broadly. *This is how motherhood acts as war's border agent.* This book shows that the increased visibility of female perpetrators of political violence on the one hand makes visible the destabilisation of gender itself as they expose the boundary of what certain bodies should or should not do. But, contemporary examples of female agency in political violence are still negotiated, communicated and made sense of, through ideas about motherhood. In this sense, *ideas about motherhood*, not motherhood itself, function to police contemporary gender norms and contemporary understandings of agency in war. This does not only mean that women are judged/read/valued based on the shape of their, maternalised, bodies, rather than what they actually do, but, overall, it means that maternalist war stories function to reiterate traditional heteronormative gender roles. This is how a 'body politics' of war is not only policing gender norms but actually writing 'sex' itself. The body politics of war told through maternalist war stories is a process in which the sexing of war means the policing of gender borders with motherhood acting as the border agent.

Notes

1 The title is borrowed from True 2012: 193.
2 For a historical account see for example Jones 2005.
3 See for example Enloe 2000b; Tickner 1992, 1997; Peterson 1992; Sylvester 2002; Zalewski 1995, 2007, 2013; Weber 2005; Cohn 1987.
4 See Wibben 2011a and Hansen 2006 for more detailed discussions on the development of critical security studies.
5 See Woodward and Winter 2006, 2007; Basham 2009, 2013; Cohn 1987, Stachowitsch 2012; Duncanson 2009; Hicks Stiehm 2001; Kronsell and Svedberg 2012; Khalili 2011; Wibben and McBride 2012.
6 On the first, see for example Alison 2004; Bloom 2007; 2011; Cragin and Daly 2009; MacKenzie 2009; Moser and Clark (eds) 2001; Parashar 2009; Eager 2008; Coulter 2008. On the second example, see Brunner 2005, 2012; Hasso 2005; Narozhna 2012; Nacos 2005; Toles Parkin 2004; Sjoberg and Gentry 2008; Gentry 2009. With regards to the latter, see for example Åhäll 2012a; Marway 2011; Sjoberg and Gentry 2007.

1 Stories of motherhood, agency and war

> A distinctive and joint creation of philosophical abstraction and sexual fantasy, war's body kills and suffers; it does not give birth.
>
> (Sara Ruddick 2002: 204)

In this chapter, I explore how motherhood is commonly understood as agency in gendered stories of war and peace. The aim of the chapter is to contextualise the nuanced way of thinking about motherhood, agency and war that this book offers, i.e. to emphasise the value of a *grammatical* rather than *material* understanding of agency and use of motherhood as an *idea* rather than a *practice*.

Within the system of signs in war, there are certain myths about male and female identities that become accentuated; female identity is seen as life-giving, whereas male identity is seen as life-taking (Skjelsbæk 2001: 220). Thus, women are designated as non-combatants and, in effect, peaceful, because of the part they play in the reproductive process. Historically, it is predominantly women who in greater numbers have organised against militarism and committed themselves to working for peace. The historical association of women, resistance, peace and non-violence is long: according to Nira Yuval-Davies the image of women resisting wars has been in existence in the Western public imagination at least since *Lysistrata* was first shown in Athens in the fifth century BC (Yuval-Davies 1997: 94). Likewise, mothering as a series of daily acts and motherhood as an idea about what those acts together should stand for each have long political histories. Cynthia Enloe argues that it is difficult to make sense of any state, past or present, without taking seriously that state's attempts to craft ideas about motherhood that pressure women as mothers to do certain things judged useful to the state (Enloe 2000a: 260).

At the same time, mothering and motherhood have also been key sites for women's efforts to resist the state through participation in civil or peace movements. Some of the more prominent examples of women's protest against war include movements such as the Women's Peace Party that drew together over a thousand women during the First World War and subsequently founded the Women's International League for Peace and Freedom (WILPF); The Greenham Common Peace Camp in Britain protesting against US military presence; the Mothers of the Plaza de Mayo in Argentina; Women in Black, an anti-war movement originated in Israel but also active in the former Yugoslavia; CodePink, a US organisation that among other things organises annual rallies on Mother's Day and Valentine's Day against US involvement in current wars, to name a few.

Indeed, women peace activists often invoke the 'natural' peacefulness of women and thereby use gendered identities provided by traditional narratives of war as a platform for political action. In this way, the gendered nature of war creates a political space for women as peace activists; peace has become a subject that women could legitimately speak about (Steans 2006: 59). In particular, women's legitimacy as peace activists has been, and continues to be, made through their roles as mothers, linking motherhood, peace and women's rights (Segal 2008: 23; Steans 2006: 59). Since all women are perceived to be potential mothers, motherhood is an attempt at unifying women involved in such transnational political activity in order to overcome other potential barriers of race, class and religious differences among activists (Steans 2006: 59).

Despite the close links between peace and femininity visible in women's political activism, however, most feminist scholarship in IR, due to a predominant constructivist orientation, is critical of such essentialist claims rendering women 'naturally' peaceful. What is more, some feminists are wary of the 'patriarchal risks' in relying on motherhood as a political idea and therefore question whether motherhood really is the best site from which to launch resistance to, for example, state militarism (Enloe 2000a: 260).

It also needs to be pointed out that similarly to how women have used traditional perceptions of gender roles in their protesting as peace activists, women also frequently utilise existing stereotypes to pursue their political objectives in warfare. Albeit this is nothing new, it is feminist scholarship that has noticed how women are not only exploiting their label of innocence in becoming spies and smugglers but also using motherhood as an explicit strategy for political violence. For example, in Northern Ireland it was women who had central responsibility for transporting, moving, hiding, cleaning and storing weapons and explosive materials simply because they were much less likely to be stopped and searched (Alison 2004: 457). In Sierra Leone, women were found smuggling weapons through military checkpoints in bags of women's underwear or hidden on their own or their children's bodies (Coulter 2008: 63–4). In Sri Lanka, Tamil nationalist women have utilised cultural expectations related to their behaviour and dress to gain access to targets as suicide bombers, hiding belt bombs under saris or dresses, as a female Black Tiger combatant did in the 1991 suicide-bomb assassination of former Indian Prime Minister Rajiv Gandhi (Alison 2004: 456). In addition, as the Improvised Explosive Device (IED) is often disguised under the women's clothing to make her appear as if she is pregnant and thus beyond suspicion or reproach, Mia Bloom argues, notions of femininity and motherhood are complicated (Bloom 2007: 143). Also, as this particular 'strategy of motherhood' has been seen in various places, Mia Bloom argues, feigning pregnancy unites women suicide bombers in places as diverse as Turkey and Sri Lanka (ibid.: 152). 'The advent of women suicide bombers has transformed the revolutionary womb into an exploding one' (ibid.: 143).

In this chapter, Caron Gentry's distinction between 'active', 'passive' and 'twisted' maternalism is offering a rough structure (Gentry 2009) as I go through how stories of motherhood, agency and war are typically told. In the first section, I build on above all Sara Ruddick's work on a Maternal Peace Thinking. This maternalist position is linked to women's peace movements and agency is understood as 'active'. The second section discusses motherhood and agency in gendered stories of war and shows how maternalist war stories are linked to militarism and nationalism. The third section focuses on maternalist stories in agency in political violence and, more specifically, on how representations of female terrorist attacks are not only gendered but rely on maternalist narratives which ultimately deny the individual women any agency of their acts. I conclude the chapter by discussing how my grammatical rather than material approach to agency and treatment of motherhood as an idea rather than a practice facilitates the telling of alternative stories of motherhood, agency and war.

Maternal peace thinking

Within IR it is contributions to standpoint feminism, sometimes referred to as 'difference feminism' that have most noticeably theorised and politicised motherhood. By shifting the study from abstract states to how *real* living women are impacted by economic and security structures within and across state boundaries, a feminist standpoint offers a way to critique traditional approaches to the study of war and peace and to tell alternative war stories (Steans 2006: 48, 58). It is 'a superior vision produced by the political conditions and distinctive work of women' (Ruddick 2002: 129). In particular, such a woman's work often comes back to mothering, care and nurturing and these scholarly contributions are, therefore, often referred to as maternalist. Here, I touch upon the work of Nancy Chodorow (1978) and Carol Gilligan (1982) but in particular I focus on the work of Sara Ruddick (1989), arguably the most relevant for the development of a feminist standpoint that in my reading have forged a link between motherhood, agency and peace.[1]

Nancy Chodorow's *The Reproduction of Mothering* is a psychoanalytic study of how and why mothering remains to be seen as a 'natural' fact and why it is 'naturally' linked to women. Chodorow argues that it is because women are the primary caretakers that mothering is reproduced as 'naturally' linked to women. This creates a focus on social relations and care rather than on women's capacity to give birth. And, as a result, being a mother is not only bearing a child – 'it is being a person who socializes and nurtures. It is being a primary parent or caretaker' (Chodorow 1978: 11).

With *In a Different Voice* (1982), Carol Gilligan builds on Chodorow and claims that women's experience of interconnection shapes their moral domain and gives rise to a different moral voice. Gilligan calls this an ethic of care, which is contrasted to a (male) ethic of justice. It is in the different voice of women, Gilligan argues, that the tie between relationship and responsibility lies. The origins of aggression on the other hand lie in the failure of connection (Gilligan 1982: 173).

Gilligan argues that while an ethic of justice proceeds from the premise of equality and that everyone should be treated the same, an ethic of care rests on the premise of nonviolence and that no one should be hurt (Gilligan 1982: 174). It is this distinctive form of ethics that has been echoed in writings that articulate a female political consciousness grounded in difference and the virtues of women's private sphere, primarily mothering. Amongst such maternalist theorising, Sara Ruddick's *A Maternal Thinking: Towards a Politics of Peace* (2002 [1989]) has most clearly emphasised the links between motherhood, agency and peace.

Ruddick argues that there is a peacefulness latent in maternal practice which means that a transformed maternal thinking could make a distinctive contribution to peace politics (Ruddick 2002 [1989]: 137). Although mothers are not intrinsically peaceful, Ruddick argues, maternal practice is a 'natural resource' for peace politics: Mothers have supported their boys and their leaders, but in the contradiction of maternal and military aims there is a dangerous source of resistance; the rhetoric and passion of maternity can turn against the military precisely because, as is shown in the next section, the ideology of militarism depends on it. 'A peace-maker's hope is a militarist's fear' (ibid.:157).

Ruddick combines a women's politics of resistance, which she defines as identified by three characteristics: its participants are women, they explicitly invoke their culture's symbols of femininity and their purpose is to resist certain practices or policies of their governors, with motherhood and a feminist politics (ibid.:222). Although neither a women's politics of resistance nor a feminist politics is inherently a peace politics, Ruddick argues that each instructs and strengthens peacemaking: 'Both politics are intricately connected to mothering, yet each also challenges just those aspects of maternal practice that limit its public, effective peacefulness' (ibid.: 222). Thus, Ruddick argues, separately and in combination they transform maternal practice into a work of peace (ibid.: 222).

Ruddick argues that by combining motherhood, with a politics of resistance and standpoint feminism, a new political identity can be constructed: the feminist, maternal peacemaker who draws upon the history and traditions of women to create a human-respecting politics of peace (ibid.: 245). As illustration, Ruddick uses the political resistance of the Madres (mothers) of Argentina to its military regime and the similar resistance of Chilean women to the Pinochet dictatorship (ibid.: 225). She calls these women the daughters, the heirs of Kollwitz's Mater Dolorosa:[2]

> As in Kollwitz's representations, a mother is victimized through the victimization of her children. These women are themselves victims ... Yet there is a sense in which, by their active courage, they refuse victimization

> ... The Latin American mater dolorosa has learned how to fight as a victim for victims, not by joining the strong, but by resisting them.
>
> (Ibid.: 233)

The maternalist position, predominant in Ruddick's work and through the activism of the women's peace movement mentioned above, might be critiqued for expressing biological determinism and essentialism as it tends to link mothering and an ethics of care to (heterosexual) women and 'real' mothers only.[3] However, Ruddick emphasises the distinction between women's *biological* capacity to give birth and their *social* work in mothering as she argues that the work of mothering does not require a particular sexual commitment or that there is any reason why mothering work should be distinctly female. Ruddick notes that while most mothering has been undertaken by women, there have always been men who mother. When mothering is construed as gender-free work, Ruddick suggests, birth-giving and mothering appear as two distinct and quite different activities (ibid.: xii). In other words, Ruddick is still critical of women's 'natural' peacefulness:

> There is nothing in a woman's genetic makeup of history that prevents her from firing a missile or spraying nerve gas over a sleeping village if she desires this or believes it to be her duty ... War is exciting; women, like men, are prey to the excitements of violence and community sacrifice it promises.
>
> (Ibid.: 154)

Although distinctly maternal desires and capacities for peacemaking exist, it is through maternal *efforts* to be peaceful rather than an achieved peacefulness that Ruddick finds 'resources for creating a less violent world' (ibid.: 136). Crucially, Ruddick does not argue that women are naturally peaceful in an ideological sense but interested in the *material* political agency of mothers (male or female).

Yet, feminist scholars have been quick to point out that Ruddick's Maternal Peace Thinking is problematic as it risks perpetuating the idea of women-as-peacemakers (Pankhurst 2004). J. Ann Tickner argues that women's political organising with peace is not necessarily a good thing as 'peace is frequently seen as an ideal, and even uninteresting, state with little chance of success in the "real" world' (Tickner 2002: 337). In this sense, the association of women with peace renders both women and peace as idealistic, utopian, and unrealistic and this is profoundly disempowering for both (ibid.: 338). Similarly, making peace feminine masculinises war. As long as peace remains associated with women, this may reinforce militarised masculinity. Thus, even though Ruddick's argument is not biologically essentialist in its use of gender, the association of predominantly women with universal practices of mothering, care and peace is still problematic as it reinforces traditional binary constructions of what certain bodies should or should not do. And, this is political.

Militarised maternalism/maternalised militarism

Cynthia Enloe defines militarisation as a specific sort of transforming process by which something becomes controlled by, dependent on, or derives its value from the military as an institution or militaristic ideas and criteria (Enloe 2000a: 291). Importantly, however, militarisation should not be seen as some form of top-down forcefully imposed ideology. Instead, as Enloe points out in numerous works, militarisation is about culture, ideas, values: 'The more militarisation transforms an individual or a society, the more that individual or society comes to imagine military needs and militaristic presumptions to be not only valuable but also normal' (ibid.: 3). Therefore, '[a] militarizing maneuver can look like a dance, not a struggle, even though the dance may be among unequal partners' (ibid.: 10).

Moreover, if militarised beliefs and values already are rooted in a society, the military itself may only have to provide legitimation, 'an encouraging nudge here, a supportive nudge there' (Enloe 2000a: 171). In other words the practices and performances of militarisation involve cultural as well as insti- tutional, ideological, and economic transformations (ibid.: 3). In her works Enloe also powerfully demonstrates where and how these practices take place and she shows just how wide-spread and overarching militarisation is as the list of what can be militarised is virtually endless: toys, jobs, the profession of psychology, fashion, faith, voting, local economies, condoms, and movie stars (ibid.: 4). Cru- cially though, Enloe argues, what has been militarised can be demilitarised. But she also warns that what has been demilitarised can be remilitarised (ibid.: 291).

Enloe is also careful to point out how militarisation relies on support from women. If militarisation were oppressive for all women in all situations, Enloe argues, militarisation would not be so potent a political process (Enloe 2000a: 297):

> It is precisely because militarization holds out such advantages to some women some of the time that it has been difficult to see the maneuvers of decision makers and difficult to detect militarization's fundamentally patriarchal consequences.
>
> (ibid.: 298)

As mentioned above, one of the iconic images of motherhood in relation to war has been the 'grieving mother'; mothers have been assigned a central role in patriarchally inspired war stories (Enloe 2000a: 249). For militaries at war, mothers are potential opponents as their children are drafted with the risk of being killed- and thus a potential threat to the war effort. By mobilising mothers into maternal organisations, the state or non-state military attempts to redirect and control mothers' anger at the drafting or death of a son or daughter (Elshtain 1995; Bayard de Volo 2004: 718). Mussolini's Italian fas- cist regime elevated the widows and mothers of dead soldiers to a special status. Israel's government has bestowed special state pensions on women who have lost either husbands or sons in its wars (Enloe 2000a: 193). Military widowhood can be an ideological boon to militarism, but it can also be a liability to the military itself. Widows can be used to symbolise the 'supreme sacrifice.' By encouraging all women in the country to identify with each military widow or grieving mother, a government can try to turn the governments' soldiers into 'our boys,' deserving of all women's support (ibid.: 193). For example, as Cynthia Weber noted with regards to President Bush's construction of the people involved on the fourth aeroplane hijacked on 11 September, 2001:

> The President's transformation of Todd Beamer from one courageous passenger into the iconic figure of all heroic Americans who opposed the terrorists on 9/11 and who would continue to do so afterwards seemed to be welcomed by most Americans. So was the transformation of his wife Lisa into the iconic figure of patriotic wife and mother whose personal loss of her husband was something Americans, including Lisa, seemed to understand as a necessary sacrifice for the nation. For this sacrifice, Lisa Beamer was enthusiastically applauded by Congress as she stood proudly next to First Lady Laura Bush. All of this was televised to the nation.
>
> (Weber 2008: 141)

Tina Managhan traces the processes of militarisation through which particular bodies emerge as *maternalised* in, around, and through specific US foreign policy moments. She treats motherhood itself as a 'discursive and inherently contested practice' (Managhan 2012: 4) and explains how 'motherhood' and 'state' are articulated through one another (ibid.: 11). One of the examples Managhan uses is Cindy Sheehan, the mother who after her son got killed in Iraq became a prominent peace activist and set up camp outside President Bush's private ranch in Texas. Managhan argues that Sheehan was marked as a white body: 'her whiteness that enabled this particular grieving mother to occupy the space of and symbolically become the grieving mother in all of "us"; a symbolic mother of the nation' (ibid.: 113).

However, militarising motherhood often starts with a conceptualisation of the womb as a recruiting station in nationalist discourses of 'heroism'. The 'Patriotic Mother' is the ever-ready womb for war (Cooke 1996; Enloe 2000a). According to this discourse, women serve their nation by 'producing' children/soldiers of the nation. Thus, women's heroism is measured in their life-giving capacities since the more children/soldiers [i.e. preferably sons] a woman gives birth to, the more significant is her heroism and the more she is contributing to 'national security'. Giving birth to sons is giving birth to the next generation of the state's soldiery (Enloe 2000a: 248). In this sense, motherhood functions as a form of 'weapon' since a multi-birthing woman will give life to many new fighters (Brunner 2005: 36). This explains why women have even been awarded medals for giving birth to a large amount of children. For example, in 1993, on the date of the 1389 defeat of the Serbs at Kosovo, Serbian mothers of more than four children were honoured with medals in a ceremony in Pristina by dignitaries of the Serbian Orthodox Church (Bracewell 1996: 30).

Another nationalist discourse is the 'Spartan Mother': a woman who raises her son as warrior ready to die for the nation. Here, it is women's *social* roles as mothers rather than their physiological and quantifiable capacity to give life that writes women as heroic in stories of war. In this rhetoric, a woman's heroism and patriotism is to urge sons and husbands to fight and thereby foster nationalism and warfare (Elshtain 1995; Varzi 2008). The Spartan Mother is heroic because she sacrifices her sons for the greater good of the nation-state. Both these nationalist discourses on women's agency in political violence are versions of what Caron Gentry refers to as 'passive maternalism', where women are denied agency as they are merely placed as idealised subjects in such discourses, which in turn means that traditionalist ideas about gender, agency and war are reinforced rather than challenged. During World War I, Canadian and Belgian male legislators, desperate to sustain popular support for male enlistment, awarded women who were mothers of soldiers with the right to vote before most other women (in Canada, only military nurses preceded mothers of soldiers in gaining the vote; most Belgian women did not gain suffrage until forty years later (Enloe 2000a: 247–8)). In the 1980s war in Nicaragua, mothers of the fallen were encouraged to 'carry on the struggle' so that their children's death had not been in vain. According to the Matagalpa Mothers of Heroes and Martyr's 1986 work plan, one of their main objectives was 'to convert each Mother into an ideological combatant who defends the principles and justice of the Sandinista Popular Revolution' (Bayard de Volo 2004: 723). In Sri Lanka the government's education policy makers adopted a policy of encouraging schoolchildren to identify with an image of the ancient queen mother Vihara Maha Devi, who according to legend inspired her reluctant son to wage war, while in the 1998 escalation of nuclear threats between India and Pakistan, Pakistan Prime Minister Benazir Bhutto evoked the myth of mother inspiring her reluctant son to demonstrate his manliness by going to war (Enloe 2000a: 244). What is important to emphasise though is that it is the combination of militarised family dynamics, a militarised popular culture, and a militarised state that makes the myths of militarised motherhood so potent (ibid.: 254). At one point, Enloe imagines masculinity and militarism as two knitting needles: wielded together, they can knit a sturdy institutional sock. But, Enloe argues, if particular concepts of motherhood and femininity – and at times, the concept of the liberated woman – are not sustained, the sock may unravel (ibid.: 235).

With this section I have tried to show how maternalism is militarised; but also how militarism relies on particular ideas about motherhood, agency and war. So far, the discussion has shown how female bodies are placed/positioned in particular, often nationalistic, discourses in order to support the war effort, to 'serve' militarisation. Next, I focus on the maternalist politics involved when women choose to take an active part in political violence.

Maternalist war stories

A different type of maternalised war story is told about women who actually engage in killing and violence directly. Historian Joanna Bourke argues that when women did kill, their ability to do so was explained under one of two mutually exclusive headings: psychosexual confusion or maternal instincts (Bourke 1999: 318). Other explanations for why women engage in violence include elevated levels of testosterone, traumatic events in childhood and excessive feminism or lesbianism (Eager 2008: 3). Hence, because women soldiers either lacked femininity or possessed too much of the maternal impulse, they were seen as uncontrollable, more ferocious and more deceitful than their male counterparts, beliefs that were endorsed and encouraged in popular fiction (Bourke 1999: 340).[4]

Analysing how women who kill, i.e. female murderesses, are portrayed, legal theorist Belinda Morrissey argues that when a woman murders, legal (mainstream and feminist) and media discourses responsible for narrating this event to the public can be read as displaying evidence of trauma (see also discussion in Chapter 5 and the Conclusion):

> [T]he vilification of women who kill attributes to these women the violence at the heart of both these discourses: it is safer to turn murderesses into monsters than to face the savagery at the core of 'the law' and the media.
>
> (Morrissey 2003: 24)

When it comes to motivations for actors' involvement in political violence, women's violence is represented differently to men's violence even though individuals from both genders are motivated by both strategy and personal politicisation. Gentry has pointed out that when the focus of studies and reports on suicide terrorism moves away from the general self-martyr, who is assumed to be male, into analysing the female self-martyr, reasons behind the person's (woman's) actions begin to change (Gentry 2009: 241). In media representations as well as some academic literature, women's motivations for turning violent are explained in personal rather than political terms. For example, Bloom argues that women are fulfilling the ultimate patriarchal ideal of motherhood by giving up her body for the collective, the nation:

> According to Hindu faith, once a woman is raped she cannot get married nor have children. Fighting for Tamil freedom might have been the only way for such a woman to redeem herself. The idea of sacrifice is ingrained in Tamil culture. Women are taught from an early age to subordinate themselves to the needs or desires of men. The self-sacrifice of the female bombers is almost an extension of the idea of motherhood in the Tamil culture.
>
> (Bloom 2007: 160)

Similarly, journalist Barbara Victor depicts Palestinian female suicide bombers as becoming perpetrators of political violence due to feminine shortcomings such as being childless, divorced or adulterous (Victor 2004). Eager argues that by portraying female suicide bombers as influenced by family members or grief-stricken over the death of a relative or a friend, these women fulfil the ultimate maternal-sacrificial code in that they want to give their own life on behalf of others' pain, grief or suffering (Eager 2008: 187). Thus, even though violent men are portrayed as rationally or logically motivated, violent women are usually not depicted as rational actors (Sjoberg and Gentry 2007; Gentry 2009). This is the case even though females committing suicide bombings tend to be older and better educated than males (Toles Parkin 2004: 84), and even if the perpetrators' own video-recorded martyrdom statements focus on their political ambitions (Sjoberg and Gentry 2007: 120). Rarely are these women portrayed as committing a suicide attack due to political motivations (Eager 2008: 187). Frances Hasso offers a detailed account of how representations by, and deployments of, the four Palestinian women who committed suicide attacks in 2002 functioned to both reproduce and undermine gender-sexual norms (Hasso 2005: 44). Alison shows that like male combatants, female combatants in nationalist conflicts view themselves as fighting to protect the political, cultural, economic and military security of their nation, community or family (Alison 2004: 458). Jessica West argues that the women referred to as 'black widows' in Chechnya are described as desperate and revenge-seeking wives and sisters of Chechen fighters who have been killed. West argues that their actions have been represented as a result of victimisation rather than agency (West 2004: 1).

> Terrorism is a political act, yet no one has stopped to ask what women's political goals are. It is just assumed that they seek personal revenge. Practically, by treating women as instruments rather than as agents of war, their political goals are likely to be overlooked in any future negotiations, when their presence is no longer needed.
>
> (West 2004: 9)

Gentry argues that when research focuses on women specifically, a relational need to belong and the participation of family and friends is emphasised. This is why women's participation is seen as based solely upon belonging, familial and friendship ties and nurturing, and less about her political motivations and beliefs. Gentry argues that this gendering both subordinates woman's agency and echoes the maternalist position (Gentry 2009: 240). Gentry refers to the writing of politically violent women in this way as 'twisted maternalism' since it continues to objectify women and deny them any agency (ibid.: 242).

Claudia Brunner uses bodily metaphors that directly refer to the gendered representation of suicide bombing in general: Virginity, Pregnancy and Motherhood (Brunner 2005: 35). She argues that the question of virginity is prevalent in many media accounts where expressions such as 'daughter of Palestine', 'Palestine's bride' and the like refer to youth and therefore innocence within the martyrdom operations that can just as easily be described as murder. Furthermore, the picture of the pregnant woman is both cited in reports to illustrate the continuing humiliation of Palestinians by Israeli soldiers at checkpoints, but it also illustrates the power over the bodies of women and children as the Palestinian nation is hindered in giving birth to itself on a symbolic level (ibid.: 36). Again, this echoes passive maternalism (mothers of nations).

Motherhood as an *idea*

The maternal thinking represented by standpoint feminists, in particular by Ruddick, as well as by women's peace activists, in Gentry's categorisation, constitutes an active maternalist position as it focuses on how real (material) women are concerned with promoting peace and anti-violent policies (mothers for peace). Passive maternalism, on the other hand, refers to situations in which women's gendered role as mother is claimed by the nation, movement or state to symbolise the collectivity. Here, women themselves are not active participants in the conflict. Instead, they are placed by others in nationalist ideology and as such subordinately held as an idealised subject (mothers of nations) (Gentry 2009: 238–9). Gentry argues that both active and passive maternalism associates women with nonviolence, but that women only have agency within active maternalism. I explain the theoretical and methodological framework underpinning my analysis in more detail in the next chapter but here I would like to draw attention to two interrelated aspects of what I mean by maternalist war stories. First of all, as mentioned in the introductory chapter, I am not interested in how and why women choose to engage in political violence. I am not using a material understanding of agency in political violence. Instead, I refer to my approach as 'grammatical', which means that I am analysing *representations* of agency. I follow Judith Butler who offers an alternative account of agency where agency is not a property of the subject, but an effect of the power of discourse; of discursive conditions. My analysis of representations of agency, thus, focuses on 'the concrete conditions under which agency become possible' within particular *discourses*, not by particular individuals or social groups (Butler 1995: 136, quoted in Morrissey 2003: 59). I study the grammar with which ideas about gender, agency and political violence is culturally communicated.

Second, I would like to emphasise that with 'motherhood', I am not referring to actual mothers' or women's 'real' embodied experience of mothering, but rather the *idea* about female bodies and their association with a naturalised life-giving identity. This makes it possible to decouple motherhood from femininity, to critique its association with a life-giving identity, and to explore motherhood through masculinity and the lack of motherhood. In the empirical chapters, I demonstrate how the ways in which female agency in political violence is communicated have everything to do with motherhood, even when this might not be immediately apparent. To me, motherhood is not just one type of narrative disciplining stories of women's violence as Sjoberg and Gentry suggest, but a foundational way of structuring our societies. And, as I will come back to in the last chapter, it functions as an expression of ideology; a myth; a meta-narrative; and as such feeds into ideas about sexuality and heteronormativity.

Notes

1 See Robinson and Confortini (2014) for a symposium on the legacy of Ruddick's maternal thinking for international relations.
2 The Mater Dolorosa is the 'mother of sorrows' who is 'weeping over the body of her son, nursing survivors, sadly rebuilding her home, reweaving the connections that war has destroyed – as she grieves over her particular loss, she mourns war itself. Where she gives birth and sustains life, his war only hurts and destroys.' The Mater Dolorosa is the 'heroine of maternal peacefulness' (Ruddick 2002: 142).
3 See Dietz (1985) for a critique of the maternalist position to citizenship.
4 Throughout the twentieth century, a fascination with female combatants developed as representations in popular culture such as novels, short stories, magazine articles and autobiographies increased (Bourke 1999: 312). See also Inness (1999) and White (2007) on women warriors and spies in popular culture.

2 Gender, security and popular culture
A methodological approach

> If a puzzle is the main research challenge, then it can be addressed with all means available, independently of their provenance or label. A source may stem from this or that discipline, it may be academically sanctioned or not, expressed in prose or poetic form, it may be language based on visual or musical or take any other shape or form: it is legitimate as long as it helps to illuminate the puzzle in question.
>
> (Roland Bleiker 2003: 420)

To explore the political puzzle, indeed what Barthes calls the 'hidden ideological abuse', involved in the way female bodies are represented, valued and understood in relation to agency in political violence, in this book I am focusing on representations in popular culture as well as mass media. This book is, thus, a contribution to Jutta Weldes' call to 'pluralise' world politics by 'going cultural', as a way to multiplying 'the sites and categories that count as political' (Weldes 2003a: 6). Today, there is a growing interest in both the study of visual representations and popular cultural artefacts in IR and Security Studies.[1] Yet, the methodological engagements and discussions as to *how* to study cultural and visual representations are still limited in IR. Subsequently, the aim of this chapter is to present a methodological framework useful to analyse and understand the political efforts that go into the construction of *common sense*. To this end, I turn to the writings of Roland Barthes. The argument made in this book builds on the writings of Barthes in two different ways: First, theoretically, his writings on myth and mythology, mainly from the essay collection *Mythologies*, inform the conceptualisation of the Myth of Motherhood and my critique of how commonsensical ideas are gendered that I develop in the concluding chapter. Second, methodologically, the analysis presented is profoundly inspired by how Barthes engages with both the visual and the cultural as 'text', as a way of 'reading' politics. While I discuss Barthes' ideas on myth and mythologies in greater detail in the concluding chapter, here I focus on disentangling a tension between Barthes' early work, of which *Mythologies* is part, and poststructuralist discourse analysis. I draw on Barthes, as well as contributions to cultural studies more broadly, also in my discussion of methods. I show how textual methods for discourse analysis can be translated to also apply to analyses of the grammar of visual representations. I start this chapter, however, by clarifying the added value of poststructuralist feminism. I show how a poststructuralist understanding of gender facilitates a separation of 'woman' as feminism's core subject and thereby enables a discursive analysis of how gendered categories are produced in the first place.

On bodies, power and gendered common sense

Poststructuralist analyses are interested in language; in communication, understanding and interpretation; how meanings are constituted through language; and, crucially, how particular constructions function to enable certain practices while excluding others. In this way, a poststructuralist analysis critiques the ways in which meaning, through discourse, is fixed and knowledge becomes 'truth', normalised, indeed, common sense. Roxanne Doty defines discourse as a system of statements in which each individual statement makes sense. Thus, a discourse produces interpretive possibilities by making it virtually impossible to think outside of it (Doty 1993: 302). By attempting to understand *how* meanings are produced rather than explaining *why* something occurs, poststructuralist research manages to problematise power; discourses are seen as practices of power because they always fix meaning temporarily. Hence, power is not only discursive but also productive of knowledge, subjectivities, social forms, cultures and institutions. To paraphrase Doty: what is explained is not *why* a particular outcome happened, but rather *how* the subjects, objects and interpretative dispositions were socially constructed such that certain practices were made possible (ibid.: 298). Thus, by examining how meanings are produced and attached to various social subjects and objects one can explore how certain possibilities are created and others precluded. The site for analysis, moreover, is representations. Stuart Hall explains:

> [R]epresentation is the production of the meaning of the concepts in our minds through language. It is the link between concepts and language which enables us to refer to either the 'real' world of objects, people, or events, or indeed to imaginary worlds of fictional objects, people and events.

> (Hall 1997c: 17)

In this sense, representation connects meaning and language to culture; it is only through the process of representation that political reality comes into being (Bleiker 2001: 512). We give meaning by how we represent something, the words we use, the images we produce, the emotions we associate with, the ways we classify and conceptualise and the values we ascribe it (Hall 1997b: 3). Thus, through language, representation is central to the processes by which meaning, but also culture, is produced (ibid.: 1). This is why cultural practices are also political practices and representation is always an act of power (Bleiker 2001: 515). Importantly, representation works as much through what is shown as through what is not. This is the case because discourses exclude or silence contesting interpretations. In this way, discourses at the same time construct the meaning, empower and fix the limits of socially recognised modes of objectivity, subjectivity and the conduct that is taken as the natural way of doing things (Ashley 1989: 282). Discourses do not merely describe objects, or simply transmit statements. Instead, discourses *do* something; discourses produce by fixing meaning, however temporarily, which 'enable us to make sense of the world' (Shepherd 2008b: 215). This is not to say that there is no reality outside discourse, only that the world does not exist intelligibly outside of the meaning that human beings ascribe to it. Discourses, as 'practices that systematically form the object of which they speak' (Foucault 1972: 49) are constitutive of 'reality'; discourses are performative. As Butler explains:

> If the power of discourse to produce that which it names is linked with the question of performativity, then the performative is one domain in which the power acts *as* discourse.
>
> (Butler 2011: 171)

In other words, "the concept of discourse is not about whether things exist but about where meaning comes from" (Hall 1997c: 45). Thus, meanings created do not reflect an already existing reality so much as they organise, construct and mediate our understanding or *imagination of it* (Sturken and Cartwright 2001: 12). Also, it is important to note, as Butler explains, there is no power, construed as a subject, that *acts*, but only a reiterated *acting* that is power in its persistence and instability. This is less an 'act,' singular and deliberate, than a nexus of power and discourse that repeats or mimes the discursive gestures of power (Butler 2011: 171, my emphasis).

Consequently, by re-politicising dominant representations, it is possible to expose the inclusions and exclusions involved in producing that which appears to be natural, fixed and timeless and to argue that the political action that follows from naturalised understandings could be pursued differently. In this way, poststructuralist analysis can offer something more than critique; it can offer a way to think differently about that which is taken for granted. It can critique that which is considered common sense. And, as I explain in more detail in the next section, it is in the critique of commonsensical ideas that I find Barthes' writings on myth particularly useful.

In a similar way to how a feminist politics has been seen as incompatible with the study of war and security studies, the combination of post-structuralist theorising with feminism has also been seen to constitute a 'contradiction in terms' (Baxter 2003: 2). This is because the poststructuralist insight that there is no, cannot, nor should there be, a singular feminine subject or a single feminist approach means that the category of 'woman' can never be fixed. In Butler's words: there was a concern that a feminist theory 'cannot proceed without presuming the materiality of women's bodies, the materiality of sex' (Butler 1992: 17) and poststructuralist feminism was seen as undermining the feminist commitment to women's agency and, thus, not compatible with a commitment to feminist politics (Shepherd 2008a: 4; Dietz 2003: 413). The emancipatory stance of feminism and the deconstructive purpose of poststructuralism seemed to clash. However, instead of constituting a contradiction, the combination of poststructuralism and feminist theorising is not only a compatible combination, but also offers new ways of thinking to identified political puzzles, especially with regards to the category of 'woman' itself:

> To understand 'women' as a permanent site of contest, or as a feminist site of agonistic struggle, is to presume that there can be no closure on the category and that, for politically significant reasons, there ought never to be. That the category can never be descriptive is the very condition of its political efficiency.
>
> (Butler 2011: 168)

I draw on Judith Butler's idea of gender as performative, which means that gender is not simply a tool for analysis, or a variable, but a much deeper logic. *Gender itself is a power relation.* Gender is written; gender is writing, which means that 'woman' does not exist coherently, there is no single discourse that produces the subject woman/female. Instead, 'woman' is 'constantly being produced anew – negotiated, subverted and embodied – by female bodies and sometimes male ones too' (Managhan 2012: 14). This also means that females always adopt multiple subject positions. Within certain subject positions, females may be powerful whereas in other subject positions they can be distinctly powerless (Baxter 2003: 10). The subject position of woman is never fixed by the signifier 'woman' as that term does not describe a pre-existing constituency, but is rather, part of the very production and formulation of that constituency, one that is perpetually renegotiated and rearticulated in relation to other signifiers within the political field (Butler 2011: 146). Combining poststructuralist theorising with feminist analysis means an exploration of how 'woman', as an effect of discourse, language and power, 'get said' (Zalewski 2000: 69) in a much broader sense than simply focusing on actual women. As Marysia Zalewski puts it: Even though feminism is often assumed to be 'only' about women's lives and experiences, it is more appropriate to think of feminism as primarily concerned with the kinds of question that are fundamentally about 'how we organise life, how we accord it value, how we compel the world' (Zalewski 2010: 29, quote by Butler 2004: 205).

Importantly, because gender is social and cultural, it varies through time and societies and is cut across by considerations of class, race, age, and so forth; gender identity can never be achieved once-and-for-all. This means that there is no direct link back to the sexed body but gender identities are, at best, naturalised fictions (rather than natural entities) always prone to dissonance and uncertainty (Lloyd 2005: 133). Acknowledging this fictiveness enables gender to be de-coupled from sex. Once gender roles are recognised as 'designated' and not natural, any necessary link between women and femininity is broken (ibid.: 21). This is how poststructuralist insights regarding gender and sex enable a critique of what is culturally considered 'normal', 'natural', 'normative', or in Morrissey's words 'hegemonic heteropatriarchal conceptions of femininity' (Morrissey 2003: 153).

Today, the combination of poststructuralist theorising with feminism is less controversial. In a recent textbook on how gender matters in global politics, Laura Shepherd divides 'feminism' into three main approaches to the study of gender and global politics depending on the relationship between bodies and behaviour: 1) essentialist understandings, which collapses gender into sex; 2) constructivist, which sees sex as biological (natural) and gender as social (cultural) and focuses on analyses of feminine and masculine; 3) and, last, poststructuralist theories, where sex collapses into gender: 'we make sense of bodies and ascribe them meaning [female or male] as a result of ideas that we have about gender: the body is not ontologically prior to gendered discourses but rather is gendered as/through part of those discourses' (Shepherd 2010: 14–15). Simply put, my poststructuralist feminist perspective means that I am interested in 'body-politics', how certain bodies are positioned and how certain bodies matter and, above all, how 'sex' is also a social construct.

A Barthesian discourse analysis

(every image is, in a way, a narrative).

(Barthes 2000b: 474)

In the essay collection *Image-Music-Text*, published in 1966, Barthes asks: 'How, according to what "grammar," are the different units strung together along the narrative syntagm? What are the rules of the functional combinatory system?' (Barthes 2000b: 269):

> Just as linguistics stops at the sentence, so narrative analysis stops at discourse – from there it is necessary to shift to another semiotics ... every narrative is dependent on a 'narrative situation' the set of protocols according to which the narrative is 'consumed'.
>
> (Ibid.: 287)

As this project is about problematising the cultural grammar that makes particular, gendered, utterances both possible and intelligible, indeed commonsensical, it is this narrative situation that I am analysing. To this end, it is useful to think about discourse as 'structures of meaning-in-use' (Milliken 1999: 231) and culture as 'shared meanings' (Hall 1997b: 1). Meanings regulate and organise our conduct and practices because they help to set the rules, norms and conventions by which social life is ordered and governed (ibid.: 4). Discourse analysis has clear political and ethical significance since in explaining discourse productivity, scholars can potentially denaturalise dominant forms of knowledge and expose to critical questioning the practices they enable (Milliken 1999: 236). To Butler, this is also about displacement and reversal:

> The argument that the category of 'sex' is the instrument and effect of 'sexism' or its interpellating moment, that 'race' is the instrument and effect of 'racism' or its interpellating moment, that 'gender' only exists in the service of heterosexism, does *not* entail that we ought never to make use of such terms, as if such terms could only and always reconsolidate the oppressive regimes of power by which they are spawned. On the contrary, precisely because such terms have been produced and constrained within such regimes, they ought to be repeated in directions that reverse and displace their originating aims.
>
> (Butler 2011: 83)

In this way, (re)-telling stories can be a powerful political practice as it high-lights the great deal of power invested in the way stories are presented (Zalewski 2000: 123). I also follow Jutta Weldes' suggestion and see discourse as enabling a process of making meaning, and, ideology as an effect of that process. This way, a discourse has ideological effects, even though they might not be immediately apparent, and is always implicated in the production and reproduction of power relations (Weldes 2003a: 20).

As a result of the focus on meaning construction through language, traditionally, discourse analysis has not only been predominantly concerned with texts as written or verbal language but most discourse analyses in IR and security studies have also focused on obvious 'political' texts such as government statements, political speeches, legal documents etc. rather than popular sites of discursive practices. However, since communicative structures and meaning-production are by no means confined to the linguistic, there is no point in limiting discourse analysis in such a way. Or, to paraphrase Roland Bleiker, the dilemmas that haunt world politics are far too serious not to employ the full register of human intelligence to understand and deal with them (Bleiker 2001: 529).

In 2001, Roland Bleiker argued that interpretations or readings of the world often come to us through the mass media and 'television is perhaps the most crucial source of collective consciousness' (Bleiker 2001: 525). Today, the visual is probably even more central to the cultural construction of social life in contemporary Western societies. Culture is increasingly permeated by visual images with a variety of purposes and intended effects, whether it is through the use of mobile phones, videogames, CCTV footage, Google Earth, Facebook, Instagram, Pinterest, YouTube or images' preponderance in the news media. From cultural studies, which has a longer history of analysing the visual than IR and security studies, we learn that the capacity of images to affect us as viewers and consumers is dependent on the larger cultural meanings they invoke and the social, political and cultural contexts in which they are viewed (Sturken and Cartwright 2001: 25). The images we interact with on a daily basis are caught up in the power relations of the societies in which we live. Similarly, a particular representation in a popular cultural text might support or undermine existing relations of power, or both at once. Thus, examining such texts helps us to highlight the workings of power (Weldes 2003a: 7).

In my reading of Barthes, myth is a set of discursive practices constituting culturally relative formation of meaning. Thus, myth cannot be said to be universal; it will not resonate similarly in all cultures. This means that myth can never be filled with one example and the arguments I make can only be made valid with reference to a specific culture in a specific time. Myth is always culturally based, as Barthes explains in the essay 'The Photographic Message', written in 1961:

> Naturally, signification is only possible to the extent that there is a stock of signs, the beginnings of a code. The signifier here is the conversational attitude of the two figures and it will be noted that this attitude becomes a sign only for a certain society, only given certain values ... the code of connotation is neither artificial (as in true language) nor natural, but historical.
>
> (Barthes 2000b: 200–1)

Also, to Barthes the power of myth is by no means confined to oral speech. It can consist of modes of writing or of representations; both written and pictorial discourse, all of which can serve as a support to mythical speech (Barthes 1993: 94). Pictures become a kind of writing as soon as they are meaningful:

> We shall therefore take language, discourse, speech, etc., to mean any significant unit or synthesis, whether verbal or visual: a photograph will be a kind of speech for us in the same way as a newspaper article; even objects will become speech, if they mean something.
>
> (Ibid.: 95)

This is why there is no need to separate between writing and pictures, or indeed any type of communication. They are both signs and they both reach the threshold of myth endowed with the same signifying function (ibid.: 100).

Drawing on Barthes' writings on myth in combination with a methodological commitment to discourse analysis is not uncontroversial however. While Barthes, through his later works, is seen as having influenced early post-structuralist theorising, his work on myth construction, which is fundamental to this book, was produced at an earlier stage of his career when he was heavily influenced by structuralist linguistics for his narrative analysis. Barthes' framework in *Mythologies* was an attempt to address the fact that semiotics, which draws on linguistics as a way to analyse signs, had been critiqued for ignoring social, political and historical factors and lacking ideology. Barthes' earlier work, thus, sought to uncover, to expose, the *singular* meaning from a multitude of situations (Saper 1997: 13). *Mythologies* concludes with a theoretical essay, 'Myth today', in which Barthes outlines semiology as a methodology for exploring the ideological function of myths and the reading of popular culture. However, the methodological quest to expose the 'true' hidden meaning through representations is not compatible with poststructuralism's reflexive approach as poststructuralism rejects the idea of an underlying structure upon which meaning can rest 'secure and satisfied' (Storey 1993: 89). In part, this might explain why critical analyses in IR that draw on Barthes are few and that poststructuralists who have used Barthes' work tend to draw on his later writings,[2] not *Mythologies*. The invisibility of Barthes' relevance for critical analyses in IR is for example demonstrated by the fact that the collection *Critical Theorists and International Relations* (2009), edited by Jenny Edkins and Nick Vaughan-Williams, includes 32 thinkers but not Barthes. Indirectly, this book might work to re-value Barthes' theorising for IR.

In order to demonstrate how the tension involved in combining Barthes early, structuralist linguistics-influenced work with a poststructuralist discourse analysis can be overcome I explain how others have 'postmodernised' Barthes. I build on Craig Saper's (1997) re-reading of Barthes' earlier work through his later ones and Cynthia Weber's (2005) discussion of 'unconscious' ideology. I also draw on some of Barthes' own explanations on how his thinking developed after he wrote *Mythologies*.

To start with, Saper simply asks what we can learn about mythology from the later works (Saper 1997: 6): "What if Barthes began over again and rewrote his mythological investigations after the later works?" (ibid.: 13)

> Interpreting his later experiments in terms of his earliest works on myth depends on a speculation that takes the form of a question: What if Roland Barthes had lived longer? What if he had continued to write after the later works, the works that broke emphatically with earlier semiotic concerns, in order to introduce paradoxical arguments and experimental presentations? What if Barthes had returned to earlier concerns with his new attitude and methodologies?
>
> (Ibid.: 5)

The background to this speculation is that Roland Barthes died prematurely in a traffic accident in Paris in 1980 and his work can therefore be considered 'unfinished'. Saper argues that while the earlier work sought to uncover the singular meaning from a multitude of situations, the later work sought 'polysemy from even the apparently most trivial details' (ibid.: 13). Most critics also agree that, with regards to his writing style, his later work abandoned didactic explanations and traditional structural analyses in favour of reflective essayistic texts that seemed to critique structuralism.

Another way to explore the tension between Barthes' mythology framework and poststructuralist discourse analysis would be to return to what we mean by 'the political'. According to Stuart Hall, one important difference between semiotic and discursive approaches is that the semiotic approach is concerned with the *how* of representation, with how language produces meaning; whereas the discursive approach is more concerned with the effects and consequences of representation – its 'politics' (Hall 1997b: 6). In this sense, a semiological approach is assumed to be apolitical. Barthes' myth framework, however, is implicitly political which, in my reading, distinguishes it from semiotics. For example he suggests that the mythical signification is never random; it is always in part motivated, and unavoidably contains some analogy (Barthes 1993: 112). Myth plays on the analogy between meaning and form. There is no myth without motivated form (ibid.: 113). In Barthes' words: 'Men do not have with myth a relationship based on truth but on use; they depoliticise according to their needs' (ibid.: 133). Hence, in my reading, the overtly political character of Barthes' mythology framework shares a common ground with poststructuralist discourse analysis because it explores the concept of power.

In 1977, only three years before his death, Barthes was appointed Chair of Literary Semiology at the College de France (a post that he was offered by Michel Foucault). In his inaugural lecture, Barthes addressed the relationship between ideology and power:

> We have believed that power was an exemplarily political object; we believe now that *power is also an ideological object*, that it creeps in where we do not recognize it at first, into institutions, into teaching, but still that it is always one thing. And yet, what if power were plural, like demons?
>
> ... everywhere 'authorized' voices which authorize themselves to utter the discourse of all power: the discourse of arrogance. We discover then that power is present in the most delicate mechanisms of social exchange: not only in the State, in classes, in groups, but even in fashion, public opinion, entertainment, sports, news, family and private relations, and even in the liberating impulses which attempt to counteract it. I call the discourse of power any discourse which engenders blame, hence guilt, in its recipient.
>
> (Barthes 2000b: 459, my emphasis)

In my reading of Barthes, it is this particular understanding of power that I would like to emphasise. Drawing from the writings of Stuart Hall and others, Cynthia Weber discusses the politics of Barthes' ideas through the concept of 'unconscious ideology', which is ideology that is not formally named and that is therefore difficult to identify. It is the common sense foundation of our world-views that is beyond debate (Weber 2005: 5). Weber argues that we use 'unconscious ideologies' to help make sense of our worlds, very often without realising it. And because we do not realise we hold unconscious ideologies or use them to make sense of our worlds, we very rarely interrogate them. We rarely ask difficult questions about them that might upset them as common sense (ibid.: 5). In this way, the reason we tend not to notice the ideological construction of our world is because ideology denies itself as an ideology. Ideology appears to be reality because it conceals its own construction (Lacey 1998: 101). Yet, as Weber notes, the process of *transforming the cultural into the natural*, which is what myth does, is a highly political practice that depends on all sorts of complex configurations of power. In a general sense, power works through myths by appearing to take the political out of the ideological. This is because something that appears to be natural and unalterable also appears to be apolitical. Yet, to Weber, such 'natural facts' are the most intensely political stories of all, not just because of what they say (what the specific myth is), but because of what they *do* (they remove themselves and the tradition they support from political debate) (Weber 2005: 7).

Again, in his inaugural lecture as Chair of Literary Semiology in 1977 Barthes explains his standing on semiotics, and how he disagrees with the methodological concerns of his earlier works. It is worth quoting Barthes at length here.

> And though it is true that very early on I associated my investigations with the birth and development of semiotics, it is true as well that I have scarcely any claim as its representative, so inclined was I to shift its definition (almost as soon as I found it to be formed) and to draw upon the eccentric forces of modernism, located closer to the journal Tel Quel than to many other periodicals which testify to the vigor of semiological inquiry.
>
> (Barthes 2000b: 457)

> I believe, indeed, that today, within the pertinence chosen here, language and discourse are undivided, for they move along the same axis of power. Yet initially this originally Saussurian distinction (the pairing was Langue/Parole) was very useful; it gave semiology the courage to begin. By this opposition, I could reduce discourse, miniaturize it into a grammatical example, and thereby hope to hold all human communication under my net ... But the example is not 'the thing itself,' and the matter of language cannot be held or contained in the limits of the sentence.
>
> (Ibid.: 470)

> Now, semiology, so far as I am concerned, started from a strictly emotional impulse. It seemed to me (around 1954) that a science of signs might stimulate social criticism, and that Sartre, Brecht, and Saussure could concur (or of describing) how a society produces stereotypes, i.e., triumphs of artifice, which it then consumes as innate meanings, i.e.,

triumphs of Nature. Semiology (my semiology, at least) is generated by an intolerance of this mixture of bad faith and good conscience which characterizes the general morality, and which Brecht, in his attack upon it, called the Great Habit. *Language worked on by power*: that was the object of this first semiology.

(Barthes 2000b: 471)

Barthes actually distances himself from semiology here. He explains how and why he wrote *Mythologies* but also why he no longer found the method used in 'Myth Today' satisfying. The method in question was a deconstruction or reading of the myth in two stages: first, denotation in which each of the signifiers of an image is decoded into a simple concept, and, then, connotation, where the concept yields a second and more elaborate and ideologically framed cultural meaning (Barthes 2000b: 114–15). However, for 'the later' Barthes, denotation is no longer a neutral level. Instead, denotation itself is a part of the production of myth. Denotation is just as ideological as connotation (Storey 1993: 89).

Language flows out into discourse; discourse flows back into language; they persist one above the other like children topping each other's fists on a baseball bat. The distinction between language and discourse no longer appears except as a transitory operation – something, in short, to 'abjure'. There has come a time when, as though stricken with a gradually increasing deafness, I hear nothing but a single sound, that of language and discourse mixed. And linguistics now seems to me to be working on an enormous imposture, on an object it makes improperly clean and pure by wiping its fingers on the skein of discourse ... semiology would consequently be that labor which collects the impurity of language, the waste of linguistics, the immediate corruption of the message: nothing less than the desires, the dears, the appearances, the intimidations, the advances, the blandishments, the protests, the excuses, the aggressions, the various kinds of music out of which active language is made.

(Barthes 2000b: 470–1)

Barthes' theorising of myths and his conceptualisation of 'text' as meaning-making offers 'a way of seeing language and text that enables citizens to grasp, and contest when need be, the covert structuring of their political thinking' (Fortin 1989: 192). Thus, despite its reliance on structuralist linguistics as part of its methodology, Barthes' theorising of myths, as well as his later work, is a highly valuable source of inspiration regarding boundaries of what counts as text, what counts as political and the inclusion of popular culture in the analysis of the political. In my reading of Barthes, I do not follow his methodological framework of denotation and connotation as published in 'Myth Today' because, as explained above, this is incompatible with poststructuralism. Instead, I draw on *Mythologies* merely theoretically, to make feminist sense of representations of female agency in political violence in the concluding chapter. Methodologically, I combine a wider range of his works with textual and visual methods compatible with poststructuralist discourse analysis. By combining the theorisation of myth with a poststructuralist methodology, a postmodernised Barthes informs this research project and the inherent tension between structuralist semiotics and poststructuralist discourse analysis is overcome.

Methods: a grammatical approach

Analyses of agency are sometimes seen as an uncomfortable fit with post-structuralist analyses. However, this is only a problem if one uses an action-based, material understanding of agency linked to political subjectivity, how individuals act. While Butler's thinking informs my poststructuralist feminist interest in body-politics, it is also crucial for my discussion of agency; to show how my theorising of gender, agency and political violence in this book differs from most other contributions on women's agency in political violence. Butler argues that agency is not related to a theory of the self but is an effect of the operations of discourse-power through which subjects are produced. According-ing to Butler, agency traditionally belongs to a way of thinking about persons as instrumental actors who confront an external political field. But, she argues, politics and power exist already at the level at which the subject and its agency are articulated and made possible, therefore, agency can be pre-sumed only at the cost of refusing to inquire into its construction (Butler 1992: 13). Following Butler, I thereby analyse agency through *representations of agency*. More specifically, I analyse *ideas* about women's agency in political violence; I am interested in the discursive construction of agency and the implications for such constructions. To reiterate, this book does not claim to explain how and why individual women choose to engage in political violence and to what extent such individuals have agency. In order to account for such explorations of agency, the way in which social actors *act*, agency is often discussed through the concept of political subjectivity (Howarth and Stavrakakis 2000: 12, 13).

In contrast, my Butler-inspired analysis of agency is interested in sub-jectivity as the constitution of subjects rather than the theorisation of self. By analysing subject positions rather than political subjectivity, this book inves-tigates how a female subject is written in a particular discourse rather than how individual women act, which most of the existing literature on female agency in political violence tends to do. Crucially, thus, subjects should not be con-fused with individuals. The concept of subject positions accounts for the *multiple forms* through which agents are produced as social actors (Howarth and Stavrakakis 2000: 12). Subject positions are used to capture the posi-tioning of subjects within a discursive structure, intelligible only with refer-ence to a specific set of categories, concepts and practices (Doty 1993: 303, 309). This means that, rather than a homogenous subject with particular interests, an individual can have multiple subject positions (Howarth and Stavrakakis 2000: 13). Similarly, there might be multiple physical individuals that constitute a single subject (Doty 1993: 309).

Moreover, all discourses construct subject positions, a place for the subject. This suggests that discourses themselves construct the subject positions from which they become meaningful and have effects. Every subject is a fluid, multiple subject (Lloyd 2005: 55). Lloyd adopts the idea of a subject-in-process, a subject that has no essential nature but is constituted in various, always incomplete ways (ibid.: 14). Particular attributes of subjects (or subject positions) may appear natural, but in reality these meanings are always already social. Their appearance as natural is the result of certain processes that attempt to make certain *ideas seem commonsensical* (ibid.: 20), and, it is these processes that I find corresponding with Barthes' ideas on myth.

> Every identity (essential or historical) is performatively produced and at the same time each performative production involves positing a constative claim. Each time, that is, feminists appeal to the idea of women they performatively invoke her, but each performative invocation produces her anew and differently.
>
> (Ibid.: 51)

To recap, I analyse agency through an ideational rather than material understanding, through subject positions rather than individuals. I think of this difference as a *grammatical* rather than the more common *ethnographic* reading of agency. The following insights from cultural studies on how to study visual representations are useful in order to explain what a grammatical approach to agency might involve.

According to Rose, interpretations of visual images broadly concur that there are three sites at which the meanings of an image are made: the site(s) of the production of an image, the site of the image itself, and the site(s) where it is seen by various audiences (Rose 2001: 16). With regards to the first one, most if not all images have a meaning that is preferred by their producers, but analysing images according to the intentions of their producers is rarely a completely useful strategy since readers have no way of knowing for certain what a producer intended his or her image to mean. Furthermore, finding out a producer's intentions often does not tell us much about the image, since intentions may not match up with what viewers actually take away from an image or text. For the other two sites at which the meanings of images are made one can either focus on issues of reception or concepts of address. The distinction between address and reception is one between thinking about the ideal viewer of an image, and the potential real viewer who looks. Address refers to the way that an image constructs certain responses from an idealised viewer, whereas reception is about the ways in which actual viewers respond (Sturken and Cartwright 2001: 72). Viewers themselves of course bring a particular set of cultural associations with them, which will affect their individual interpretation of an image (ibid.: 45–6). For this reason, the focus lies on the site of the image itself. I focus on address only, which means that I am not interested in how audiences actually interpret an image. I am not trying to find the 'real' meaning of an image, but how an image constructs certain responses from an idealised viewer. Visually, one way to think about this is to focus on the 'gaze', but more specifically the gaze of the narrative. In other words, how the narrative is constructed, how the story is told, through particular camera positions, voices and angles.

Next, I first focus on three specific methods used in textual discourse analysis that I have 'translated' to also 'read' visual representations. My point here is to show that in the same way as we can read and analyse the grammar of a written text, through subjects and objects, we can also read visual representations. I suggest that the cultural grammar of visual texts has a similar structure, a structure that makes particular expressions both possible and intelligible. I also explore a few additional theoretical concepts useful for my analysis. Again, I build on Barthes' thinking on how to read images but the discussion of abjects and the idea of interpellation are also very important for my eclectic methodological toolbox.

Predication, presupposition and subject positioning

In 1993, Roxanne Doty used the concepts of predication, presupposition and subject-positioning, understood as textual mechanisms, to discursively analyse US counter-insurgency policy in the Philippines (Doty 1993). Here, I illustrate how those concepts can also be used to inform a discourse analysis in which 'language' includes visual language and where popular culture is read as 'text' (see also Åhäll and Borg 2012). Again, it is important to remember that these methodological concepts concern *subjects*, rather than 'individuals' or 'states', as positions within particular discourses and intelligible only with reference to a specific set of categories, concepts and practices (Doty 1993: 303). As Doty summarises, '[t]aken together, these methodological concepts produce a "world" by providing positions for various kinds of subjects and endowing them with particular attributes' (ibid.: 307). It needs to be stressed, however, that although these concepts, for analytical purposes, are discussed separately, in actuality of course all three work together and simultaneously.

Predication refers to how nouns are endowed with certain properties. As Jennifer Milliken puts it: 'Predication of a noun construct the thing(s) named as a particular sort of thing, with particular features and capacities' (Milliken 1999: 232). It involves the linking of certain qualities to particular subjects through the use of predicates and the adverbs and adjectives that modify them (ibid.: 231). A predicate affirms a quality, attribute or property of a person or thing. Attributes attached to subjects are important for constructing identities for those subjects and for telling us what subjects can and cannot do. This is linked to whether the subject is ascribed agency or not. For example, let's think about how some states might be described as 'democratic' or 'free' and as a result ascribed a certain amount of legitimate agency within 'international society'. Others might be described as 'failed' or 'rogue' and will subsequently lack legitimate agency in the international community. Taken together these attributes produce a state as a particular kind of actor, able to do certain things and unable to do others.

Presupposition concerns background knowledge in place when reading a text, written, verbal or visual. It is about what is taken for granted in the particular representation; what kind of world the representation is construct-ing, and what is considered true in that constructed world. As Doty explains:

> Statements rarely speak for themselves. Even the most straightforward and ostensibly clear statements bring with them all sorts of presupposi-tions or background knowledge that is taken to be true. In the absence of the 'truth' of the background knowledge and the world it presupposes, the statement would not make sense.
>
> (Doty 1993: 306)

Presupposition, therefore, is an important textual mechanism that by creating background knowledge constructs a particular kind of world in which certain things are recognised as true. In this way, it is through presupposition that the naturalisation/ normalisation of discourse occurs. This is a political process.

The final concept covered in this section is *subject-positioning*. I use the concept of subject-positioning in a grammatical sense by which I mean the way in which subjects are positioned within discursive practices and read as 'text', even though the 'text' chosen for analysis is not limited to written or spoken words. In other words, subject-positioning means to analyse the way in which texts create a 'reality' by linking particular subjects and objects to one another. The two previous textual mechanisms – predication and pre-supposition – not only endow subjects with properties and construct a world in which they make sense; they also create relations between various kinds of subjects and objects. Hence, meaning constructed through discursive practices is relational, which entails that subjects and objects emerge by either being produced as similar to, identical to, opposed to, complementary to etc. other subjects and objects (Doty 1993: 306). Moreover, subject-positioning also involves agency as a subject is ascribed various amounts of agency whereas an object is not. In this way, subject-positioning facilitates analysis of how a subject is positioned in a 'text', written, verbal or visual. Subject-positioning reveals the subject's relation to objects, who is passive, who is active, who is looking at who etc., which in turn suggests whether or not the subject is ascribed agency and acts as the authoritative subject of the 'text'.

Interpellation and the abject

As mentioned, the method of subject positioning involves a degree of agency ascribed to the subject, as well as its relation to the object and other subjects.

But, as theorised by Foucault, subject position is also the place that a particular discourse asks a human subject to adopt within it (Sturken and Cartwright 2001: 368). In this sense, subject position is a term used to define those
ways that images designate an ideal position for their intended spectators. There
is an ideal spectator of a film regardless of how any particular viewer might
make personal meaning of the film. In this way, subject positioning facilitates
analysis of not only how a subject is positioned in an image, its relation to
objects, if the subject has agency in the image, who is passive, who is active,
who is looking at who etc., but also in order to analyse a discourse's ideal
position for their intended spectators; what subject positioning the image, or
'text', tells us to take.

This book explores cultural grammar, the communicative processes of how
representations of female agency in political violence are culturally intelligible
through gender. It is interested in what happens when two logics, of gender and
security, meet. In the essay 'The Third Meaning' written in 1970 (published in
the collection *Image-Music-Text*) Barthes address what he calls 'the obtuse
meaning'. The obtuse meaning is different from the 'obvious' meaning. The obtuse
meaning is about disguise, and, more importantly, the obtuse meaning is about
emotions. Caught up in the disguise, Barthes argues, such emotion is never sticky, it
is an emotion that simply designates 'what one loves, what one wants to
defend'. The obtuse meaning is about 'an *emotion value*, an evaluation' (Barthes
2000b: 324). In order to explore the politics of the 'obtuse meaning', I find the
concepts of interpellation and abjection useful. To start with, interpellation is a
term coined by Louis Althusser (although borrowed from Jacques Lacan) to
describe the process by which ideological systems call out to or 'hail' social
subjects and tell them their place in the system. Stuart Hall explains:

> We are constituted by the unconscious processes of ideology, in that
> position of recognition or fixture between ourselves and the signifying
> chain without which no signification of ideological meaning would be
> possible.
>
> (Hall 1985: 102)

Interpellation is when we come to recognise ourselves and identify with the
ideal subject in the subject position offered in a particular visual representation (Sturken and Cartwright 2001: 203). Interpellation is similar to how
subject positioning of a discourse works but interpellation also refers to how
these representations work to hail individuals so that they come to accept the
representations as *natural* and *accurate* (Weldes 1999: 163). In my reading,
this resonates strongly with myth construction and the concept of [uncon-
scious] ideologies because, as I explain in greater detail in the concluding
chapter, the essential function of myth is the naturalisation of the concept. By
accepting representations as natural and accurate, myths are hidden and
ideologies at work are kept unconscious. This is how we interpret representations as common sense. Thus, I find interpellation useful to unpack

commonsensical ideas as myth construction. However, as Hall points out, Althusser discusses interpellation through ideological system*s*, plural: 'Ideologies do not operate through single ideas; they operate, in discursive chains, in clusters, in semantic fields, in discursive formations' (Hall 1985: 104). To clarify, I use the concept of interpellation, rather than just subject positioning, in an attempt to dig deeper into how common sense, as part of unconscious ideology, is communicated through discursive practices.

In addition, I find Julia Kristeva's notion of the abject useful to make sense of processes in which subjects are interpellated *not* to identify with the subject position, but rather in opposition to the subject position. As I discuss in greater detail in Chapter 5 and in the concluding chapter, such processes are about borders and boundaries, but it is also about emotions. I would like to emphasise that I use these two concepts in particular ways. Paraphrasing Imogen Tyler, the point is not to remain obedient to the orthodox psychoanalytic logic and conservative political agenda that inform the development and application of the concept of abjection in Kristeva's writing. Instead, the intention is to prise abjection out of the theoretical and political frames in which it is positioned in her work (Tyler 2013: 13). In this sense, Tyler sees herself as an unfaithful reader of Kristeva. In this book, I, too, am an unfaithful reader, not only of Kristeva and Althusser, but of Barthes too. Thus, similarly, the concept of interpellation is only used in the context of unconscious ideology, not as linked to ideology in a traditional (Marxist) sense but informed by Stuart Hall's reading of Althusser's reconceptualization of ideology, and also Butler's ideas about social abjection.[3]

In *Powers of Horror*, Julia Kristeva explores, through literature, different ways in which abjection, as a source of horror, works within patriarchal societies. Here, I will draw on her discussion of abjection in its construction of the human subject constituted through transgression of borders and through exclusion of what is different or other. Like the object, Kristeva argues, the abject is opposed to the subject, but the difference is as follows: 'What is abject, on the contrary, the jettisoned object, is radically excluded and draws me toward the place where meaning collapses' (Kristeva 1982: 2).

> Abjection ... is immoral, sinister, scheming, and shady: a terror that dissembles, a hatred that smiles, a passion that uses the body for barter instead of flaming it, a debtor who sells you up, a friend who stabs you ...
> (Ibid.: 4)

Kristeva defines the abject as that which 'disturbs identity, system, order' and 'does not respect borders, positions, rules' (ibid.: 4). Ultimately, the abject is part of ourselves. We reject it, locating it as that which we are not. Because of this, the abject may reveal as much about ourselves as it does about external reality. The abject both fascinates and horrifies because it thrives on ambiguity and the transgression of taboos and boundaries. This is how the abject reveals our own conceptions of the world and our normative disposition (ibid.: 10). In this sense, the abject has transgressed the borders and rules and, as a result, [unconscious] ideologies call out to social subjects not to identify with the subject/abject position but rather to connect individuals as different from it, in this case within the boundaries of normalised and thereby deemed appropriate behaviour. This is how the abject not only highlights the border/s of the myth but also challenges its content to a point where meaning risks collapsing. As I develop in the concluding chapter, there is a politics of emotions involved in the way in which these borders and boundaries are represented, communicated and ultimately policed.

The cultural grammar of body-politics

To sum up, a poststructuralist understanding of gender means that the unit for analysis is not the fixed category of 'woman' but instead about 'body-politics' where the social category of 'woman' is seen as produced through practices, institutions and discourses. It is about the writing of female bodies as 'women'. As such, rather than analysing whether or not *individuals* have (material) agency within a particular cultural context, I analyse the way in which the *subject* of 'woman' is positioned with agency in various discursive practices and, more importantly, the meanings attached to such ideational representations of agency. This facilitates an analysis of how 'woman' as a discursive subject is written in discourses of agency in political violence.

Barthes suggests that if we can understand how a narrative is seen and consumed as common sense, we can expose underlying hierarchical structures. He refers to the 'narrative situation' as the protocols according to which the narrative is consumed. Therefore, although the arguments I make here could potentially be applied elsewhere, the scope of this book is limited to understandings of female agency in political violence in the cultural context in which I live and have access to, where the issue of terrorism was brought to the forefront of Western security thinking and resulted in the declaration of a global 'war on terror' by the George W. Bush administration and its allies. This book is about the politics involved when two logics (gender and security) meet, it is about the cultural grammar with which such a tension is communicated and made sense of. This is how my analysis of female agency in political violence is also an analysis of the cultural grammar of body politics.

Notes

1   See for example Grayson *et al.* 2009; Hansen 2011; Williams 2003; Weber 2002, 2005; Weldes 2003b; Neumann and Nexon (eds) 2006; Muller 2008; Buus 2009; Grayson 2012; Rowley and Weldes 2012; Shapiro 2013; Shepherd 2009, 2012c.
2   See for example the edited collection by Der Derian and Shapiro (1989).
3   See Hall (1985) for a more detailed discussion on discourse, representation and ideology; the compatibility of Althusser and poststructuralism.

Cast: empirical cases and supporting roles

Faye Turney

Faye Turney was one of fifteen British sailors and marines who, while patrolling the waters between Iraq and Iran, were arrested and subsequently held captive in Iran for two weeks in the spring of 2007. When the *Sun* revealed that the only woman involved was also a mother, both British media and the Iranian government focused their attention on Turney. In the UK, a broader debate regarding women's roles in the military service was ignited. After two weeks, the captives were dressed in suits, taken to see the Iranian President, pardoned and released. They arrived in the UK with 'goody-bags' from the President. In a rare attempt to control the media, the Ministry of Defence allowed the members of the group to sell their story to the media. As a result of the focus on herself, Turney was offered and accepted close to £100,000 to talk about 'her ordeal' in the *Sun* and in an hour-long interview with one of the UK's main terrestrial television channels, ITV.

Female agents

Female Agents is a French/British film from 2007 inspired by the women who fought as secret agents during the Second World War when France was occupied by Germany. As such, *Female Agents* is a film that retrospectively attempts to re-value women's roles as heroines in war. The film was promoted with the slogan: 'In times of war, heroism is not just for men' and the subtitle on the DVD-cover, 'D-day depends on them', indicates their importance. The film follows a group of four female agents who are put together by the British Special Operations Executive (SOE): Louise, Jeanne, Gaelle and Suzy. Louise's brother Pierre leads the group in their first mission to rescue a British geologist from a German military hospital in Normandy. Their second task is to kill an influential Nazi officer, Heindrich, in Paris but all agents except Jeanne are soon arrested or killed. Gaelle commits suicide in prison, Suzy is shot and killed by Heindrich, her former fiancé, and Louise is tortured while in captivity. By the end of the film, Louise successfully completes the mission, but only thanks to Jeanne who diverts the attention to herself in an act of sacrifice. Jeanne is subsequently arrested and hanged, whereas Louise is the only one amongst the group of agents who survives the war.

Janis Karpinski

Janis Karpinski became the first female US General to command soldiers in a combat zone when she took control of the 800th Military Police Brigade tasked with running all prison facilities in Iraq in June 2003 (Karpinski with Strassner 2005: 4). Their mission was prisoner of war operations in 16 different facilities spread all over Iraq. Abu Ghraib prison was the biggest and the only one in which interrogations were carried out, by military intelligence officers. During the autumn of 2003, however, the control of Abu Ghraib prison was transferred from Karpinski's Military Police Brigade to a Military Intelligence Brigade. Crucially, however, military police officers were still working at Abu Ghraib. This created a blurry chain of command structure, which in effect meant that while Karpinski was no longer in charge of Abu Ghraib, some of her soldiers were still working in that facility. Karpinski was often referred to as the highest officer to be punished for the prisoner abuse scandal but she was actually cleared of any involvement in the abuse. Instead, Karpinski was punished for weak leadership and for not having disclosed a false shoplifting accusation before she was promoted to General. Janis Karpinski is the first General ever to have been demoted in US military history (Karpinski, *Signal City*, 13 November 2005). Other higher-ranking officers, such as General Sanchez who was the Head of the Army in Iraq, have since also been punished (although not demoted).

Lynndie England

In May 2004, the *New Yorker* ran the story 'Torture at Abu Ghraib: American soldiers brutalized Iraqis' (Hersh 2004) and soon thousands of photos seemingly depicting US soldiers abusing and degrading Iraqi prisoners at Abu Ghraib prison in Iraq, many with sexual connotations, were released. Lynndie England was one of three female army personnel in a small group of US military police officers who were punished for the Abu Ghraib scandal. England is the most well-known of the people involved, by far the most published and written about. At the time, England was in a relationship with Charles Graner, one of the MP's tasked with 'preparing' prisoners for interrogations by military intelligence officers during the night shifts. She was actually not working when the photos were taken. When the news story regarding prisoner abuse broke, as well as during her trials, England was pregnant with Graner's child. (At this point, Graner had already left England for one of the other women involved.) In order to receive a lower punishment England initially agreed to plead guilty, but after a witness statement by Graner, who said that England was only following orders by superiors, the deal was thrown out. In her second trial, England was sentenced to three years in prison for 'posing' in photos, the third highest sentence. Graner and another senior officer received ten-year sentences whereas the other low-ranking soldiers received much shorter sentences (Morris 2008; Sjoberg 2007).

Nasima

Nasima is the main female character in *Britz*, an award-winning two-part television drama shown in 2007 at primetime on one of the UK's mainstream terrestrial television channels, Channel 4. It is about a brother and a sister's contrasting experiences as British Muslims during increasing tensions between counter-terrorism laws and civil liberties in a post-'9/11' and '7/7' 'war on terror' society. While the first part, 'Sohail's story', follows the brother as he joins the Security Service (MI5) and takes part in surveillance operations of terrorist suspects within Muslim communities, I focus on how the transformation of Nasima into a suicide bomber takes place in the second part, 'Nasima's story'. Nasima becomes radicalised after her best friend, Sabia, commits suicide after being mistreated by police, and because she is not allowed to be with her secret boyfriend, Jude. Nasima becomes involved in a terror attack in London that her brother is trying to prevent. At the end, just as Nasima is about to push the button and ignite her bomb (which she is wearing under a maternity suit), Sohail reaches for her, hugs her and asks her not to do it. In the epilogue of 'Nasima's story', a martyrdom statement is read out where Nasima explains her political motifs.

Ulrike Meinhof/Gudrun Ensslin

Ulrike Meinhof and Gudrun Ensslin are the two main female characters in the Academy Award-nominated German film *The Baader-Meinhof Complex* (2008) about the German left-wing terrorist organisation Red Army Faction (RAF) and their activities in the 1970s. The organisation is often referred to as the Baader-Meinhof group as Ulrike Meinhof was seen as a leader together with Andreas Baader, the main male character in the film and also Gudrun Ensslin's boyfriend. The film shows how the members of the core group meet and how Ulrike, an established journalist at the time, joins Baader and Ensslin in the new formation named the Red Army Faction. After West Germany declared 'its own war on terror' (Colvin 2009: 14), most RAF members were either killed or arrested within a couple of years. The trials of Meinhof, Baader, Ensslin and a few others in the core group went on for several years and during this time the prisoners were mostly held in isolation. The relationship between Meinhof on the one hand and Baader and Ensslin on the other was estranged and Meinhof, who never saw the end of the trials, committed suicide in prison. While the film continues with the newer formations of the RAF and while a majority of the RAF members were women, my analysis is centred on the film's representation of Ulrike Meinhof and Gudrun Ensslin, particularly Meinhof's transformation from an

outspoken journalist committed to non-violence to a perpetrator and insti-
gator of political violence. To me, the main thread of the film is the inherent
tension between Ulrike and Gudrun throughout the film; how the writing of
one informs the writing of the other in a dichotomised positioning, whereas
Baader merely plays a supporting role. Crucially, the positioning of the two
leading female characters as well as Ulrike's transformation into a 'terrorist'
is communicated through ideas about motherhood.

In supporting roles

Adam – Faye Turney's husband.
Andreas Baader – one of the main characters in *The Baader-Meinhof Complex*.
He is in a relationship with Gudrun Ensslin.
Arthur Batchelor – the youngest of the sailors and marines held hostage in
Iran in 2007. He was the only other member of the group besides Faye
Turney to sell his story to the media.
Buckmaster – a character in *Female Agents*, the head of the British Special
Operations Executive (SOE) set up by Prime Minister Winston Churchill.
Dutschke – a character in the *Baader-Meinhof Complex*. He is a union leader
and friend of Ulrike Meinhof's who gets shot. The shooting of Dutschke
triggers Ulrike Meinhof's radicalisation.
Heindrich – 'the bad guy' and as such one of the main characters in *Female
Agents*. Was engaged to Suzy before war broke out.
Jude – a character in *Britz*. Nasima's secret boyfriend.
Molly – Faye Turney's daughter.
Pierre – a character in *Female Agents*. The Special Operations Executive
(SOE) agent who puts together a group of female agents tasked with rescuing
a British geologist from a German military hospital in Normandy. Pierre is
Louise's brother.
Sabia - a character in *Britz*. Nasima's best friend who is imprisoned under
terrorism laws and subsequently commits suicide.
Sohail – the main male character in *Britz*. Nasima's brother but while his sister
Nasima becomes radicalised, Sohail starts working for the British intelligence
service, MI5, and is working to prevent the attack his sister is part of.
Trevor McDonald – the journalist who interviews Faye Turney for ITV.

3 Victimised objects

'I feared being raped by Iranians.'
Subheading on one of the *Sun's* front covers about Faye Turney's 'ordeal'

In this chapter, I build on a rich contribution of feminist scholarship that has shown how in traditional narratives of war, men make war and women keep the peace; men go to the front and women stay at home; men fight and women are fought for. In this war story, man is constructed as violent and aggressive and woman as nonviolent and pacifist. Because of these categorisations, women are seen as incapable of protecting themselves, and this subsequently serve as the grounds on which to persuade men to exercise their masculinity and defeat the enemy; they are the reason why men fight (Kumar 2004: 298). Women become at once the victims of war and the causes for war. Jean Bethke Elshtain has referred to these binary constructions of men and women's roles as the personae of 'Just Warriors' and 'Beautiful Souls' and termed the relationship the Myth of Protection (Elshtain 1995). Here, I focus on three main ways in which women are written as victims through the Myth of Protection: by being referred to in passive terms; by being associated with children and thereby infantilised; and by being emotional. I refer to these tropes as *passivity, 'womenandchildren'* and *emotionality* throughout the chapter.

The Myth of Protection

According to the Myth of Protection the most prominent role that women can play is that of the victim. Women can suffer rape, torture or death during war, giving the male soldier the special duty to protect her from such consequences (Kumar 2004: 297). The binary constructions of war stories in this way proclaim that the sex segregation is justified for biological reasons: the men are strong, therefore, they must protect the women who are weak. It is written in their genes that men shall be active and women passive; men are the subjects and women are the objects represented as being acted upon (Cooke 1996: 16; Young 2003: 8).

Feminist scholars have done much to expose the politics of the Myth of Protection by showing how it has been an important motivator for the recruitment of armed forces but also to 'sell' wars to the public. For example, feminist scholars were quick to point out how the Bush administration's security rhetoric in the 'war on terror' was underpinned both by the fact that women appeared to disappear from view domestically immediately after the attacks on September 11th 2001 but also because, in order to justify the invasion of Afghanistan, the women of Afghanistan were written as the ultimate victims, putting the US in the position of the ultimate protector. Ann Tickner noted how, despite having the first female national security advisor, 'our TV screens after 9/11 were full of (mostly white) men in charge briefing us about "America's new war" both at home and abroad' (Tickner 2002: 335). Tickner argues that this functioned as a re-masculinisation of society and points out that gender is a powerful legitimator of war and national security in times of crisis and uncertainty (ibid.: 336). However, as for example Jan Jindy Pettman and Laura Shepherd have shown, women were not invisible completely but visible in traditional demonstrations of agency along the gendered war story, as 'mothers', 'sisters' and 'daughters' (Pettman 2004; Shepherd 2006). Moreover, the 'war on terror' was also launched in the name of women's rights through a narrative of chivalry where those who respect their women are civilised, while those who do not are barbarians (Ferguson 2005). Shepherd argues that this construction of woman-as-victim marked the enemy abroad as the 'Irrational Barbarian' in need of rectification and punishment from the 'Figure of Authority' (Shepherd 2006). As symbols of 'otherness', then, the women of Afghanistan were utilised as 'our men setting out to rescue their women, from their men' (Pettman 2004: 89). However, despite the use of a women's rights rhetoric, the Bush administration was unwilling to listen to the same women they were seeking to 'liberate' (Steans 2008: 164).

Krista Hunt and Kim Rygiel argue that a similar rhetoric of 'victimized women to be rescued', 'hyper-masculine rescuers' and 'cowardly oppressors' was later used to convince the American public that the war in Iraq would liberate the Iraqi people from a brutal dictator (Hunt and Rygiel 2006: 9). In these gendered war stories women, when and if they appear, were typically represented as being acted upon rather than as actors themselves, as casualties of terror attacks, mothers of fallen soldiers, victims of repressive dictators, and widows rebuilding their lives in the aftermath of war (ibid.: 1).

In addition to being written as passive objects, women are also being written as victims in war by being infantilised. Feminist scholars have shown how, in a whole range of policy documents, activist discourses, speeches by politicians, press statements and media representations, women are usually intimately linked with children and other groups deemed particularly vulnerable, such as disabled and elderly. Indeed, such representations are often critically referred to as 'womenandchildren'. For example, Laura Shepherd notes how in a speech by the then First Wife Laura Bush the combination of 'women and children' twice in close succession infantilises the women of Afghanistan, 'denying them both adulthood and agency, affording them only pity and a certain voyeuristic attraction' (Shepherd 2006: 20).

Claudia Brunner's research on the representation of female suicide bombers in Israel/Palestine offers another example. Brunner argues that while male martyrs are mostly named by their full name and treated as grown-ups, even if they are only 16 years old, in the media coverage, female suicide bombers are mostly cited by their first names and treated as little girls which underlines their young age and supports an interpretation of innocence (Brunner 2005: 43). In this way, women are being treated as equivalent to children, both having the status of victims, which means that women are removed from being seen as active political agents (ibid.: 36). The writing of women as vulnerable victims in need of protection through the unit of 'women-and-children' is problematic not only because women are repeatedly associated with victimhood, and in effect denied adulthood, but also because gendered ideas surrounding perpetrators and victims are reinforced with the implication that men as victims of sexual violence in war for instance remain invisible.

A third way in which women are written as vulnerable victims through the Myth of Protection is by being portrayed as 'emotional'. Again, the legacy of feminist scholarship across the Social Sciences has done much to highlight how we think about the world in dualistic ways and, importantly, that these dualisms are characterised by both hierarchy and opposition. As Zalewski explains, this means that the first term is hierarchically positioned with regard to the second and also that they are perceived as opposed to each other: 'In simple term, good is better than bad and one is the opposite of the other' (Zalewski 2000: 46–7). This is why, when emotions and emotionality are commonly associated with feminine characteristics and defined in opposition to reason and rationality associated with masculinity, emotions and emotionality operate on a gendered spectrum involving processes of valuing. Thus, when a woman is written as 'being emotional' she is disciplined along assumptions of traditional gender roles (see also Åhäll 2012b).

The feminist literature on female 'terrorists' has demonstrated how such actors are often viewed as engaging in such actions due to personal connections and grievances rather than to focus on their political ambitions (Brunner 2005; Eager 2008). To paraphrase Eager, while women engage in political violence for all types of reasons, it is perplexing why the so-called 'personal reasons' consume much of the public's and media's fascination (Eager 2008: 4). In media representations of female suicide bombers in Israel/Palestine, for example, the use of political martyrdom statements is common but the coverage and analysis of their behaviour often still focuses on their personal lives and feminine shortcomings such as a divorce or a miscarriage, rather than their agency in a political cause (Sjoberg and Gentry 2007: 120). In this way, media representation of the first female Palestinian suicide bomber in 2002, Wafa Idris, focused on the fact that she was single, living with her mother after a compulsory divorce as a result of her infertility. Wafa Idris was a 'tainted woman', a 28-year-old sterile divorcee who seemed to fit the picture of a desperate woman, a social outlaw, who might have thought of committing suicide anyway (Brunner 2005: 32). This is particularly problematic if we take into account that men too are motivated to engage in political violence and terrorism through a combination of ideological and personal motivations (Eager 2008: 4).

In the next section, I focus on these three main themes, or narrative tropes, that function to deny female bodies agency and thereby write them as victimised objects: *passivity; 'womenandchildren'*; and *emotionality.* It is important to note, however, that these themes are only separated out in order to emphasise a particular point. As will become clear, themes often overlap in order to make the representation as a victim as strong as possible.

Faye

Womenandchildren

The immediate focus on Faye Turney's identity as a mother with headlines such as 'Topsy, **the mum who went to war**' (Ingham and Flanagan, *Express*, 28 March 2007); 'Iran **mum hostage**' (Hughes, *Mirror*, 27 March 2007); 'LOVING MOTHER' (Linge, *Daily Star*, 28 March 2007); 'The **Mother held captive** in Teheran' (Unattributed, *The Times*, 28 March 2007); 'A **mother on parade** in Iran's propaganda war' (Kennedy, Webster and Sanderson, *Times*, 29 March 2007) automatically emphasised her identity as a woman. Soon, a debate whether or not mothers should be allowed to serve in the military services was intersected with discussions regarding women's roles in the military all together: 'Should women in the armed forces be allowed to serve on the front line?' (Sengupta, *Independent*, 30 March 2007), 'Frontline women: The great debate' (Hickley, *Daily Mail*, 30 March 2007), 'Woman at war in numbers' (Unattributed, *Mirror*, 3 April 2007) and 'Should women serve on the front line?' (Unattributed, *Daily Mail*, 4 April 2007). A former Commander in the Gulf War discussed mothers in relation to men, not fathers:

> I feel there is a problem with **mothers** in the frontline. Just imagine if Faye Turney had been mistreated like the Tornado pilots in the first Gulf War. There would be an eruption, and **it would not be the same if a man had been mistreated**.
>
> (Unattributed, *Daily Mail*, 6 April 2007)

Another commentary was simply titled: 'Faye should not be in the frontline':

> The plain fact is that **women are physically vulnerable in a way men are not**. I may be old-fashioned, but I feel ashamed that Faye Turney has been put in this peril to fight on my behalf. A woman's place may no longer be in the home, but neither is it at the sharp end of an AK-47.
>
> (Heffer, *Daily Telegraph*, 31 March 2007)

Leaving aside questions as to how any woman could voluntarily leave her young child for such tours of duty, Faye's capture highlights the real risk of women in the front line, not just to themselves but to their comrades in arms. **They put their male combatants at greater risk of harm**, not because they are weaker than them, but **because they are a far more valuable trophy of war**, a prize to be used as blackmail against her comrades and her country.

(Platell, *Daily Mail*, 31 March 2007)

Besides focusing on how women are more vulnerable than men, the debate also centred on how the inclusion of women would impact negatively both upon the armed forces but also on society in general:

[A] mother's love is one of the strongest of human forces. To deny it when we recruit men and women to our armed forces is to **make our society as a whole vulnerable**.

(Parkin, *Daily Mail*, 30 March 2007)

[J]ust how effective are women in the Armed Forces? We still don't really know the truth about how men feel alongside women in the front line. Is there some part of them which isn't concentrating on winning and surviving but on **protecting a female** colleague? These instincts go much deeper than politically-correct legislation, right into the chemistry of the body and the structure of society, and my guess is they are not so easily suppressed.

(Ibid.)

[T]he presence of women in risky situations was a distraction, because many servicemen were still **inclined to protect women** and would be more distressed by the death of a woman. Such distress can only be heightened where the woman is a mother.

(Kirby, *The Times*, 1 April 2007)

The mere presence of women also has a dramatic effect on the ability of men to be combat soldiers, as has been proved in those situations around the world where female soldiers serve on the front line. For example, when a soldier sees a female colleague lying injured, he immediately feels his first duty must be to **protect her** rather than to stick to the military plan.

(Webb, *Daily Mail*, 7 April 2007)[1]

In addition to the explicit focus on how [all] men seem somehow biologically trained to protect women, what I would like to emphasise with these quotes is the use of women and mothers interchangeably in contrast to how men are just men; fatherhood remains invisible.

Initially, the Iranians made assurances that Faye Turney, as the only woman, received proper treatment by being held separate from the male hostages. In fact, the Iranian foreign minister ensured that Turney would be 'released as soon as possible' (Borger and Wintour, *Guardian*, 29 March 2007). In other words, it is because of Turney's identity as a woman that she should be released before the others. However, a few days later the Iranians changed their mind and, again, Turney's identity as a woman was highlighted:

> As a result of Britain's 'wrong behaviour' the release of the woman sailor had been 'suspended' … A No 10 source said: 'It is cold and callous to be doing this to **a woman** at a time when she is being detained in this way.'
> (Borger and Wintour, *Guardian*, 30 March 2007)

Faye Turney's vulnerability was also addressed directly in the ITV interview: Trevor McDonald asks: 'How vulnerable did you feel?' Faye replies: 'Initially, very vulnerable … It wasn't until like a four days into it that I started to become strong and I can and I will get through this' (ITV 2007). To illustrate Turney's vulnerability as a mother, McDonald at one point interrupts her to clarify his point: 'They actually said that to you, do you wanna see your daughter again?' McDonald then asks: 'It made you angry?' Turney replies: 'Yes.'

Passivity

Faye Turney's capture highlighted women's alleged vulnerability, but the issue of women on the frontline was most often about the impact upon male soldiers, arguments that emphasised men as active subjects and women as passive objects:

> Men **put women** in a 'special' category. That is why, perhaps, when two women died under my command I found myself deeply upset. On one occasion it rendered me incapable of coherent thought for some time.
> (Colonel Bob Stewart quoted in Unattributed, *Daily Mail*, 6 April 2007)

> When I was Chief of Defence Staff, I always thought it was a risky business because I felt **they could be used** as propaganda trophies and that there was a danger that if women started **getting hurt and killed** it might have a greater effect on the **men fighting**.
> (General Charles Guthrie quoted in Hickley, *Daily Mail*, 30 March 2007)

By describing women as 'put', 'used', 'hurt', 'killed' etc. they are written in passive tense, which means that they are written as objects rather than subjects. The arguments regarding women's impact on male soldiers' capacity to do their jobs are also interestingly echoing the Ministry of Defence's own justifications for excluding women in combat roles (which at the time of writing is under review). After having opened up more and more positions to women during the 1990s, the MOD published the first exclusion policy on women in combat roles in 2002. Women are excluded from so-called ground close combat roles defined as 'roles that are primarily intended and designed with the purpose of requiring individuals on the ground *to close with and kill the enemy*' (MOD 2002, my emphasis). Legally, the exclusion policy is exempted from EU sex discrimination legislation by referring to combat effectiveness.[2] Crucially, the reason why women are excluded is not because of their perceived physiological and/or psychological differences to men such as physical strength or aggression, but because the presence of female bodies is seen to constitute a potential risk to team *cohesion*. A lack of cohesion in turn is assumed to impact negatively upon combat effectiveness. The ban therefore means that women are excluded as a social category because of the shape of their bodies, and ideas about those bodies, rather than their actual individual competence. It also means that the exclusion policy on women in combat roles is actually all about men: the exclusion policy is justified with regards to *how men might react*, their feelings and ability to do their job (see also Woodward and Winter 2006, 2007; Basham 2009, 2013; Åhäll 2013).

Echoing arguments on the 'othering' of the enemy and/or women already put forward by various feminist scholars, visually, another way in which Faye Turney was effectively written as a passive vulnerable victim was the focus on the fact that Turney was wearing an Islamic headscarf while in captivity. On 29 March 2007, the *Independent, The Times*, the *Guardian*, and the *Daily Mail* all have a photo of Turney wearing the headscarf on the front page. The title of the *Daily Star* is 'Mum **paraded** on telly by Iran: She's **forced** to confess and wear Muslim head-dress' (Burchell, *Daily Star*, 29 March 2007). In the *Daily Mirror*, a photo of Turney in the headscarf takes up two pages accompanied with the headline 'A sick charade' (Hughes and Prince, *Daily Mirror*, 29 March 2007). Similarly, in the *Sun*, the leading article focuses on Faye-the victim, seemingly terrified and despicably **paraded**:

> Strain and fear were etched on the face of Faye Turney as she 'confessed' to straying into Iranian waters ... By picking on the **terrified** young mum, the mullahs showed how low they are ready to sink. Parading her before TV cameras was a despicable act of aggression.
>
> (Pascoe-Watson, *Sun*, 29 March 2007)

The following day, the *Daily Mail* publishes three photos of Faye Turney on the front page. In addition to the images previously dominating the media coverage of mother/child photo and soldier photo there is an image from the television coverage from her capture in which Turney is veiled. The caption reads 'mother', 'fighter', '... **pawn**' (Seamark, *Daily Mail*, 30 March 2007).[3] Faye Turney now has three distinctive subject positions in these discursive practices. Moreover, the televised ITV interview was titled 'A Tonight Special: **Captured, paraded** and **exploited**: the inside story of Leading Seaman Faye

Turney's ordeal' (ITV 2007); and an article in the *Sun* had 'STRIPPED, WARNED and THREATENED' emphasised in bold caption and capital letters (Newton Dunn and Moult, *Sun*, 9 April 2007a). The representation of Turney, visually and textually in passive tense, means that Turney is no longer the subject of the story but an object being used by men. In this story the subjects are all male whilst Turney, the lone female, is a vulnerable victim, a passive object.

The story of the white vulnerable woman of course taps into a long history of postcolonial and orientalist discourses and thereby resonates with other stories discussed in this book: the story and rescue of US soldier Jessica Lynch in Iraq but also the rescuing of 'other' women to emphasise the West as 'good'/ 'protector' etc. as in the case of how the women of Afghanistan were portrayed as passive and silent victims in burkas. The visual emphasis on Turney as veiled therefore resonates with a much larger set of discourses about 'the war on terror', British national identity, increasing islamophobia, secularism, legacies of colonialism and of course the gendered representation of Iran's government as 'the enemy', 'evil', 'irrational', 'coward' and so on. While such discourses reach far beyond the aim of this book, it is important to highlight, as feminist scholars have done, the politics involved in how narratives of women's rights play out in imperialist narratives intersecting gender with race, religion or ethnicity.[4]

Yet another way Faye Turney's vulnerability was portrayed was her reliance on her fellow male sailors and marines:

> As the only woman in the group, Faye heaped praise on her fellow hostages. She said: 'I could never have got through this without them'.
>
> (Newton Dunn, *Sun*, 10 April 2007)

Similarly, in the ITV interview, Faye Turney says: 'The lads on my boat were fantastic. Every time I looked at them they were winking at me, just to like give me ...' At this point, McDonald fills in the gap: 'Trying to **reassure you**?' Faye answers 'yeah' (ITV 2007).

The Myth of Protection is about vulnerability and how, in combination, these writings of Turney reinforce traditional gendered war stories of active males and passive female victims. Turney is used as a tool of communication between not only the UK and Iran but between different masculinities. There is a body-politics involved in the way in which Turney is represented as an object rather than a subject in her own story. Turney's body is not only gendered in the sense that she is coded female but motherhood also acts as a border agent by making visible the cultural boundaries that are not just disciplining, but sexing and essentialising female bodies in a male-coded environment.

Emotionality

Another way in which Turney is powerfully written as a victim is through a focus on her fear. In both the interviews with the *Sun* and ITV, Faye Turney's fear while being held hostage is put to the fore, in particular her fear of being raped. One of the *Sun's* cover pages (the story was divided into two parts) had 'I **feared being raped** by Iranians' as a sub-heading. Inside the paper, the article describes how 'Faye desperately tried to hide the fact she was a woman – **fearing she would be raped**':

> Terrified of being discovered, she mouthed to Captain Air: '**Are they going to rape me?**' She said: 'I mouthed it to him again and again. He didn't answer but he winked and smiled at me which reassured me everything would be OK. Looking back it was unfair of me to have asked him. But I wanted to know. I wanted to be prepared for whatever was going to happen to me.'
>
> (Newton Dunn and Moult, *Sun*, 9 April 2007b)

Other headlines and stories include '**I was stripped** and **feared I'd be raped**, says Faye' (Ballinger, *Daily Mail*, 9 April 2007) and 'Ms Turney said that initially she had tried to cover her hair and **hide the fact that she was a woman, fearing that she could be raped**' (Hodgson, *Guardian*, 9 April 2007).

Remarkably, even in Arthur Batchelor's story (he was the only other hostage to sell his story although for a much smaller sum of money), Turney's fear of being raped dominates: The front page reads: 'Faye: **I feared they'd rape and kill me**' and 'Arthur: My 3 days of hell in solitary' (Unattributed, *Daily Mirror*, 9 April 2007). Inside, the biggest headline reads '**Faye feared they'd rape and kill her** ... they called me Mr Bean'. In the text, Batchelor is quoted saying 'The blood drained from her face and Faye whispered **there's going to be a rape involved in this**' (Stansfield and Hughes, *Daily Mirror*, 9 April 2007). Here, not only does the representation of Turney's fear dominate the story, but the males' fear is marginalised. In fact, in the *Daily Mirror* article, Batchelor expresses his own fear of being raped: 'I was absolutely exhausted by the pressure – so much I could barely move. There were times when I feared being **raped** or killed' (Stansfield and Hughes, *Daily Mirror*, 9 April 2007). He also described an incident where another soldier's hair was gently caressed and then sprayed with aftershave: 'We all thought he was about to be sexually abused' (Stansfield and Hughes, *Daily Mirror*, 9 April 2007). This article is supposedly conveying Batchelor's story but the headlines concern Turney's fear of being raped, whereas Batchelor's fear is only mentioned briefly in the text. Turney's fear of rape is emphasised and Batchelor's fear of rape is marginalised. Turney's fear ultimately resonates better with traditional assumptions about women as victims; the fear of rape makes more 'sense' in the story of Turney than in the story of Batchelor.

Women's alleged vulnerability for rape was emphasised again in the representations of the hostages' return to the UK:

> The first thing I told Adam and my mum and dad was that **nobody had touched me**. I knew that would have been in their thoughts and I wanted to put their minds at rest.
>
> (Moult and Newton Dunn, *Sun*, 10 April 2007b)

The focus on Turney's fear of rape only ignores that rape is used as a weapon of warfare against both men and women and that female soldiers, at least Western, are actually more likely to be raped or sexually assaulted by their fellow soldiers than by 'the enemy'.[5] An interesting parallel can be drawn to the case of US soldier Jessica Lynch, who was held hostage in Iraq in 2003. I discuss the attempts at constructing Lynch as a heroine in more detail in Chapter 4 but here I just want to flag up that 'raped by the enemy' played a significant role in such narratives. Melisa Brittain argues that the writing of Jessica Lynch as a modern-day heroine is an example of how colonial memory and fear of the Other have been effectively evoked to rally support for Bush's 'war on terror' (Brittain 2006: 74). For example, by suggesting that Lynch was anally raped, Arab masculinity is reproduced as not only sexually violent, but also 'unnatural' and 'perverse' (ibid.: 83). Crucially, not only did Lynch herself claim that it was unlikely that she had been raped while unconscious but such narrative did not circulate with regards to the other two women, an African-American and a Native-American (ibid.: 82). Brittain suggests by creating a narrative of vulnerable white femininity and Arab hypermasculinity at a time of crisis with rising Iraqi resistance against the US occupation, the Lynch story meant that the Pentagon managed to divert attention away from their loss of control (ibid.: 81).

To return to Faye Turney, again, I am not questioning whether or not she actually feared being raped during captivity, but the focus on her fear in the media representation, and in particular her fear of rape, positions her in the traditional role for women as victims and undermines her authority and agency as a soldier.

Another way in which Turney was written as a victim was through her actual display of emotions. When the ITV interview begins, Faye Turney is already tearful. As the interview continues, it becomes clear that the focus is on Turney as an emotional, weak and vulnerable mother, not a brave soldier. We (the audience) are watching Turney as she is watching the television footage of herself during captivity for the first time. We see her face in profile with Trevor MacDonald, the interviewer, sitting on the other side of her. As she watches the pictures of herself, Turney is biting her lip, seemingly trying not to cry. She gets tears in her eyes. She is emotional. At this point, McDonald asks: '**How do you feel** Faye, seeing that back now?' Turney answers it upsets her deeply. The next question from McDonald is '**What were your emotions** on being separated from the rest of your colleagues?' Turney replies it was horrible and that she had a panic attack after being put in her cell (ITV 2007). When Faye Turney describes the moment her Iranian captors told her that her colleagues had been sent home and that she was the only one left, she says: 'It was just [Turney sighs] … what a feeling'. She seems to get emotional and the camera zooms in. She swallows. McDonald asks 'So you felt you were in this alone?' Here, the close-up on Turney's face emphasises her emotionality. Then, McDonald asks another bizarre question: 'Did you ever **cry yourself to sleep**?' Again, Turney gets emotional as she answers in the affirmative.

The display of emotionality in the moment Turney was told she was the only one left was reported in the newspapers as when she 'totally lost it':

All I could think of was how completely alone I was … At that moment I just **totally lost it**. All I could think of was what my family must be going through. What would my husband Adam be telling Molly? Did they even know I was missing? **I cried my eyes out**. I asked the guards about my friends but all they did was laugh at me.

(Newton Dunn and Moult, *Sun*, 9 April 2007a)

Even though this quote concerns her feelings about being alone, commentaries focused on her role as a mother:

Faye Turney goes on to say that, once in Iranian custody, she '**totally lost it**' when she thought about what her three-year-old daughter Molly would be going through. '**I cried my eyes out**,' she told the *Sun*, 'but all the guards did was laugh at me.' It is hardly surprising that her interrogators then began to ask her whether she wanted to see her daughter again.

(Lawson, *Independent*, 10 April 2007)

Here, the focus is on a mother's feelings. Crying her eyes out is linked to her role as a mother as she is portrayed as having lost it when thinking about her daughter when, in fact, she was expressing her feelings about being 'completely alone'. This is not accidental but instead shows how intimately linked 'being emotional' is with ideas about a naturalised femininity which itself is based on women's capacity to give life.

Moreover, speaking of the moment when she had to reveal that she was female, Faye Turney's emotional experience is described:

I **had tears welling in my eyes** because I knew this was the point they would discover I was female. But I was determined not to give them the satisfaction of seeing me cry and I pulled myself together. There was a look of total disbelief and they kept staring at me and repeating 'woman, woman'.

(Newton Dunn and Moult, *Sun*, 9 April 2007b)

Similarly, much of the media coverage of the hostages' reunions with friends and families focused on Turney's emotional reunion with her husband but above all with her daughter. The *Sun*'s headline on the front page is '**Hello Molly!**', a reference to her daughter. In the text, we learn that 'Hostage Faye Turney was reunited with little daughter Molly yesterday – amid **tearful scenes**' (Newton Dunn and Moult, *Sun*, 6 April 2007). Later, in the *Sun*'s second day coverage of 'Faye Turney's ordeal' based on the interview with Turney, the front page reads '**Mummy mummy!**' and a photo of Turney lifting up her daughter Molly is covering the whole page. The caption reads '**Tears** as Faye holds her little Molly again. FREED Navy hostage Faye Turney lovingly kisses the little daughter she feared she might never see again. Faye, 25, told last night how she **wept** at being greeted by cries of "**Mummy, Mummy**" at an emotional reunion with Molly, three' (Moult and Newton Dunn, *Sun*, 10

April 2007a, b). Inside the paper, it is mentioned that 'throughout her time as a prisoner of the fanatical Iranian regime, the thought of her only child growing up without a mother had reduced her to **tears**' (Newton Dunn and Moult, *Sun*, 10 April 2007). Another article was titled: 'Smiles that say Mummy is home: **Tears** and laughter in the sunshine at hostages' reunion'. In the text it is mentioned that 'some chatted with their families, while others were over-come with the emotion and **broke down and wept**' (Kelly, *Daily Mail*, 6 April 2007). However, the story does not tell us who broke down and wept. Con-sidering the attention to Turney's emotionality in the overall coverage, it is likely that if it was Turney who was 'overcome with emotion and broke down and wept' she would have been named.

Again, I do not suggest that Faye Turney should not have been emotional, but, the interviews are set up to portray her emotionality and by doing so the representation of Turney follows essentialist assumptions of gender behaviour. For example, with regards to the ITV interview, if the interviewee had been male both the questions and the set up would have been different. If Turney had been showed the footage of herself in captivity beforehand, the desired out-come of her emotionality might not have happened. By emphasising Turney as emotional, these representations function to reinforce the link between emotionality and female bodies which not only writes Turney within the boundaries of naturalised femininity but also, as a victim of the masculinised context of the military, her emotionality is also associated with weakness:

> [W]e are the **more compassionate sex**; instinctively **more nurturing** and **lacking** the **thirst for aggression** that drives our male counterparts … [T]he strong **emotional ties of motherhood** cannot be underestimated. All this makes women **less effective** than the men with whom they stand on the battlefield. And the **consequences** to a fighting unit which must be tightly focused are potentially **catastrophic**.
>
> (Webb, *Daily Mail*, 7 April 2007)

There is a valuing of emotions here. The thirst of aggression is, in this parti-cular context, 'positive', whereas the 'strong emotional bonds of motherhood' is not only 'instinctive' but again, in this context, 'negative' in the sense of 'less effective'. Consequently, in these writings of Faye Turney as a victimised object, men's emotionality is anonymous, invisible, or 'positive', whereas a single woman's emotions are identified, highly visible and/or 'negative'.

Ulrike/Gudrun

To me, it is the contrasting positioning of Ulrike and Gudrun that is most useful in order to analyse understandings of gender, agency and political violence in *The Baader Meinhof Complex*. There is an inherent tension between Ulrike and Gudrun, which is displayed through ideas about being active/passive; through motherhood; and also displays of emotionality. Above all these expressions of difference are communicating agency versus a lack of agency. Moreover, as the aim of this chapter is to trace constructions of victimised objects, my main focus here is on how Ulrike is written through a dichotomised positioning of the two main female characters. Again, this particular case from popular culture works as a reminder of how the chosen themes overlap and interlink; they are only separated out for analytical clarity.

Womenandchildren

Perhaps the most obvious way in which Ulrike and Gudrun are positioned against each other is through motherhood and mothering. In this section, I focus on scenes in which Ulrike and Gudrun's roles as mothers are contrasted.

The film starts with Ulrike, her two children and husband on a beach in northern Germany, which immediately puts focus on Ulrike's role as a mother. Soon, there is a scene where Ulrike leaves her home with a bag and her daughters. Bleak slow music (violin chords) starts to play communicating seriousness and sadness. The next scene shows when Ulrike moments earlier had walked in on her husband having sex with another woman and the audience understands that this is the reason Ulrike has left her husband.

Because of this personal trauma, Ulrike seems to be searching for a new meaningful purpose in life. And what she finds is Gudrun Ensslin. As a journalist, Ulrike is covering a trial of some activists, including Gudrun Ensslin and her boyfriend Andreas Baader. At the trial, Ulrike listens in when Gudrun's parents are interviewed on the radio:

JOURNALIST: How has your relationship to your daughter changed with this act?
FATHER: It was surprising for me to see how Gudrun, who was always very rational, reached a state of almost euphoric self-realization through this act. A holy self-realization.
MOTHER: I sense that she has achieved something liberating, even in the family. Suddenly, I myself feel liberated from a constriction and the fear that previously dominated my life. She released me from my fears.

In the next scene, the music intensifies and Ulrike, clearly inspired by what she has learnt about Gudrun, is shown energetically writing an article about resistance for a political journal. Ulrike decides to arrange a meeting with Gudrun. What I would like to emphasise here is that from the beginning of the film the two women's political conviction seems to stem from different places. We learn how Gudrun's political conviction is almost religious, whereas for Ulrike it is a failed marriage, a cheating husband and, as a result, ultimately a search for another calling that drives her. Their different views on motherhood are portrayed in their very first meeting:

ULRIKE: What about your son?

GUDRUN: If you are serious, you have to be able to **make** such **sacrifices.**
    Andreas has a little girl as well.
ULRIKE: I could **never leave my children**

This scene communicates first of all that the difference between these women is placed within their roles as mothers. Gudrun has sacrificed her motherhood-role in order to pursue her political aims and in order to function as a perpetrator of political violence. Ulrike, however, says she could never make such a sacrifice. The scene also emphasises the film's central focus on motherhood rather than fatherhood. In the film, we see both Gudrun's son and Ulrike's two daughters, whereas Andreas' daughter is only mentioned once and never shown. In this sense, similarly to how 'fatherhood' was often invisible in the representation of Faye Turney's story, the two women's motherhood is visible whereas Andreas Baader's fatherhood is invisible

Furthermore, as the film progresses Ulrike's identity as a suitable mother is compromised. When some of the most prominent RAF members travel to Jordan for guerrilla training with the Palestine Liberation Organization (PLO), Ulrike's children are being looked after by other members in Sicily. In Jordan, there is a meeting between Andreas, Gudrun, Ulrike and the camp organisers regarding Ulrike's children:

GUDRUN: We have a problem with Ulrike's kids. They are in Sicily now but
    they cannot stay there any longer. Is it possible to send them to Jordan to
    one of these camps for Palestinian orphans?
MAN: Generally speaking yes, but if we accept them, she will never see them again.

Gudrun answers the man 'yes'. During the discussion, Ulrike remains quiet and passively looks down. She seems shocked by what has been arranged, yet, she does not protest. These scenes not only show Ulrike's passivity towards Gudrun and Andreas but it also constructs her as weak and unable to protect her children. She seems to accept the decision for her children to be sent away to become resistance fighters, despite her earlier declaration that she would never be able to leave her children. There has been a shift: Ulrike's willingness and capability to mother has changed; motherhood is no longer her 'first duty'. The change is portrayed as a personal failure and a process told through, and enriched by, her escalating mental ill health and subsequent suicide. In contrast, Gudrun Ensslin's sacrifice of motherhood is unproblematic, a rational decision, due to her political conviction; religiously justified by her parents, a sacrifice that has to be made.

Passivity

Another way in which Ulrike and Gudrun are positioned against each other, with Ulrike as the victimised object, is their conversations about, and capacity for, political violence. In their very first meeting, Ulrike's commitment to non-violent political action is questioned by Gudrun:

GUDRUN: If they shoot our people like Ohnesorg and Dutschke then we are going to **shoot back**. That is the logical consequence.

ULRIKE: You are not serious?

GUDRUN: All over the world armed comrades are fighting. We must show our solidarity.

ULRIKE: But we do.

GUDRUN: Even if the Fascists throw you in jail? Such sacrifices have to be made. Or do you think that your theoretical masturbation will change anything?

Perhaps in response to Gudrun's criticism, Ulrike agrees to act as the cover for the freeing of Andreas Baader. Through her role as an established journalist, she manages to organise a meeting with Baader outside of prison to 'work on a book'. The plan is for armed members of Baader's group to free him and for Ulrike to act surprised in order not to blow her cover. She changes her mind, however, and follows the RAF members by jumping out of a window. My point here is that in preparation for the freeing, Gudrun says to Ulrike: 'Just write about it afterwards. That's all you're good for anyway.' Similarly, when Gudrun tells Ulrike that her theoretical masturbation is not working, she is critiquing Ulrike for passivity, not real action. This is one scene in which Gudrun is written as the active masculinised subject, whereas Ulrike is the passive feminised object (see also discussion in Chapter 4).

As the film continues, the division between the two women increases and it is this rift that is portrayed as the main tension within the core group of the RAF. In prison, Gudrun starts to write the group's statements instead of Ulrike:

ULRIKE: Why are you changing my texts?

GUDRUN: Because the stuff you write is depressing.

ULRIKE: I don't understand why you are doing this. You swoop on every mistake I make! I can't take it! Your deceit drives me up the wall!

GUDRUN: You wait! I'm so sick of your bouts of exhaustion! I'm so fed up with them! You want me to snap!

In the following scene, the two women are yet again arguing. Then, Andreas is seen reading a letter from Gudrun:

GUDRUN: You want to know about Ulrike? It's sinister. A vampire, trembling with bloodlust. Ulrike's two laughs during work were necrophilic, hysterical, absolutely ugly and clearly directed against me... Although I still say it's directed less against me than against you.

When Ulrike shows the group a new statement she has written, Andreas reads it, says 'it's crap' and tears it apart. Gudrun is sitting with her back turned towards Ulrike.

ULRIKE: You are giving me false information or Gudrun completely rewrites my stuff. Why do you do that? (She asks Gudrun.) To torment me? Still with her back facing Ulrike, Gudrun says:

GUDRUN: To pay back your tormenting. (Gudrun turns her head, looks Ulrike in the eyes.) An eye for an eye.

ULRIKE: I don't get it, or I don't want to. But I can't take it anymore.

GUDRUN: **I'm no witch, but I've learned to be brutal**.

After one of the trial sessions, Gudrun whispers to Ulrike:

GUDRUN: You are the knife in the RAF's back.

Ulrike never goes back to the trials, she takes her own life. The tension within the RAF, portrayed as a split between Gudrun and Ulrike, ultimately pushes Ulrike towards mental ill health and suicide. By portraying the tension between Ulrike and Gudrun as one between femininity and masculinity, however, the film reinforces traditional ideas about gender, agency and political violence where masculinity is associated with power, rationality, aggression, brutality, agency, violence, strong etc., whereas femininity is associated with not only emotionality, passivity, weakness and non-violence, but also hysteria and mental-illness.

Emotionality

Motherhood is also a key thread when it comes to the way Ulrike is written as a victimised object through emotionality. First, Ulrike's hesitation about the use of political violence is in part communicated through what I refer to as 'maternal insights'. For example, this is the case in the scene depicting the freeing of Andreas Baader. In the scene, Baader is accompanied by two armed guards. Aware of the plan to free Baader, and that the RAF members might use violence, Ulrike asks a policeman:

ULRIKE: Are you married? Do you have children?

POLICEMAN: Yes, wife and children.

ULRIKE: Oh.

The tone in her voice is disappointed. Ulrike is expressing doubt over the possibility of making a child fatherless. Aware of the risk that the officer might get injured or killed, Ulrike's hesitation about violence is communicated through maternal feelings with connotations to nurturing, caring, affection and attachment. By depicting Ulrike as showing maternal feelings, her role as a woman and a mother is emphasised which enables the writing of her as the feminised subject for whom participation in violence is not natural.

This resonates with how, as discussed in Chapter 1, representations of female terrorists tend to portray their justification for turning violent in personal terms such as that they could not have children or in other ways had failed in their traditional roles as women. Similarly, as touched upon above, Ulrike's motivation to join the RAF is portrayed as a result of her failed marriage and cheating husband. Later, when a friend, Peter, questions her decision to play a part in the freeing of Andreas Baader (discussed below): 'This is crazy!', Ulrike responds 'I have to do it'. Thus, the freeing of Baader, and for Ulrike to play an active part in it, is personal. Both Ulrike and Peter know that this decision is a shift, from her previous commitment to non-violence to actively supporting the use of political violence.

Moreover, the writing of Ulrike as the weak, feminised, passive object and Gudrun as the active, masculinised subject is made through the display of emotions. For example, when the two women, on different occasions, are arrested, they are portrayed in contrasting ways. Gudrun is arrested for carrying a gun in a clothes shop. She violently tries to resist and the music in the background is fast, energetic and action movie-like. When Ulrike is arrested, however, she collapses and starts to cry. She makes no attempt to resist while despondent background music starts to play. Overall, Ulrike is shown crying several times, whereas Gudrun is not.

Another personal relationship that seems to convince Ulrike about a 'turn to violence' is her relationship with Rudi Dutschke, a union leader. We see Ulrike attend a meeting where Dutschke is speaking. He recognises that she is there and smiles at her, they seem to be close friends. Soon afterwards Dutschke is shot by a right-wing extremist. He survives, but is brain-damaged. When Ulrike hears about the shooting on the radio she starts to cry. This seems to be yet another personal trauma for Ulrike. In combination, what is communicated is that Ulrike ends up as a female perpetrator of political violence due to personal traumas and failures.

Lynndie

Womenandchildren

As mentioned above, women's gendered bodies are also denied adult status by being associated with children. This is how Lynndie England was belittled and written as a victim, especially by her own defence team during the trials. A psychologist who examined England as a child was called to give evidence and portrayed her as a '**blue baby**', deprived of oxygen at birth, and also suffering from a malformation of her tongue that required it to be clipped. The psychologist also found her suffering 'from an inability to process information, an ailment affecting fewer than **2 children** in 100' (Blumenthal, *New York Times*, 4 May 2005). The defence team's argument was that she in this way was a victim who could not tell right from wrong and was only doing as she was told:

> 'The entire case, what this has always been about, is authority,' Captain Crisp said. 'Pfc. England's **blind compliance toward authority** and her **lack of authority** in any context.'
>
> (Cloud, *New York Times*, 27 September 2005)

Lynndie England's insinuated low level of intelligence was also echoed by the judge:

> Then he [Judge Colonel Pohl] turned to Private England. 'Maybe you think we forgot about you,' he said, trying to explain the ruling to her but realizing, he said, **'I'm not sure you'll understand**.'
>
> (Blumenthal, *New York Times*, 5 May 2005)

> Standing **just over five feet tall** and speaking almost inaudibly, with little emotion, Private England testified in court at Fort Hood that she went along with the demands of a fellow soldier, Specialist Charles A. Graner Jr., thinking 'it was just for his personal amusement.'
>
> (Levy, *New York Times*, 3 May 2005)

In an interview with Tara McKelvey, published as 'Lynndie England in love', Janis Karpinski recollects her memory of when she first met England:

> I shook her hand. I remember that her hand was very small. She was small, you know. Not assertive or aggressive. She seemed nondescript. Honestly, she was young and innocent.
>
> (McKelvey 2007: 213)

Karpinski, trying to explain how someone like England might have ended up where she did, also comments on England's intelligence:

> She probably felt inferior because she was working alongside military police. They seemed more important than she did. Also, she recognized her own mental limitations. I don't mean she's retarded. But she's slow.
>
> (McKelvey 2007: 214)

Passivity

In one of her first interviews, Lynndie England said that she was only following orders. In the *Daily Star* this story got the title 'Lynndie **told to pose**' (Unattributed, *Daily Star*, 13 May 2004). Again, the title suggests passivity rather than agency and England is written as an object in a story in which Graner is the subject and main character:

> 'Did you think any of this was wrong?' the judge asked. 'Why were you doing it?' **He asked me to**, she said, referring to Specialist Graner.
>
> (Levy, *New York Times*, 3 May 2005)

> Her lawyer Capt Jonathan Crisp said: Her role in this is not what it was initially thought to be. **She was a pawn**.
>
> (Unattributed, *Daily Mirror*, 30 April 2005)

The focus on her height, her insinuated low level of intelligence and the alleged lack of authority associates Lynndie England with childhood and writes her as a passive victim who is denied adulthood. This is how the writing of England as an object denies agency in political violence. This is how victim stories are told as inversions of motherhood.

> [S]he is, as she says, weak and passive and the sort of woman who is an **easy mark for a man with the gift of fibbery**. This was Charles A. Graner Jr., her superior and boyfriend, father of her child, and stock character in every country-western song: He left her and the baby for another woman. As is very often the case in life and literature … the perpetrator is often also a victim. No reading of England's life story can stand any other interpretation. She is one of life's losers.
>
> (Cohen, *Washington Post*, 1 October 2005)

Emotionality

In Errol Morris' documentary *Standard Operating Procedure* (Morris 2008) England defends her actions at Abu Ghraib prison by saying 'it was all because of a man'. This was also a common thread in the media representation during the trials:

> I was embarrassed because I was used by Private Graner; I didn't realise it at the time … I **trusted** him and I **loved** him.
>
> (Unattributed, *The Times*, 28 September 2005)

> England's defence countered that England was only trying to please her soldier boyfriend, then-Cpl. Charles Graner Jr., labelled the abuse ringleader by prosecutors: 'She was **a follower**, she was an individual who was **smitten** with Graner,' Crisp said. 'She just did whatever he wanted her to do'.
>
> (Gutierrez, *USA Today*, 26 September 2005)

> [S]he was **under the influence of Charles Graner**, an enlisted man who was her boyfriend and who oversaw an Abu Ghraib cellblock … 'Those pictures don't show the absolute amazing trust she placed in him **because she loved him**.'
>
> (Cloud, *New York Times*, 22 September 2005)

By emphasising England's emotionality, the defence team tried to put focus on England's identity as a woman and highlight that it is alien for a woman to participate in such activities. By associating her behaviour with emotionality, however, England is also associated with a lack of authority. While this is likely to have been the defence team's desired outcome, it was also a predominant representation of England in the media at the time of her trials. By being portrayed as a victim of her own emotions and lacking authority, England is disciplined as 'just a woman' who could not help herself but was blinded by love. In fact, England was not even allowed the right to plead guilty because a court determined that she 'could have been so manipulated by her boyfriend as to have lost her sense of right and wrong' (Sjoberg 2007: 96).

Female Agents

Female Agents is a film, supposedly, about heroines in war. While I show in the next chapter how such heroism is mainly communicated through motherhood, here I focus my discussion on scenes in which the main characters are written as victimised objects. In particular, I discuss *passivity* and *emotionality* as ways in which gender, agency and political violence are communicated.

Passivity

Similarly to the way Faye Turney is represented, Louise, the main character in *Female Agents*, is, as soon as one learns she is pregnant (see discussion on motherhood in Chapter 4), often portrayed in passive tense. For example, at two different occasions, Louise's life is saved by other agents; she misses her shot at Heindrich and is subsequently captured. In captivity, she is tortured before being saved by her brother Pierre and towards the end she is rescued by Jeanne, twice. In these scenes, Louise is acted upon rather than acting; she is the object, rather than the subject of these scenes. To develop this argument, I start by discussing the torture scene:

When Pierre, who initially formed the group of female agents, is brought into the room where Louise is being 'interrogated', Louise is sat on a chair with her arms tied behind her back in handcuffs. Louise, wearing her underdress only, is visibly tortured; her legs shivering at times. Heindrich, the German Nazi officer asks:

HEINDRICH: Why have you tried to kill me twice, Louise?

Louise says nothing, looks down, whereupon another officer hits her so that she falls off the chair. She gets pulled back up. By letting Pierre watch the torture of his sister, Heindrich and his men are trying to make Pierre give up secret information about the resistance movement. The communication of this scene is mainly between the two male characters – Heindrich and Pierre – but, importantly, the 'conversation' is taking place through/on Louise's female body. Thus, in these scenes, Louise's body is a tool for communication between the two male bodies involved.

For example, when Louise has been hit and is pulled back up on the chair, Heindrich sits down in front of Pierre. At this point, the camera angle is from behind Pierre, depicting Louise and an officer in the background behind Heindrich. The gaze of the narrative is thereby told from Pierre's perspective.

Pierre is the main character in this scene. Heindrich keeps asking Pierre the same questions, yet, he refuses to give in. We watch Louise's head being held under water (a practice that resonates to infamous interrogation techniques such as waterboarding forming part of 'war on terror'-discourses). Pierre still does not speak.

HEINDRICH: I thought a brother and a sister's love was the strongest. (Louise is still being held under water). I wish I had a sister like Louise. I would hate to have a brother like you.

In the next scene in the torture chamber, Pierre is in a stress position with his hands tied in handcuffs attached to the ceiling (again, something the audience would be familiar from infamous practices at Guantanamo Bay and Abu Ghraib). Two officers in the background are hitting Louise in the stomach. These torture scenes are overlapping with scenes in which Gaelle, who is held in a cell in the same building, is preparing to take her own life. Choir-like sacral music interlinks the two scenes powerfully as Gaelle is taking her own life and Pierre is reflecting over whether or not to save his sister (who never asks him to do so).

In the room next door, Gaelle naked lies down on the floor. She tells a prayer and swallows a cyanide pill. The music intensifies and the camera shots from the ceiling show Gaelle as Jesus on the cross, arms out to the sides. The religious references are very strong, both visually and through the music. A power over life is communicated in the collage of images moving from Pierre and Louise's situation in the torture chamber and Gaelle's in her cell. In the torture chamber, Pierre has power over Louise's life and by taking her own life, Gaelle is retaking control over her own. As I return to below, the overlap between the two scenes later also sees Pierre take his own life, and the audience later learns that Louise loses her unborn baby as a result of the torture. Thus, the overlap between the scenes functions to create a narrative of life, death, sacrifice but also agency.

HEINDRICH: She can't take much more. You can still **save her**. (The same sacral music is still playing).
PIERRE: If I talk, do I have your word she will live?
HEINDRICH: I give you my word.
PIERRE: I want your word as an officer.
HEINDRICH: Stop! (the torturing).

As he finally gives in, Pierre starts sobbing.

HEINDRICH: I'll keep my promise. Your sister's life will be spared.

Pierre looks at Louise, she moves her lip slightly in a covered smile of gratitude, she seems thankful. What is communicated in these torture scenes is that, despite Louise's endurance and bravery, she is still saved by her brother. Pierre's heroic act of protecting his sister has overshadowed Louise's heroism. This is how, despite Louise's bravery, it is Pierre, the male subject, who through the Myth of Protection is protecting Louise, the passive victim in need of protection. The focus in this scene, moreover, is the 'dialogue' between Pierre and Heindrich. They are the subjects (male) whereas Louise (female) is a silent and passive object in the background. Also, the fact that Heindrich is willing to 'let the woman go', despite the fact that she is the one who has tried to kill him twice shows how much more of a valued 'asset' Pierre is (see also earlier discussion on 'letting the woman go' in the case of Faye Turney). In other words, even in a film emphasising women's heroism, male characters are still the main actors.

Emotionality

In *Female Agents*, Suzy is the only one of the agents who has no previous military training. Instead, although Suzy herself is unaware, she was chosen for the mission because she had had a relationship with Heindrich. This is how the SOE planned to get close to the enemy and, ultimately, to affect him. However, the plan backfires. In a similar way to how Lynndie England is represented as a victimised object for being in love, and therefore naïve/ irrational enough to end up in the situation she did at Abu Ghraib prison, Suzy fails to control her feelings for a man.

When Louise and the other agents have been captured or killed, Suzy is Buckmaster's (the Head of the SOE) last chance to assassinate Heindrich. The plan is for Suzy to meet, seduce and subsequently kill him, her former lover.

HEINDRICH: Liliane, (Suzy's real name) … for three years I refused to believe you were dead. Why did you leave? (Suzy turns around, faces him.)
SUZY: Our love was doomed.
HEINDRICH: Give us another chance. Come with me. I am leaving for Germany tonight.

Suzy pulls out her gun and points it at him.

HEINDRICH: Did Buckmaster send you? You are one of his agents? Don't let them sully the beauty of what we had.

Heindrich takes a few steps closer, Suzy hesitates. He takes her hand with which she is holding the gun, gently puts her down on the bed with him on top. He takes the gun from her hand and unloads it. He seduces her, holds her hand and they kiss. In the next scene, from a car on the street outside Jeanne hears a shot, and then a sole melancholic violin tune starts to play. We see both Heindrich and Suzy lying on the bed with their eyes closed but we do not know who is dead. Then, watching from a car outside, Jeanne sees a body bag being carried away and Heindrich appears. At this moment, the music intensifies with darker lower keys associated with danger. It seems that 'evil' in the shape of Heindrich has won this battle. Heindrich reaches for the body in order to touch Suzy once more but blood evaporates from the sheets. He is clearly upset about what he had to do and we understand that he is still in love with her. Importantly, however, Heindrich manages to not let his (personal) feelings for Suzy interfere with his role as a military commander at war. While Suzy was unable to perform her task, too weak and emotional, Heindrich killed his former love interest when he realised her intentions. In this sense, Suzy is the emotional victim, unable to kill because she is unable to control her feelings, whereas Heindrich is the rational subject, able to control his emotions and, as a result, able to kill.

Suzy's failure to execute her mission also has serious consequences for the others in the group. Furious, Henidrich returns to Louise and Pierre in the torture chamber and changes the initial agreement to let Louise go.

HEINDRICH: You should never have used her! You will be transferred to La Roquette prison. I am taking your brother to Germany with me. It is probably the last time you will see each other. Take him away!

Pierre fights loose and manages to pick up a sharp object and slit his throat. Louise screams 'No, No, No!' as she watches her brother die.

HEINDRICH: The only thing I can do for you now is to commute your death sentence to deportation. What do you choose?
LOUISE: Execution!
HEINDRICH: I will make the arrangements. Take him away. (Louise is looking at Pierre's dead body).

In this scene, Louise defiantly opts for execution rather than imprisonment. However, as it is represented, she does this because her brother just killed himself. Louise has now nothing to live for. Again, Louise's decision is influenced by her private relationships.

The display of emotions and emotionality is also a noticeable change when it comes to how Gaelle is portrayed before and after her capture. While in the beginning of *Female Agents*, Gaelle is most often positioned as a tough and committed agent, an explosive expert. In captivity, however, Gaelle is instead positioned as the ultimate weak female subject. For example, when Heindrich and his men bring Gaelle into the room where Pierre is also held, Gaelle is stripped of her clothes until she is standing in her underwear only. She is crying quietly. Heindrich asks Pierre:

HEINDRICH: Where are your accomplices hiding? And the Phoenixes? What are they for?

While Pierre says nothing, Gaelle wets herself. At this moment, there is an extreme close-up on her underwear that takes up the whole screen. As mentioned above, close-ups are used to emphasise an object's qualities and to draw attention to what makes it different. The close-up, Mitry argues, 'appeals to the emotions but these can only be felt, experienced by seeing it' (Mitry 2000: 67). Therefore, by showing her underwear in a close-up as she wets herself, an emphasis on Gaelle's fear, weakness and vulnerability is communicated. This scene is also yet another reminder that women cannot control their emotions. An officer puts Gaelle on a chair and pulls out one of her finger nails. Gaelle screams out loud. Again, there is a close-up on her face as she immediately gives up information regarding where the female agents were meeting up:

GAELLE: The Duroc Institute for the Blind. (Gaelle is crying). We were to meet there to await orders for a new mission.

The next scene focuses on Pierre's face as he looks down visibly disappointed. Later, when the two prisoners are chained to the walls of the same room, Pierre asks Gaelle about her cyanide pill, insinuating that she should have taken her own life instead of being put in a situation where she would give up information. There is a close-up on Gaelle's face as she turns away and says:

GAELLE: I am scared. You don't know what that means.

Later, when Heindrich enters the room, he offers Gaelle a white tissue but she refuses. The camera is filming from Gaelle's perspective. Heindrich crouches down to be level with Gaelle and the camera.

HEINDRICH: I am going to need your services again. Your friends got away from me. Where and when was the back-up?
GAELLE: The back-up?
HEINDRICH: Don't act dumb. I know the SOE methods.
GAELLE: Louise knows that I betrayed them. She won't come to the rendez-vous. (Gaelle defiantly looks Heindrich in the eyes).
HEINDRICH: She is a woman who likes to take risks.
GAELLE: If I talk, what is in it for me?
HEINDRICH: Your freedom.
GAELLE: To be tried and sentenced by the SOE?
HEINDRICH: You prefer that we torture you? (Gaelle looks down, her nose starts to bleed.)
GAELLE: Tomorrow noon. Concorde Metro, Pont de Neilly platform.

The agents had been told that, in the event of a capture, they must endure at least 48 hours of captivity, even if they are being tortured, before they can reveal any secret information in order for the other agents to get to safety. Gaelle, however, gives up the information almost immediately. What is interesting is that in earlier scenes, when Gaelle was mainly positioned/written in relation to other female characters, she was positioned as a subject. In captivity, however, when she is positioned against male characters, she is written as the ultimate female victim. More specifically, Gaelle's fear is visually communicated through her body; it is her body that ultimately reveals her feelings. Again, she fails to hide/control her emotions. In addition to the emphasis on the physical effects of her fear, Gaelle's fear is also highlighted by the use of particular camera angles. The display of fear and vulnerability through Gaelle's body, in combination with the fact that she gives up secret information almost immediately under duress, resonates with common assumptions that women's presence risks endangering the mission. In this sense, the narrative gaze is telling a familiar story of women's unsuitability for war due to their inability to control their bodies and their emotions, which ultimately makes them weak and therefore a liability. This, of course, resonates strongly with the cultural grammar involved in the media coverage of Faye Turney's capture, particularly the focus on Turney's fear in captivity. Read in combination, these two stories of fearful female bodies, whether 'true' or not, contribute to reinforce traditional understandings of gender, agency and political violence about male subjects and female victimised objects.

Furthermore, in a similar way to how *The Baader-Meinhof Complex* starts by showing Ulrike as a mother and a wife, i.e. her private role and relationships, *Female Agents* starts by showing Louise as responsible for her husband's death. In this scene, Louise is a sniper in a group of resistance fighters. At one moment, Louise is supposed to give fire in order to cover one of the others. However, her weapon jams and as a result the man whom she was supposed to protect is shot and killed. Louise looks up from the rifle sight, takes a sharp breath of air, seems shocked but has to run off in order to save her own life. In the next scene, Louise meets up with her brother Pierre, who offers his condolences to Louise for the death of her husband. Thus, we understand that the man killed in the initial scenes that Louise failed to protect was her own husband.

Female Agents also includes a couple of emotional displays of what one might call 'irrational grief'. I call these displays irrational as they, to me, stand out in the overall portrayal of a particular character that in most other scenes are portrayed as calculating and rational. This is the case with Jeanne in the scene when she realises that Heindrich has killed Suzy.

Watching from a car, Jeanne sees Heindrich walking out from the hotel where Suzy was supposed to kill him. She understands that the dead body brought out is Suzy's. Upset and overcome with feelings for revenge, she tells the driver of the car:

JEANNE: Give me your gun!
MAN: What for?
JEANNE: The mission is to kill him.
MAN: You're **mad**. Not here!

Jeanne calms down and quietly agrees, puts her head in her hands. In an earlier scene, it is Louise who, as she watches her brother Pierre's capture, acts distraught and irrational by attempting to shoot at the Germans, an act that would have endangered the whole group of agents' survival. What is interesting in these two examples is that in both scenes it is only because others intervene and physically stop them to shoot that they manage not to blow their cover. In Louise's case, it is one of the other agents that physically stops her from firing her weapon, in Jeanne's it is the [male] driver. In both cases, these characters are out of control, i.e. not in control of their emotions.

The scene in which Jeanne 'loses it' is particularly interesting as she, in comparison to all the other female agents, is most often portrayed as the strongest and in many ways the 'true' heroine in *Female Agents*. In this scene, however, the male driver has to calm her down and to force her to reconsider her urge to kill Heindrich; to act rationally. In this scene, Jeanne is positioned in relation to two other male subjects: Heindrich and the driver. It seems, therefore, that the writing of Jeanne as a heroic subject is limited to discursive contexts in which she is positioned in relation to other female bodies. The subject positioning of this scene shows that in relation to male subjects, Jeanne is still written as the emotional and irrational stereotypical female, while male bodies are written as rational subjects.

Janis

Womenandchildren

In a similar way to how Jeanne is allowed agency in relation to other female bodies but not in relation to male bodies, it is interesting how Janis Karpinski was represented in comparison to male colleagues. She was portrayed as not being in control of her soldiers and as a naïve leader unable to understand the implications of her leadership: 'MP Commander: "No knowledge" of alleged abuse' (CNN, 4 May 2004). The same day, the *Sun* headlined an article 'JAIL BOSS IN DENIAL' (Unattributed, *Sun*, 4 May 2004). A few days earlier, the *Daily Mail* published an article titled 'They love it here said General Janis' (Unattributed, *Daily Mail*, 30 April 2004). Not only does this article imply that Karpinski has no idea about what is actually happening at Abu Ghraib and is, therefore, lacking control and authority, but interestingly it also refers to Karpinski by using her first name only. As mentioned above in relation to female suicide bombers in Palestine, the representation of a first name only indicates that the subject lacks authority, a step towards being infantilised. This is repeated in the text of the article where 'colleagues', who are anonymous, critique 'Janis':

> **Colleagues** of the tough, super-fit officer last night described her as a woman with one mission to raise her own profile. One colleague said: '**Janis** sees herself as making way for women to get to the top in the US

Army. But many of her soldiers said she had been promoted beyond her ability because she was a woman.'

(Churcher and Graham, *Mail on Sunday*, 2 May 2004)

In the independent panel's report (the Schlesinger report) about the Abu Ghraib scandal, published in the *New York Times*, Karpinski was portrayed as an incompetent leader in need of mentoring:

We believe Lt. Gen. [Ricardo] Sanchez should have taken stronger action in November when he realized the extent of the leadership problems at Abu Ghraib. His **attempt to mentor** Brig. Gen. [Janis] Karpinski, though well-intended, was insufficient in a combat zone in the midst of a serious and growing insurgency.

(Unattributed, *New York Times*, 25 August 2004)

According to Karpinski, her leadership abilities were never in doubt:

Gen. Sanchez never once – not once did he ever mention to me his concerns about my leadership ability. He never mentored me, he never suggested that I try something differently, he never criticized me, not once.

(Karpinski, *Signal City*, 4 July 2004)

The *Washington Post* quoted an unclassified report by an Air Force psychiatrist who studied 'physical abuses by US military police of Iraqi prison detainees':

Nelson said Karpinski had difficulty delegating work, dismissed punishments of lesser officers that were recommended by her staff, and was ineffective in resolving problems with personnel, logistics, administration and supplies, of which she was aware. Karpinski '**felt herself a victim** and she propagated a negativity that permeated throughout' the area of her command responsibility, Nelson wrote.

(Smith, *Washington Post*, 24 May 2004)

Furthermore, after Karpinski left the Army, she was described as an abandoned child. An article published in The *Times* was titled 'My army life: **lonely**, restless and **afraid**'. The author suggests that she is lonely and 'now that she has lost the crutch of the Army, feels somewhat **abandoned**.' The article says: 'She lives alone in South Carolina and **never had children**.' Karpinski is quoted saying: 'If anybody wanted kids more than the other, George did. Not that I didn't want them. It just wasn't on the cards. And you have to be together occasionally' (de Bertodano, *The Times*, 13 August 2004). Here, Karpinski is written as a victim, both according to her own supposed feelings and by being associated with childhood. In addition, her choice of not having children is turned into a punishment as she is assumed to be lonely when she has left/been kicked out of the 'family' of the army. By representing Karpinski as in need of mentoring and as a victim herself, she is associated with childhood and a lack of authority. Ultimately, she is denied agency in these discursive practices.

Approximately a year after the images were released and Karpinski had been framed as a weak leader, she received her penalty. Her rank was reduced to colonel and she was issued a reprimand and relieved of her command. However, she was not officially punished for what happened at Abu Ghraib:

> The Army said Karpinski was guilty of dereliction of duty and shoplifting. Investigators did not substantiate allegations that she made a false statement to an investigating team and failed to obey a lawful order. Karpinski was relieved of command of the 800th Military Police Brigade on April 8. President Bush had to approve the Pentagon's action against Karpinski.
>
> (Moniz, *USA Today*, 6 May 2005)

> 'Though Brig. Gen. Karpinski's performance of duty was found to be seriously lacking, the investigation determined that no action or lack of action on her part contributed specifically to the abuse of detainees at Abu Ghraib,' according to an Army news release.
>
> (White, *Washington Post*, 6 May 2005)

Despite having been officially cleared from the abuse at Abu Ghraib, Karpinski is commonly referred to as the highest ranked officer to have been punished for the scandal. She also remains the only General ever to have been demoted in the US army (Karpinski, *Signal City*, 13 November 2005).

Emotionality

The display of emotions and emotionality also played an important role in the representation of Karpinski, both by the way in which her feelings were used to construct her as a weak leader, in effect to make her a scapegoat for the prison scandal, and by herself in an attempt to revalue such emotionality as leadership skills. For example, Janis Karpinski was considered 'extremely emotional' by General Taguba in the investigation of the 800th Military Police brigade:

> BG Karpinski was **extremely emotional** during much of her testimony. What I found particularly disturbing in her testimony was her complete unwillingness to either understand or accept that many of the problems inherent in the 800th MP Brigade were caused or exacerbated by poor leadership and the refusal of her command to both establish and enforce basic standards and principles among its soldiers.
>
> (Taguba 2004)

Karpinski defended being emotional by arguing that she is a caring boss who indeed will get emotional when defending her soldiers. However, Karpinski also claims that she was not the only person involved being emotional:

> But it wasn't me who was overwhelmed. Every man in that room – and there were six of them – was in tears when my statement was finished. Every one of them. Including Taguba. And I think that they were embarrassed by that, and that's why he made that comment in the report.
>
> (Karpinski, *Signal City*, 4 July 2004)

If true, this echoes displays of emotions in the Faye Turney story, where her feelings were first-page news whereas the men's feelings and fears remained invisible or at least sidelined. That this has to do with femininity/masculinity (rather than women/men) is also shown in the example from *The Baader-Meinhof Complex* where displays of emotionality are associated with the feminised character, Ulrike, but absent in relation to the masculinised subject, Gudrun.

The construction of Karpinski as a weak leader was made through a strategy of feminisation. Karpinski was not only feminised but also infantilised by the fact that she 'felt like a victim' herself; by being referred to by first name only; by not being in control and therefore in need of mentoring by male colleagues; and by being 'extremely emotional'. True or false, the shoplifting incident could be seen to add yet another layer to her feminisation. This gendering was vital in order to construct her as a weak leader.

Nasima

Emotionality

In the story of the female suicide bomber in the television drama *Britz*, Nasima is written as a victim through emotionality in two main ways: by being motivated by personal relationships and by the insertion of doubts and maternal insights. First, by describing her motivations as personal, Nasima is portrayed as acting out of desperation. In the beginning of *Britz*, however, Nasima is acting out her dissatisfaction with the situation for British Muslims in non-violent ways. She takes part in demonstrations and she voices concerns about the radicalisation of British Muslims and the resort to violence as a means for change. Similar to how the story of Ulrike Meinhof in *The Baader-Meinhof Complex* begins, Nasima is convinced political issues should be solved through democratic means. At the end, however, Nasima has become radicalised and transformed into a suicide bomber. In particular, Nasima's radicalisation takes place as a response to two failed personal relationships: her relationship with Sabia, her best friend, and Jude, her secret boyfriend. Sabia, whose brother is under surveillance by counter-terrorism agencies, ends up being incarcerated for buying a larger amount of spices. In prison, she is humiliated and later tells Nasima she was 'touched'. Once released, Sabia is put under a control order and not allowed to see her friends or leave the house. As a result of the trauma, Sabia eventually commits suicide. The second failed personal relationship is with Jude, one of her fellow medical students. Nasima is afraid her family will not accept Jude as her boyfriend because he is black and so their relationship is secret. As expected, when Nasima's father finds out, she is sent off to Pakistan to meet and plan a marriage to a local man.

Jude finds Nasima in Pakistan, but members of Nasima's 'new family' attack him. Nasima flees, assuming Jude has been killed. Nasima now finds herself in a desperate situation as she has run away from the family she was supposed to marry into, her father thinks she has put shame upon their family because she has had a (sexual) relationship with a man without being married, she believes her boyfriend has been killed and her best friend has committed suicide. Before leaving the UK Nasima had made arrangements to train as a fighter in Pakistan and because of her flight from her new 'family', this route is now Nasima's only choice. Although the meeting was arranged before Jude showed up, the latest trauma for Nasima seems to function as another push towards violent resolutions and no turning back. When training is over and Nasima needs to make up her mind about the suicide mission, the camp organisers reveal that they have faked her death. Nasima is shown a photo of her family attending her funeral. In effect, Nasima now has no choice. She cannot go back to her old life in Britain any more. She has got nothing to lose.

Nasima's personal motivation for her actions is also demonstrated when the man who is helping her prepare for her mission says 'You'll sit at God's right hand'. Nasima replies: 'That's not why I'm doing it'. Instead, Nasima is taking revenge for her friend but she is also acting out of despair. Although Nasima's martyrdom statement issuing her political reasons is shown in the epilogue, Nasima is written as desperate. This representation is ordered by *emotionality* because by representing Nasima as motivated by personal rather than political reasons, her agency is denied and she is but a victim. This portrayal also echoes how female 'terrorists' are represented in mass media as discussed above. It 'makes sense' that a female perpetrator of violence is driven by personal motivations.

Second, in a similar way to how Ulrike hesitates about the use of political violence through maternal insights in the beginning of *The Baader-Meinhof Complex*, Nasima is expressing concerns about the target of her attack. When she finds out about the location, she asks: 'Who will be there?' The man helping her with her final preparations says it is bankers on a lunch-break with their families. Nasima looks up, seems troubled and says: 'I didn't realise there would be children there.' At this point, a simple melody which will run until Nasima reaches her target starts to play. Background music is usually used in order to establish a specific mood or emotion. In these scenes, the music is played in minor keys giving a sparse, bleak and serious impression which functions to enrich the emotional communication of the scenes.

Nasima's hesitation about hurting children is an example of how the tension between life-giving (Myth of Motherhood) and life-taking (agency in political violence) materialises. By showing her hesitation through maternal feelings, the audience is reminded that her [a woman's] proper role is to give life, not to take it. Thus, by portraying the female subject as having maternal insights or in doubt, essentialist ideas about gender, agency and political violence are reinforced and female agency in political violence is, subsequently, rendered 'unnatural'. Moreover, the hesitation about the use of force in gendered terms in itself writes the subject as, not only emotional rather than rational, but as weak. In *Britz*, Nasima hesitates about the use of violence right until the end of the programme. For example, at a meeting with the camp organisers in Pakistan, Nasima says she has only agreed to training in the camp, not yet about 'the other', meaning the suicide mission. Moreover, shortly before Nasima leaves the house in London where she has been staying for her final mission, she phones her brother Sohail's mobile phone, but he does not answer it. The audience is reminded that Nasima hesitates about the violent mission.

Inversions of motherhood

The scenes analysed and the stories told about victimised objects in this chapter, through the three narrative tropes of *passivity*, *'womenandchildren'* and *emotionality*, means that there is a particular cultural grammar to how gender, agency and political violence are communicated in these stories. To me, this is about motherhood, or more specifically, about the way in which all three narrative tropes communicate inversions of motherhood.

This is the case when female characters are being portrayed or written in passive tense, such as when Faye Turney and Lynndie England are described as captured, paraded, veiled, exploited, told to pose and so on; infantilised such as when Janis Karpinski is in need of mentoring or Lynndie England is described as a 'blue baby'; when the female character's fear is highlighted whereas the male characters' fear is not, such as in the case of Turney's fear of rape or the zooming in on Gaelle wetting herself in *Female Agents*; or when the subject positioning writes the female character as an object in a story of male subjects, such as the torture scene in *Female Agents*.

What these scenes have in common is that female characters are understood as vulnerable and in need of protection simply because of the shape of their bodies. Sometimes this is because they are mothers, sometimes because they are, 'by default', represented as emotional/irrational/weak and in any other way feminised and thus deemed inappropriate or inadequate for whatever it is that they are doing. This is how the idea of the Myth of Protection writes these characters as victimised objects denied of agency.

Overall, this book aims to make a tension between life-giving and life-taking in representations of female agency in political violence visible. However, with this chapter, I have shown how, if one takes a closer look, in many examples of what appears to show female agency in political violence, female subjects are actually denied agency. Instead, the female body is positioned as a victimised object. My argument is that it is because of the fact that the female characters in these scenes are written as victimised objects rather than subjects with agency that there is no tension between life-giving and life-taking. The writing of the female subject as a victim, means its life-taking identity is 'removed' and agency in political violence is denied. The victimised object remains in the life-giving sphere and a normative femininity associated with motherhood is reinforced. The cultural grammar with which stories of victimised objects are communicated is maternalist and, more specifically, the type of maternalist war story told is an inversion of motherhood due to the lack of agential potential.

Notes

1 Parkin's and Webb's commentaries in the *Daily Mail* published a week apart are very similar. Not only are the arguments echoing the Myth of Protection similar, but they also use the same examples. For example, both articles quote (without referencing) an Israeli medical study that highlights women's physical limitations and both articles emphasise that the inclusion of women in combat roles will make our society weaker and more vulnerable as a whole.
2 According to EU regulations, the exclusion policy has to be reviewed every eight years.
3 With all the focus on Faye Turney wearing the headscarf, the *Daily Mail* was also quick to point out when she was not wearing it: 'the only captive woman, is shown for the first time not in an Islamic hijab'. The caption says: 'On film: Iran releases images of some hostages, apparently looking relaxed. This time, Faye Turney is not wearing the hijab' (Seamark and Chapman, *Daily Mail*, 4 April 2007).
4 See Yuval-Davies 1997 and Enloe 2000a for discussions of the historical positioning of 'other' women in tourist, nationalist and other discourses; see Brittain 2006; Kumar 2004; Ferguson 2005; Richter-Monpetit 2007; Shepherd 2006 and Steans 2008 on othering practices in the 'war on terror'; see Spivak 1999 and Said 1997 on postcolonial reason and orientalist practices; and see anthropologist Abu-Lughod on the rhetoric of 'saving Muslim women'.
5 See for example Williams 2006 for an honest description of a woman's experience as a soldier in the US army, including problems regarding not only sexual assault by fellow soldiers but also stigma attached to reporting such incidents.

4 Heroic subjects

'In times of war, heroism is not just for men.'

Slogan promoting the film *Female Agents*

'In 1949, Louise returned to France and married an architect. She was awarded the Croix de Guerre and the Légion d'Honneur. She died in 2004 at the age of 98, **childless.**'

Epilogue to *Female Agents*

In this chapter, I discuss stories of war where female bodies are written as heroic subjects in representations of political violence. The term 'heroic', however, is not meant as a value judgement of the stories and scenes covered in this chapter. We have already seen in Chapter 3, for example with *Female Agents*, that characters portrayed as heroines might in fact, if one analyses the cultural grammar, be read as victimised objects. Instead, I would like to re-emphasise the discussion in Chapter 2 on the difference between political subjectivity and subject positioning; the difference between studying how individuals act and how particular subjects are positioned with or without agency. In other words, 'heroines' is not necessarily the same as 'heroic subjects' in the sense that where the first one refers to individuals, the latter refers to subjects that in a grammatical reading of a scene or story is positioned with agency. As mentioned above, and as illustrated with the structure of this book, a particular character or person is written in multiple ways, i.e. multiple subject positions. Moreover, due to the fact that we tend to distinguish legitimate political violence, as in authorised by the state, from illegitimate political violence, which we often call terrorism, most contemporary stories about heroic female subjects in the context of political violence concern female soldiers. Likewise, a similar reasoning might explain why female 'terrorists' are often denied agency by being written as victimised objects as discussed in Chapter 1 and 3.

Here, I trace how displays of female agency in political violence (as in subjects with agency) rely on and reproduce a naturalised femininity associated with motherhood. To this end, I start by drawing on feminist scholarship on heroism and heroines more broadly in order to identify key themes or narrative tropes. I discuss three main ones that can be summarised as communicating 'before', 'through' and 'instead of' motherhood. I refer to them as the *Vacant Womb*, the *Protective Mother* and the *Masculinised Subject*. In some of these scenes with heroic subjects, motherhood is present as a naturalised constitutive other. Accordingly, the aim of this chapter is to show how the ways in which female agency in political violence is enabled have everything to do with motherhood, even when this might not be immediately apparent. The aim of this chapter is to show how a tension between identities of life-giving and life-taking needs to be removed or somehow overcome in order for agency of female bodies to be enabled.

Rambettes

First, in stories about female heroism in popular culture, the central positioning of the empty, vacant womb is common. According to Sherrie Inness, the stereotypical female heroine in popular culture is likely to be muscular but not too muscular, independent, but not as tough as the males around her, and she is typically childless (Inness 2004: 12). In her discussion of Lara Croft, the virtual heroine in the computer game 'Tomb Raider', Claudia Herbst argues that Lara Croft's body is designed to trigger sexual impulses leading up to reproduction. For example, Lara Croft's tiny waist is considered seductive because it indicates she is not pregnant and thus 'available' for the act of procreation. However, Herbst argues, Lara Croft's presence denies everything related to reproduction; the question of menstruation, pregnancy and potential for motherhood. Biologically, Lara Croft is not capable of reproducing (Herbst 2004: 28–35). The tension between life-giving and life-taking for female bodies is also cemented in military service drafts. For example, in Israel, women have been drafted for military service, but only to age 24 *or motherhood*, whichever comes first, whereas it is life-long for men (Goldstein 2001: 86). As wives or mothers they are not suited for military service, for risking their life. Instead, their role is to give life. Both of these examples emphasises agency in violence *before* motherhood.

Another famous example of the writing of a war heroine is the mass media representation of US soldier Jessica Lynch, the first American heroine of the war in Iraq in 2003. Lynch was involved in an incident that left eleven US soldiers killed and seven captured. Lynch was injured, captured and then rescued by Special Forces from the Iraqi hospital where she had been treated. Lynch was immediately constructed as a heroine: a 'maintenance clerk turned woman-warrior' (Priest *et al.* 2003: 1). However, there were in fact three American women involved in the incident and, consequently, there were three potential heroines: Private Jessica Lynch, Private Lori Ann Piestewa and Specialist Shoshana Johnson. Pietstewa died from her injuries. Like Lynch, Johnson was taken hostage. Like Lynch, Johnson was also rescued. Even though Johnson was held hostage much longer than Lynch and even though she had engaged in fighting, it was Lynch who was constructed as a

'Rambette' even though she had actually been hiding for cover when her weapon jammed (Sjolander and Trevenen 2010: 159; Kampfner 2003). In this sense, the writing of Lynch as the heroine meant not only that the others' stories remained untold and their agency denied but the writing of Lynch as the heroine also highlighted how her whiteness was crucial to the story. Various scholars (see for example Sjoberg 2007; Kumar 2004; Brittain 2006) have argued that the exclusion of Piestewa, a Native American, and Johnson, who is African American, exposes the racial aspect of appropriate femininity; within the discourse of white supremacy, neither Johnson nor Piestewa could figure as all-American heroines:

> As 'women of color', they do not fit into the category of femininity worth saving. Unlike Jessica Lynch, they cannot signify as vulnerable to the threat of inter-racial rape, and they could never be made to stand in for the violation of the US by a foreign male threat.
>
> (Brittain 2006: 83)

Many have also critiqued the political purpose of the Lynch story. The rescue of Jessica Lynch was made with references to popular culture, it was referred to as an action movie. The US special task force filmed the entire rescue (Sjolander and Trevenen 2010: 164). Krista Hunt and Kim Rygiel argue that the political purpose of official war stories such as the one associated with Jessica Lynch is to camouflage the interests, agendas, policies, and politics that underpin the war in order to legitimise and gain consent for the 'war on terror' (Hunt and Rygiel 2006: 4). Kumar, furthermore, suggests that Lynch was used by the military to enable a controversial war being talked about in emotional rather than rational language, i.e. as war propaganda (Kumar 2004).

Here, I would like to add that in comparison to Piestewa and Johnson, Lynch was also easier to frame as a heroine because she did not have children. Piestewa was a single mother of two who left her four-year-old son and three-year-old daughter with her parents while she went to Iraq (Younge 2003). Johnson has a daughter. Both of them were described in the media as 'single mothers' (Prividera and Howard III 2006: 33). Lynch on the other hand, was not a mother and as such she fits into stories about female heroines *before* motherhood. In my reading, the writing of Lynch as the heroine at the expense of the agency of Piestewa and Johnson can also be understood as a maternalist war story because as a *Vacant Womb*, the tension between life-giving and life-taking is removed. This is how Lynch's empty womb enables a narrative as a heroine, while in the cases of Piestewa and Johnson the tension could not be as easily removed. In this way, intersecting with race, motherhood adds another piece to the puzzle of the writing of Lynch as a heroine.

In addition, there is also a religious dimension to the writing of [childless] heroines. For example, heroines are often associated with virginity, such as Joan of Arc and Queen Elisabeth I.[1] Similarly to how Gaelle is presented through religion in *Female Agents* as discussed in the previous chapter, Lynch's faith in God was presented again and again as evidence of her position as an exemplar of American values and bravery (Sjolander and Trevenen 2010: 168–9).

Importantly, the empty womb signifies 'vacant'/'free', ready to be filled. It signifies potential for fullness and is thereby communicating heteronormativity. Thus, despite being 'empty' the story of the *Vacant Womb* still reproduces a normalised femininity associated with motherhood. As such, the female heroine written as a *Vacant Womb*, as before motherhood, does not transgress boundaries of appropriate gender behaviour. In fact, my point is that it is precisely because the subject has not utilised her life-giving capacity, yet, that it/she does not challenge essentialist understandings of gender and as such risk disrupting the normative association between femininity and motherhood.

The second theme identified in how female bodies are written as heroines in war stories is *through* motherhood. I refer to this trope as the *Protective Mother*. As seen in Chapter 1, most often, women are portrayed as unable to kill because they are, or could be, mothers. This is how the capacity to kill (agency in political violence) is juxtaposed with the capacity to give life, i.e. motherhood. However, in stories of violent women where motherhood is key, it usually forms part of either a revenge- or a 'protecting-the-family' narrative. For example, in the story of the Celtic queen Boudicca who led a rebellion against the Romans around AD 60 it is mentioned that she did so after her husband had been killed and her daughters raped (Goldstein 2001: 118). Furthermore, historian Joanna Bourke mentions the American frontier where hand-to-hand combat with Indians was considered to be appropriate behaviour for the good American wife and mother (Bourke 1999: 311). Even more importantly, however, femininity is also claimed as the reason for women's participation in violence. According to this logic, women kill because they are super-feminine. Miriam Cooke argues that although such female combatants are sometimes caricatured and often feared, they command a much higher social prestige (Cooke 1996: 36). Explanations for why women kill have also been linked to their maternal nature. According to this narrative, maternal passions, biological urges, transform women into fearsome killers. The argument is that women would have little difficulty killing in the defence of their husbands, lovers and children (Bourke 1999: 318, 321). Similarly in popular culture, if the female heroine does have a child, her aggression is shown as a manifestation of desire to save him or her (Inness 2004: 12). This is how the narrative trope of the *Protective Mother* works to explain women's participation in violence as performances of what is considered normal and natural because it echoes dominant ideas about women's roles as caring, nurturing, protecting their children, husband or lover.

The *Protective Mother* organises stories of heroines where the subject performs normative femininity along a maternal role. However, the maternal relationship does not have to be biological. As an example, Sigourney Weaver as 'Ripley' in Ridley Scott's Hollywood blockbuster *Aliens* is a fierce protector of a young girl called Newt, 'promising her own death if need be to save the girl from the Alien Mama' (Bundtzen 2000: 105; Cooke 1996: 36). Thus, the *Protective Mother* influences stories where female agency in political violence as heroism is explained in their maternal relationship to others.

The third way in which female bodies are written as subjects in representations of agency in political violence is as *Masculinised Subjects*. Here, heroic subjects are written in opposition to motherhood. Thus, in contrast to cases where the subject performs femininity through a naturalised life-giving identity, here female subjects' agency is enabled through masculinity and a lack of motherhood. These subjects are communicating agency in political violence *instead of* motherhood. This is how the tension between life-giving and life-taking is removed. These subjects interrupt boundaries of femininity as associated with life-giving, however, crucially, they are not deemed threatening to those boundaries.

More specifically, the masculinised subject departs from the norms and boundaries of femininity and a naturalised life-giving identity by being, for example, childless by choice, masculine, gay or a prostitute. Such representations incorporate a number of different and distinctive subject positions, but the common denominator is that the subject is already acting outside the boundaries of femininity as associated with life-giving and is therefore not considered a 'normal' or 'real' woman anyway. These subjects are masculinised. Stereotypically, the gay woman is not interested in the act of 'natural' (heterosexual) reproduction, the masculine woman can 'do it as a man', and the prostitute is not using her womb for the act of procreation but her body for economic gain and is in this sense empowered. To give an example from popular culture, Terrell Carver notes the masculinisation of the female body in the film G.I. Jane (1997), about the first (fictional) woman to undergo training with the US Naval Special Warfare Group. In order to turn G.I. Jane's soft, feminine body into a hard machine, it needs to be militarised – and this means masculinised:

> O'Neil has to train hard, and she loses her period (the female physician describes this as 'normal' for female athletes). In the end she does well enough humping a very large man off a battlefield, albeit with buddy-assistance, and well enough to pass all the other physical hurdles, including pain endurance and psychological resilience. When she shouts 'Suck my dick!', context and metaphor triumph over all, and she's in.
>
> (Carver 2007: 314)

In this way, subjects are disciplined as subjects with agency through references to their lack of/difference from a naturalised femininity associated with motherhood. This is why it becomes important to emphasise that the lead character loses her period, the symbol of her life-giving capacity. Thus, these subjects are not using their capacity to give life, but are in fact 'unable' to perform motherhood. These subjects have agency in political violence precisely because they are already acting outside the boundaries of a naturalised femininity. My point here is that the writing of these subjects as heroines and subjects of political violence depends on the fact that the subject is lacking femininity coded as natural for female bodies, being caring, maternal or using her womb for procreation. In other words, in these discursive practices, agency in political violence is enabled at the expense of a life-giving identity; agency is enabled *instead of* motherhood. As I develop further below, I suggest that these subjects whose agency in political violence is enabled at the expense of their motherhood are seen to constitute a minority and are thus reassuringly marginalised as different from – but ultimately not threatening to – the norm of a naturalised femininity. Importantly, this means that motherhood and a naturalised life-giving identity are still communicated as that which is different from the violent subject. Thus, even where representations of female agency in political violence are constructed as heroine stories at the expense of motherhood, motherhood is still present as a naturalised constitutive other and the female subjects are acting out the masculinised norm.

Faye

The Protective Mother

Perhaps the most obvious way in which female bodies are written as subjects in representations of political violence as maternalist war thinking is through motherhood and the trope of the *Protective Mother*. Faye Turney's heroism was constructed with reference to her motherhood. Front pages were headlined as 'A **mother undaunted** by 17-hour shifts and a macho world' (Judd, *Independent*, 28 March 2007); 'Faye knew the risks when she **left Molly** to serve in Iraq: **courage** of sailor held captive in Iran' and '**Bravery: Faye holds daughter Molly**' (Lyons, *Daily Record*, 28 March 2007). It was reported that she '**loves being a mum** and her greatest concern right now will be for her little girl and how badly she is being affected by this' (Newton Dunn and Parker, *Sun*, 27 March 2007; Beeston and Kennedy, *The Times*, 27 March 2007). In the *Sun* she is the '**Hero Mum**' pictured cuddling her daughter. The photo of Turney holding her daughter, however, is of a new-born baby, not depicting the fact that Turney's daughter was three years old at the time. This photo not only implies inappropriateness because her daughter is so young, but the photo of Turney and her new-born daughter also signify the icon of motherhood, the natural bond between mother and child and, thus, the naturalisation of femininity with motherhood.

Moreover, as mentioned above, maternal relationships do not have to be biological. The trope of the *Protective Mother* also influences the representation of Faye Turney's agency in political violence through her relationship with her fellow soldiers. Arthur Batchelor was the only sailor except Turney who sold their story to the media. Interestingly, even in his story, which was published in the *Mirror*, most focus is on Turney. The article is titled: '**Faye saved me**: Brave colleague got me through my kidnap horror'. Batchelor describes how Turney was comforting him when they had just been arrested and were transported to Iranian mainland:

> Topsy [Turney] kept on whispering to make sure I was okay, she just **reassured me** that we were all together. The guards got really aggressive whenever they heard us communicating. Topsy really **put her neck on the line** to make sure I was holding up.
>
> (Hughes and Stansfield, *Mirror*, 9 April 2007)

Then, speaking of the moment when they were reunited Batchelor said:

> I missed Topsy [Turney] most of all. I really **love her, as a mum and a big sister** and I can't describe how that felt … just every emotion rolled into one. I ran up to her, threw my arms round her and **cried like a baby** … When I'd calmed down, she asked, 'Do you need another hug, a **mother hug**?' and I said 'damn right' … Topsy said she'd always be there for me, to **protect me** and look after me.
>
> (Hughes and Stansfield, *Mirror*, 9 April 2007)

Faye Turney's maternal role in their relationship was portrayed in the *Sun* as: 'Touchingly, Arthur, the youngest Brit, said: Faye was like a big sister or a mum to me, she gave me hugs when I needed them' (Moult, Newton Dunn and Lazzeri, *Sun*, 7 April 2007) and echoed by Turney in the ITV interview:

> My boat crew had the youngest member, Arthur Batchelor, and I remember I put my arms around him and told him that **if you ever need a mum** or a sister or a hug, he was to find me and **I would be there for him**.
>
> (ITV 2007)

At this stage, Trevor McDonald, the interviewer, says: 'I think he has since said that you were **like a mother to him**.' Faye Turney responds: 'yeah, he was my main concern. He was the youngest of the group, **he was the baby**' (ITV 2007).

The writing of Faye Turney's agency as a soldier in a maternal language means that Turney is performing appropriate femininity in these discursive practices. As a woman and also a mother she is expected to be caring and nurturing and her heroism as a soldier is, therefore, dominated by such traits. By being represented in this way and by giving herself such a maternal role, Turney is acting within the boundaries of naturalised femininity.

During and after Faye Turney's captivity, voices were raised that she was perhaps a bit too willing to collaborate with the Iranians (see also the discussion in Chapter 3 on how Gaelle is represented while in captivity in *Female Agents*). In her defence, Turney used her identity as a mother to justify her actions:

If I confessed to being in Iranian waters and wrote letters to my family, the British people and the Iranian people, I'd be free within two weeks. If I didn't, they'd put me on trial for espionage and I'd go to prison for 'several years'. I had just an hour to think about it. If I did it, I feared everyone in Britain would hate me. But I knew it was my one chance of fulfilling a **promise to Molly** that I'd be home for her birthday on May 8.

(Newton Dunn and Moult, *Sun*, 9 April 2007a)

When Turney accepted a huge sum of money to sell her story to the media she was perceived as a greedy monster. However, again, the action was justified in the name of motherhood: In the *Daily Star*, the headline reads 'I **sold my story for Molly**; Hostage Faye fights back as fury grows over her decision to cash in' (Lawton, *Daily Star*, 9 April 2007).

Faye is a working-class, low-ranking sailor who has to worry about paying off her mortgage and **securing a future for her daughter**.

(Sharp and Judd, *Independent*, 15 April 2007)

Adam and I never intended to spend the money on ourselves. It's **for Molly**. It will be for her education and anything else we can do to give her the best start in life.

(Moult and Newton Dunn, *Sun*, 10 April 2007a)

In this sense, Turney's value as a fellow soldier is related to her role as a woman and a mother, not in her capabilities as a soldier. Turney's response with reference to her motherhood repositions her within the *Protective Mother* narrative trope as she performs femininity linked to motherhood. By emphasising Faye Turney's life-giving identity and role as mother these discursive practices are told as maternalist war stories.

Janis

The Protective Mother

In the initial media coverage of Janis Karpinski it is often mentioned that she is childless. Despite, or perhaps because of, Karpinski's childlessness, however, she was still also written in maternal language. The maternal language used in representations of Karpinski indicates that she was valued as a military leader through essentialist understandings of gender. Karpinski is written as a subject in representations of agency in political violence through maternalist stories. First, being the only female General in Iraq, Janis Karpinski was interviewed and written as a 'caring commander' months before the Abu Ghraib scandal emerged:

'She's really **caring**,' says Sgt. 1st Class Philip J. May of Pinellas Park. 'She doesn't just talk the talk, she walks the walk.' She sends **personal** letters to the families [of lost ones] and tries to attend all memorial services in Iraq. '**I love my soldiers**,' she says. 'When I ask if there's a problem or I hear of a problem, I make every effort to resolve it, and if I can't, I tell them why I can't or why the system can't, there is no lip service.'

(Taylor Martin, *St Petersburg Times*, 14 December 2003)

When the initial coverage of the Abu Ghraib scandal begun and Janis Karpinski was mentioned as in charge of the soldiers shown in the photos, it was stories of the caring commander that were used in her defence:

A captain and a lieutenant colonel from the Army Reserve, both of whom served with Karpinski during her stint as commander, praised her leadership. They described her as **caring** and in charge. 'She is very **personable** and she's very soldier-oriented,' says Lt. Col. Dennis McGlone, commander of the 744th MP Battalion, one of the subordinate units to the 800th MP Brigade.

(Copeland, *Washington Post*, 10 May 2004)

I love my soldiers, she said. When I ask if there's a problem or I hear of a problem, I make every effort to resolve it, and if I can't, I tell them why I can't or why the system can't.

(Unattributed, *Daily Mail*, 30 April 2004)

Answering to criticism, one of Karpinski's attorneys said Army investigators had ignored statements by officers in her brigade 'replete with praise and admiration of her clear guidance, firm, fair and common-sense enforcement of standards, [and] her **caring** for the soldiers' (Smith, *Washington Post*, 24 May 2004). Similarly, when Karpinski was described as 'extremely emotional during much of the interview' in General Taguba's investigation, the response was made with reference to her maternal caring role as an expression of good leadership:

And if I'm emotional about my troops, then that's a credit to my leadership abilities and my leadership skills and my **compassion** for my soldiers. But, I did what I needed to do as a leader. And I know how to lead, and I know how to **take care of soldiers**.

(Karpinski, *Signal City*, 4 July 2004)

Karpinski says she gets **passionate** when speaking of her soldiers, and rightly so. It is not only her reputation she is defending, she says, but the reputations of the thousands of good soldiers serving at the prisons who were not involved in wrongdoing. 'If you don't **get emotional** when you're talking about your soldiers who served with you for a year, there's something wrong with you,' she says.

(Copeland, Washington Post, 10 May 2004)

In addition to the framing of Karpinski as a caring commander through maternal narratives, another maternalist story is present in the writing of Karpinski as a strong and feisty leader defending her soldiers:

> He made it sound like I was blubbering and crying the whole time I was being interviewed, like I was an out-of-control, emotionally distraught woman. Well, I can tell you this: that the only time there were tears in my eyes, and I did get emotional, was when I was **defending my soldiers**. And I would do it again today, I would do it again next week, I will always do it. Because they deserve it. And I felt like all of their accomplishments were being pulled away from them, by design, for something that they didn't do or have any participation in, with the exception of the six or seven who were so vividly photographed.

(Karpinski, Signal City, July 2004)

However, Karpinski also defended the soldiers being depicted and punished for the scandal:

> Well, they've been accused of being responsible for the photographs. But if we take it down to the very basics, Lynndie England did not deploy to Iraq with a dog collar and a dog leash. So obviously somebody gave her those props that we see in those photographs that are now seen around the world.

(Karpinski, Signal City, 13 November 2005)

> I think the MI people were in this all the way. I think they were up to their ears in it … I don't believe that the MPs, two weeks onto the job, would have been such willing participants, even with instructions, unless someone had told them it was all okay.

(Higham, Stephens and White, Washington Post, 23 May 2004)

Refusing to single-handedly take the blame for what happened at Abu Ghraib, Karpinski also spoke out on behalf of reservists in general:

> We're disposable, she said of the military's attitude toward reservists. Why would they want the active-duty people to take the blame? They want to put this on the M.P.'s [Military Police] and hope that this thing goes away. Well, it's not going to go away.

(Shenon, New York Times, 2 May 2004)

In addition, Karpinski's childlessness was compensated as she was written in maternal language in her relationship to a parrot:

> She and George have **no children**, but they have kept an African gray parrot named Casey for 26 years, and she delights in telling of him. He can bark and meow; he can say 'hello' when the phone rings. He is so used to flying with Karpinski on her various assignments, he can even say 'Delta is my airline.' On Saturday, Karpinski pulls from her bag a rather large framed photograph. It is of Casey. She says she brought it with her because she hasn't been able to spend much time with him lately, and this way, he's with her all day.
>
> (Copeland, *Washington Post*, 10 May 2004)

The focus on Karpinski's maternal relationship to her soldiers and to her parrot[2] attempts to compensate the fact that she and her husband decided not to have children. By showing Karpinski as the caring, nurturing mother, even though she is childless, the narrative gaze tells a familiar maternalist war story. The representation of Janis Karpinski as the caring commander, both by media and by Karpinski herself is a result of essentialist ideas about gender as traits such as emotionality, care and nurture are traditionally associated with women. As discussed in Chapter 3, when Karpinski was constructed a bad leader through accusations of being emotional, it was in gendered language. Similarly, when Karpinski responded to such claims, it was in gendered language. Karpinski's defence was influenced by the narrative trope of the *Protective Mother* which enables agency within the boundary of naturalised femininity associated with motherhood. By protecting and defending her soldiers, Karpinski was seen as performing femininity according to traditional ideas about gender. Her leadership skills were measured in their maternal value and her 'natural' emotionality was a valuable asset in a female commander.

The Masculinised Subject

As already mentioned, in the initial media coverage of Janis Karpinski, before the Abu Ghraib prison scandal had erupted, it is often mentioned that she has a husband of 29 years, but that they have no children:

> Karpinksi understands the trials of separation. She has **no children**, but her husband of 29 years, a lieutenant colonel, works with the US embassy in Oman. [She] has not seen him in recent months. Her blond hair is braided and coiled in a tight bun; her ice blue eyes, devoid of makeup, fix listeners with a friendly, if unflinching gaze.
>
> (Taylor Martin, *St Petersburg Times*, 14 December 2003)

The information regarding her childlessness immediately puts focus on the fact that Karpinski is different. The fact that she is married signifies hetero-sexuality, but 'childless' means that she has sacrificed her life-giving identity and is therefore not acting according to her gendered 'essence'. Karpinski defends her choice not to have children in her autobiography:

> Choosing a military life did require sacrifices. My husband and I **decided we would not have children**. As career Army people, we were always on the move and often flying off to different assignments. Even when we were based together, as a Special Forces officer George spent most of his life in the field. If we had kids, I knew I would have to take most of the responsibility for raising them. But I could not do that and also meet the responsibilities of a full-time officer in the Army. I also needed George's calmer temperament to make me a better person; his parenting skills would have exceeded mine ... but I couldn't ask him to become my househusband.
>
> (Karpinski with Strassner 2005: 82)

The focus on Karpinski as childless constructs her as different and the fact that she defends her decision not to have children in her autobiography highlights the break with normalised femininity intimately linked to mother-hood. Karpinski's childlessness emphasises the tension between life-giving and life-taking identities. Karpinski has sacrificed motherhood for her career. She has sacrificed her life-giving identity for her life-taking identity. Similarly as discussed above, the message that is communicated is that these two identities are not compatible. Agency in political violence is enabled at the expense of/ instead of motherhood. This also explains why Karpinski was commonly referred to as 'a dyke' or a 'bull dyke' despite the fact that she had been married for thirty years. Laura Sjoberg argues that this categorization, of Karpinski's sexual preferences, is not about whether or not Karpinski sleeps with women. Instead, it implies that Karpinski is somehow less of a woman; less pure and therefore less female because she coordinated prisoner abuse. Importantly, Sjoberg argues, the depiction of Karpinski as a dyke because of her (alleged) involvement with prisoner abuse at Abu Ghraib implicitly characterises real women as incapable of that sort of violence (Sjoberg 2007: 89).

Female Agents

By highlighting the secret role women played in the resistance movement during the Second World War, *Female Agents* is a film specifically about women's heroism. Here, I show how such displays of heroism, however, how the writing of heroic subjects in *Female Agents,* is communicated through motherhood or through an absence of motherhood. Interestingly, all of the females are non-mothers, yet, each character has their own motherhood-story. Thus, what is communicated overall is not only that the writing of heroic subjects depends on a removal of motherhood, but also that because several of the agents either are, have been, or want to be pregnant, heterosexuality and maternal reproduction is seen as the foundation for being female.

Vacant Wombs

As mentioned in Chapter 3, Suzy, was chosen as an agent because she had had a relationship with Heindrich, the Nazi officer that the group is trying to assassinate. We learn that she left him because 'she didn't want to belong to a man'. We also learn, however, that she was pregnant at the time she left him but that he was unaware of it.

SUZY: He never knew I was pregnant. (sobbing).
JEANNE: You have got a kid? (Suzy shakes her head).
JEANNE: You gave it up?
SUZY: A family in Liverpool. No more Nazi dad and collaborator mum. (Louise is listening in).
SUZY: For him, the slate is clean. (Jeanne puts her hand on Suzy's shoulder to comfort her. Louise sighs.)

Suzy claims that she would have made a bad mother so she gave the baby up for adoption. I argue that it is precisely the fact that Suzy is unsuited for a life-giving role that opens up for the writing of her as a heroic subject, potentially capable of a life-taking role. The two identities of life-giving and life-taking cannot co-exist and by informing the audience that Suzy would have been a bad mother anyway, Suzy's identity of life-giving is 'removed' without complications. Suzy is a *Vacant Womb* despite having been pregnant and given birth, precisely because her previous pregnancy also functions to sign-post Suzy's heterosexuality. This is important because it signifies a potential for fullness that offers a reassurance that Suzy, once the war is over, might be able to return to a mothering role. In other words, Suzy's empty womb does not indicate difference in the same way as a masculinised subject. Suzy does not signify a break with heteronormativity and a naturalised femininity but is very much following such norms.

Louise is the main character in *Female Agents* and initially portrayed as the leader of the group. On a train to Paris, Louise finds out that she is pregnant. She goes to the toilet and looks at herself in the mirror, feels her breasts, wondering if they have become larger. She looks down on her belly in the mirror, takes a step back and moves her hands from her breasts to her belly. She takes a deep breath and gives an uncomfortable facial expression. In cinema studies, mirrors can function to signify ambiguity or duplicity (Hayward 1996: 4). Here, this mirror scene also represents a shift in the way in which Louise is portrayed in *Female Agents*. Pregnant, Louise no longer fits the *Vacant Womb* and from this scene onwards Louise is often represented as a passive and emotional victimised object rather than a heroic subject. And, it is her pregnancy that is used to construct her as such. The following conversation takes place when Louise and Jeanne have found out that Suzy has had a child but given it up for adoption:

JEANNE: Suzy's cut up about what she did.
LOUISE: Why? Maybe she would have been a terrible mother.
JEANNE: How can you say that? Except dying, nothing worse can happen to a kid.
LOUISE: There is always worse.
JEANNE: Pity is not your strongest point. Try to be a little bit human for once.
LOUISE: On the train, I found out that I was three months pregnant. I can't
　　be more human. My husband and I had been trying for kids for years.

For a female body, then, this conversation implies that being pregnant somehow makes you more human. The essence for a female body is to give life. As discussed in Chapter 3, when Louise has been captured, she is bravely enduring torture. Later, we learn that she lost her unborn baby as a consequence. The following conversation takes place when Jeanne has rescued Louise from the transport that is taking her to her execution:

JEANNE: What about Gaelle?

Louise shakes her head. Jeanne reaches for Louise's belly, Louise embraces her and we understand that Louise has lost the baby. At the end of the film, Louise goes to a church to light candles for the other girls. As she walks out of church the following text is shown on the screen:

In 1949, Louise returned to France and married an architect. She was awarded the Croix de Guerre and the Legion d'Honneur. She died in 2004 at the age of 98, **childless**.

Louise's heroism is valued in relation to her sacrifice of motherhood, which seems even greater due to the fact that Louise and her deceased husband had 'been trying for years' to get pregnant. At the end, 'childless' functions to remind the audience of Louise's sacrifice but it also signifies that all heroines portrayed in the film are empty wombs, even though some of them had actually been pregnant. As such, what is communicated in this discursive practice is female heroism's association with childlessness. This is how heroism is associated with empty wombs and heroines constructed through the discourse of the *Vacant Womb* where the tension between life-giving and life-taking has been 'removed'.

As discussed in Chapter 3, Ulrike Meinhof is written as a victimised object through a comparison to Gudrun Ensslin (and vice versa). In *Female Agents,* Gaelle and Jeanne are written as subjects in relation to each other. As mentioned above vacant wombs are often written through associations to religion and morality. In *Female Agents*, it is Gaelle who signifies such traits and

Jeanne their opposites. More specifically, the two characters are differentiated through ideas about religion, capitalism and agency in political violence. Whereas Gaelle finds moral guidance through religion, Jeanne – as a prostitute – is driven by an interest in making money. These differences are key also in the writing of them as subjects capable of killing. At the beginning of the film Gaelle refuses to take an active part in killing with reference to her faith. For example, in preparation for their mission the women receive a cyanide pill, which they are meant to use as a last resort if they are captured. When Gaelle boards the plane that will take them to France, she drops the cyanide pill on purpose. On the plane, Pierre approaches Gaelle:

PIERRE: You lost this.
GAELLE: It does not matter. I would never use it. It is **against my religion**.
LOUISE: God does not care what goes on down here.
GAELLE: Do you say that because of your husband? (Louise looks at Pierre assuming he must have told Gaelle that her husband had been killed.)
GAELLE: My brother was shot on his 20th birthday, but **I never lost my faith**.

As a moral subject, Gaelle initially refuses/avoids to use violence herself, yet, she is still positioned as brave and heroic and she still takes part in the act of killing indirectly. For example, at the military hospital in Normandy where the group rescues a British geologist, Gaelle assists Pierre to shoot a soldier. After their successful mission, in which the agents killed several German soldiers, Gaelle reflects on the use of force:

GAELLE: When the war is over I will light a candle for you in church. Promise me you will do the same.

Most often, it is the dichotomised writing of Jeanne and Gaelle that communicates morality and strength of character, where Gaelle's faith positions her with high morals and Jeanne's interest in money, as a prostitute, positions her as its opposite. On their way to Paris after their first successful mission in Normandy, the agents stop at a safe house. Gaelle argues with Jeanne:

GAELLE: You are used to humiliation. I am not! I refuse to crawl to the Germans! (She grabs Jeanne by the neck and pushes her to a wall.)
GAELLE: Pierre has been arrested, Rene is dead. It is our duty to take their place.

Soon afterwards, the agents hear cars stopping outside the safe house and ensuing shooting. Louise walks up from the safety of the cellar whereupon she is attacked by a German officer. However, just as the German officer is about to stab her, Gaelle appears, shoots and kills him. Despite her moral beliefs, Gaelle too has now killed. She does not move and takes a long look at her victim, seemingly shocked by what she has done.

The writing of Gaelle as a heroine with references to her faith continues: When the group of agents are on the train to Paris, Jeanne seizes an opportunity and gets off the train with the suitcase which is full of money. Again, it is Gaelle who notices, catches up with her and forces her to get back on the train:

GAELLE: Jeanne!
JEANNE: Louise is with a Kraut. We are fucked. Come with me.
GAELLE: Running won't win over your mum.
JEANNE: Or save my dad from Verdun. Don't get preachy with me. (Gaelle blocks Jeanne's way and points a gun at her from underneath coat.)
JEANNE: What is that? **"Thou shall not kill?"**
GAELLE: Who is getting preachy now?

In these scenes, Gaelle is written as a heroine through her faith; her high morals make her loyal to Louise and the mission. Her empty womb in combination with the religious references emphasise virginity; in these scenes, Gaelle is a *Vacant Womb*.

The Masculinised Subject

In *Female Agents*, Jeanne is the most obvious heroine due to the fact that she is the one most often presented as an active subject rather than a passive object. She is the one who rescues Louise from prison; she is the one who sacrifices herself for the mission by drawing attention to herself as armed in order for Louise to assassinate Heindrich. At the end, we learn that due to such an act of heroism, Jeanne was arrested and taken to a concentration camp where she was hanged. Jeanne paid the ultimate price.

In an article discussing the capture and rescue of US soldier Jessica Lynch, Veronique Pin-Fat and Maria Stern argue that Lynch (see also discussion in Chapter 3) 'symbolically stands for what the soldier is protecting; she is that for which the soldier sacrifices and, therefore, cannot be sacrificed herself' (Pin-Fat and Stern 2005: 42). In contrast, Jeanne could be. There are two things in particular that enable the writing of Jeanne as a heroic subject with agency in political violence, which at the same time means that she could also be sacrificed: the fact that she is a childless prostitute and her already demonstrated capability to kill. The two are intimately linked because, as the next conversation shows, it is the fact that she is a childless prostitute that enables the writing of her as capable of killing. Jeanne is the first person Louise and Pierre approach when they are setting up the team of agents. The following conversation takes place when Louise and Pierre visit Jeanne who is in prison in London.

LOUISE: Your sentence has been put on hold.
JEANNE: It's not a mistake? **I killed** a man.
LOUISE: Your pimp? I don't call that a man.

JEANNE: Nobody forced me into anything.

PIERRE: Stop being silly. If not for us, you would have been hanged. That's your only alternative to our proposition.

JEANNE: I knew there would be a catch. What is this?

LOUISE: We need you for a mission in France.

JEANNE: Who do I have to fuck?

PIERRE: We are reliably informed that you used to perform nude in Soho.

JEANNE: You need a girl who will get her leg over, so here I am? You must be desperate.

LOUISE: We also **need a girl who can kill**.

JEANNE: What do I get out of this? … I'm not the type who works for nothing. Thanks anyway. (Jeanne walks away. Louise approaches again.)

LOUISE: You will die like a whore who never had a chance. Is that what you want? If the mission is a success, you will be pardoned. (Jeanne stops and turns around, now clearly interested.)

In the next scene, Louise and Pierre are discussing Jeanne:

LOUISE: I am sure she is the right choice.

PIERRE: We can't trust her, she is **a nutcase**.

LOUISE: A rope round her neck and she still said no. That takes hell of a nerve.

The prostitute, similarly to the 'Femme Fatale', is a key figure in the cinematic articulation of gendered identities in relation to constructions of independence, self-reliance and sexuality (Tasker 1998: 5). Traditionally, female bodies have things done to them, but prostitutes are often seen as agents, written as [capitalist/immoral] subjects. The visibility of the prostitute is therefore about status. The prostitute asserts herself within spaces from which other women are excluded, but her visibility, Tasker argues, at the same time suggests the lack of any other place to go (ibid.: 5). What is communicated in *Female Agents* is that Jeanne, as a prostitute, has already transgressed the boundary of femininity as naturalised through life-giving and is therefore not a 'real' woman. Acting outside the boundary of normative femininity, her agency in killing is allowed, and, in fact, welcomed. Importantly, the fact that Jeanne is capable of killing is not deemed threatening but seen as a rational act. Because her victim was a pimp who probably was using her, Louise (and the audience) understands Jeanne's motivations. In addition, not only is Jeanne 'using' her womb outside the boundary of naturalised femininity focused on giving birth, but she is also using her body as a commodity in order to make money. Thus, the writing of Jeanne as a heroine is through her masculinised 'thirst' for money as a prostitute. She is a masculinised subject.

As mentioned above, her role as a prostitute is, moreover, often juxtaposed with Gaelle's religious identity. The role makes explicit that 'femininity' – and the prostitute's distance from it – is a raced and a classed concept (Tasker 1998: 5). For example, in the first safe house the agents stay in, Jeanne's identity as a prostitute and her obsession with money surfaces in an argument with Gaelle:

JEANNE: A freezing cellar and rotten apples when we have millions in cash. What better time to **spend our cash**?
GAELLE: How can you think of money now?
JEANNE: It is **the way I am. I am a whore**, not a choirboy. Never forget it.

When the agents are walking to the aircraft that will take them to France, Suzy asks Jeanne if she has ever been blessed. Jeanne responds: 'Never. If I get down on my knees it is not to pray'. When the agents are on the train to Paris, it stops abruptly, whereupon a man puts his hands on Jeanne's breasts.

JEANNE: Who do you think you are?
MAN: Don't play hard to get.
JEANNE: Call me **a slut**, why don't you.

My point is that the writing of Jeanne as a prostitute facilitates the writing of her as a heroic subject capable of killing. Later, during a conversation with Louise in a safe house in Paris, Jeanne expresses her eagerness to kill:

JEANNE: In the metro, I sat next to a Jerry. His holster was open and he hadn't even noticed. But nothing happened.
LOUISE: What should have happened?
JEANNE: Nothing. But it gives you ideas. **We should kill** all the Krauts!

The writing of Jeanne as a heroine is intimately linked with her identity as a prostitute. As a prostitute, Jeanne does not represent the norm of naturalised femininity. This is what enables the representation of Jeanne as the true heroine, as capable of killing. As an isolated case, Jeanne is allowed agency in political violence because it does not challenge a 'real' woman's life-giving identity as associated with life-giving. In fact, emphasising Jeanne's identity as life-taking (agency in political violence) in order to write her as a heroine also means that her identity as a life-giver is denied: When Louise and Jeanne are preparing the shooting of Heindrich, Jeanne asks Louise, who at this point is still pregnant, if she is OK. Jeanne looks at and touches Louise's belly.

LOUISE: I am fine, I am not ill.
JEANNE: **I just wish I was in your shoes**.

As mentioned above, the prostitute asserts herself within spaces from which other women are excluded, but, according to Tasker, she does not have any other place to go. In other words, it is precisely because Jeanne is a prostitute that she can occupy spaces and roles from which other women are excluded; she is already acting outside the realm of normative femininity as maternal reproduction. She is allowed to be a masculinised subject. Crucially, however, this also means that she is denied an identity of life-giving. As a masculinised subject Jeanne's agency in political violence is enabled, she is capable of killing but she 'cannot' have children. This is how the tension between a life-giving and a life-taking identity is 'removed' and how Jeanne is written as the ultimate heroine in *Female Agents*.

Gudrun/Ulrike

The Masculinised Subject

Similarly, in *The Baader-Meinhof Complex*, Gudrun is written as a masculinised subject in contrast to Ulrike who is the emotional victim. As already mentioned, this is demonstrated in their first meeting, which takes place as Ulrike, as a journalist, visits Gudrun in prison. Here, I return to that scene in order to focus on how gender, agency and political violence is communicated through the positioning of Gudrun.

GUDRUN: This time we won't sit idly as Fascism spreads like under Hitler. This time we will put up resistance. We have a historical responsibility ... I'll never resign myself to do nothing. Never. If they shoot our people like Ohnesorg and Dutschke then **we are going to shoot back**. That is the logical consequence.

ULRIKE: You are not serious?

GUDRUN: All over the world armed comrades are fighting. We must show our solidarity.

ULRIKE: But we do.

GUDRUN: Even if the Fascists throw you in jail? Such sacrifices have to be made. Or do you think that your theoretical masturbation will change anything?

Here, a violence/non-violence dichotomy is used in order to position the two women against each other. Being the masculinised subject, action and the use of force is uncomplicated to Gudrun, whereas for Ulrike, who in this scene represents femininity and non-violence, it is not. To emphasise this divide, Ulrike is dressed in light, beige clothes while Gudrun is wearing dark clothes. Gudrun is looking Ulrike straight in the eyes, argues very powerfully with much conviction, whereas Ulrike mostly looks down at her papers, which gives an insecure, passive impression. In addition, Gudrun is most often portrayed with very dark make-up that creates a harsh impression in contrast to Ulrike who is not wearing make-up at all and, thereby gives a softer, more feminine, appearance. Visually, the contrasting use of clothes and make-up feeds into the two subjects' capacity to use violence. To Ulrike, the feminised subject, violence is alien, whereas to Gudrun as the masculine subject it is a rational choice.

While the writing of the characters in *Female Agents* as heroic subjects depends on them having, in one way or another, sacrificed motherhood, the writing of Gudrun as a masculinised subject includes a similar motherhood story in the sense that her identity as a life-giver is removed: Gudrun leaves her son and thereby gives up her role as a mother in order to pursue her political ambitions. The first time we meet Gudrun she is watching a televised debate, where Ulrike Meinhof is one of the panellists, together with her parents, fiancé and infant son. When Gudrun's father (a priest) criticises Ulrike's argument, Gudrun defends it:

GUDRUN: Well, why don't you preach that over half the world's population are starving while others bathe in luxury! That there's no use in just praying for a better world! That they **have to fight back, damn it!**

Agitated, Gudrun leaves the room, whereupon her father tells Gudrun's then fiancé: 'You two should get married soon!' The link between an expression of violence and 'getting married' is interesting. Marriage seems to function not only as a rescue plan for Gudrun but it also illuminates the polar choices: marriage, motherhood, domesticity on the one hand and political activism and violence on the other. Of course we already know which route Gudrun chose to take. The next time we see Gudrun, we realise that she has left both her fiancé and her son. What I would like to draw attention to is that Gudrun's sacrifice of motherhood is not made visible however. Gudrun's sacrifice of motherhood is not only made rational but also portrayed as uncomplicated:

GUDRUN: What we need is a new morality. You have to draw a clear line between yourself and your enemies. Free yourself from the system and burn all bridges behind you.
ULRIKE: **What about your son?**
GUDRUN: If you are serious, you have to be able to **make** such **sacrifices. Andreas has a little girl** as well.

The way in which Gudrun and Ulrike are positioned against each other, through dichotomies of being active/passive, rational/emotional, dark/light, hard/soft and violent/non-violent, emphasises the tension between the identity of life-giving, which Ulrike represents, and the identity of life-taking (agency in political violence) which Gudrun represents. The juxtaposition between Gudrun and Ulrike also implies that Gudrun is an exception from the norm. Gudrun is different to the norm of 'natural' femininity; instead, she shows us what we are not. What I would like to emphasise here though is the need for a 'removal' of motherhood for the masculine subject, a removal that is somewhat trickier, yet as the next section shows, still present in non-fictional empirical cases.

Faye

The Masculinised Subject

I would like to end this chapter by returning to the case of Faye Turney. This is because while the distinctions between active/passive, violent/non-violent, rational/emotional and so on are relatively easy to make, or at least to emphasise, in fictional cases such as with regards to contrasting make-up and clothing as mentioned in the case of *The Baader-Meinhof Complex*, even 'real' cases include juxtapositions. Because Turney was a mother, the story about her did not fit the *Vacant Womb* trope. When her identity as a woman and a mother was revealed under the headline 'Let Mummy Go' (Newton Dunn and Parker, *Sun*, 27 March 2007), there was confusion; the representation of Turney visually split into two identities: the soldier *and* the mother. The tension between her life-giving and her life-taking identities dominated the media coverage: 'I really do love my job – **but** I love my daughter also' (Coles, *Sun*, 28 March 2007). Another caption read: 'Action Woman: Faye on guard duty in Sierra Leone in 2000, far right; in the middle of an inflatable during training prior to being sent to the Middle East; with Adam and Molly as a new mum' (Lyons, *Daily Record*, 28 March 2007). In stories like these, the tension inherent in the two Faye Turneys is underscored by the choice of images and their composition. On the one hand, there is the 'Action Woman'; on the other, the 'new mum'. In another article, the captions to the two photos read: 'gun girl' and 'proud parents'. As the 'gun girl', Turney was described as a brave heroine who could 'do it as a man', i.e. a masculinised subject:

> You can't sit back just because you're a girl. I love the satisfaction of being able to walk away from a job and know that I've coped and completed the task **just as well as a man** would have done it.
>
> (Kennedy 2007)

Hence, in the discursive practices where Turney is 'the soldier', portrayed as the masculinised subject who can 'do it as a man', her heroism is organised through discursive practices at the expense of her identity as a mother, despite the fact that Faye Turney is an actual mother. Thus, in order for the story of Faye Turney-the-soldier to make sense as the masculinised subject, her role and identity as a mother is side-lined. In these discursive practices, Turney's life-giving identity is temporarily put on hold. Subsequently, the tension between identities of life-giving and life-taking is also temporarily 'removed'.

In a similar fashion to the way in which Jeanne, as a prostitute, was allowed agency in political violence by being an exception to the norm of femininity as a naturalised life-giving identity, it seems that Turney is allowed agency in political violence because she is seen as a cultural exception; she belongs to a minority:

The world has watched in horror as the brave mum has been paraded in front of the cameras by her Iranian captors. Faye's courage has shone through during her ordeal, but she remains one of only a small **minority of women** in the military.

(Smith and Jackson 2007)

The headline 'Mother Set Her Heart on Life in the Royal Navy' was accompanied by 'Leading Seaman Faye Turney is one of a **small number of mothers** who are serving in the war against terror' (Payne and Britten, *Daily Telegraph*, 28 March 2007). While the quote from the *Daily Telegraph* communicates a message of reassurance to the public that there are not many *mothers* serving in the war against terror, in the text we learn how many *women* are serving in the armed forces, in what roles, where they can serve and where they are excluded, and how many who have been killed. What is interesting here is not only that 'mother' is used interchangeably with 'woman' (see also discussion in Chapter 3), but also that it is deemed important, possibly to offer reassurance, to showcase that Faye Turney is in a minority.

Another way in which the tension between Faye Turney's two identities of life-giving mother and life-taking masculinised subject soldier is made obvious is when the writing of Turney as the masculinised subject is 'interrupted' by her 'natural' feelings as a mother. In particular, feelings of guilt caused by her 'sacrificing' her daughter were used to emphasise her 'real' identity as a life-giver rather than a life-taker. A front-page headline in the *Independent*, accompanied by a photo of Faye Turney as a soldier in Sierra Leone in 2000, proclaims: 'My Little Girl Is Growing Up Every Day. I'm Missing That':

But it was Molly, her three-year-old daughter that she spoke of most. She described the **guilt** of leaving behind her 'bubbly, headstrong' little girl to be looked after by her husband, Adam, also serving in the Navy but based in Plymouth. But she believed emphatically that this sacrifice would give her daughter every opportunity in life. The 25-year-old mother, one of 15 sailors and marines captured, said: 'I know by doing this job I can give my daughter everything she wants in life and hopefully by seeing me doing what I do, she'll grow up knowing that a woman can have a family and have a career at the same time.'

(Judd, 28 March 2007)

One commentator expressed the tension between these identities specifically:

Faye Turney should not receive any criticism for having the **natural feelings of a mother** – or for expressing them; but they were clearly in conflict with what she knew was her duty as a member of the armed forces in an extraordinarily stressful situation.

(Lawson, *Independent*, 10 April 2007)

In 1991, Laura Marks comments on the increased visibility of female US soldiers in the news leading up to the Gulf War and finds that the figure of the young servicewoman tearfully leaving her children behind is a particularly repeated figure who is 'applauded for her toughness and patriotism, adored for her maternity, even made out to be a conventionally sexy figure'. But, Marks argues, there is also a focus on her tears, which 'show the strain of this multiple identification- and signify the punishment she faced for abandoning her first duty as a mother' (Marks 1991: 64, quoted in Managhan 2012: 91). While such representations at first glance might seem to describe these soldiers' value in the sense of the larger the sacrifice, the greater the hero, what they actually do is communicate the temporal limitations to such constructions of heroic subjects. These women are expected to return to their 'first duties' as mothers. 25 years or so later, a similar story is told when Faye Turney and the other fourteen Royal Navy personnel are freed and back in the UK: Turney, the soldier, was returning to her [proper] role as a mother. The return was described as emotional:

> It was the moment she had prayed for during her darkest hours in captivity. Yesterday Faye Turney the young mother who became the face of the hostage crisis was finally reunited with her three-year-old daughter. The ecstatic 26-year-old wrapped her arms around little Molly, who had spent the last fortnight oblivious to the trauma that her mother was enduring thousands of miles from home. Cradling her delighted daughter, Leading Seaman Turney was also reunited with her husband Adam, who could barely contain his relief that the ordeal of the previous 14 days was over.
>
> (Kelly, *Daily Mail*, 6 April 2007)

More specifically, the emotional coverage of the homecoming was of an apologetic Faye Turney; it was about a mother's guilt. One of the *Sun*'s front-page headlines reads 'Mummy Mummy' and depicts Turney kissing her daughter. Inside the paper, the article headline is 'I Burst Into Tears and Told Family **I'm Sorry**'. Here, 'I'm Sorry' is printed in capital letters in contrast to the rest of the text. The words are printed in a much larger font and are located at the centre of the page. There are also two smaller photos of Faye Turney, her husband and their daughter on the same page. Faye Turney is quoted as saying:

> Adam had hold of Molly and we ran to each other. We all hugged and I said, 'I'm sorry, I love you'. **I felt guilty** for what I'd put them through.
>
> (Moult and Newton Dunn, *Sun*, 10 April 2007b)

In addition to portraying Turney's apologies to her family and her feelings of guilt as a mother, the representation of Turney was also of a woman who through her ordeal had realised what her *true* role was – that of a mother:

Mum Faye Turney said last night she had cashed in on her hostage ordeal in Iran for the sake of the daughter she feared she would never see again … now [she is] considering quitting the forces to be a full-time mum.

(Lawton, *Daily Star*, 9 April 2007)

In the article, an 'anonymous friend' of Turney's is quoted as saying:

This has shaken her to the core. She had a long time to think about her life and what is really important. She's **just a mum** who loves her daughter and her job. But she has to think of Molly and the future … The way she feels right now, she can't see herself going back to the frontline. She loves the Navy, but after what has happened she has to consider giving it up and **just being a mum**.

(Ibid.)

One of the photo captions reads 'Love of her life: Faye holds on tight to Molly, the precious daughter she thought she would never see again' (ibid.). Similarly, the *Sunday Star*'s headline reads 'Faye: I'm Back to Being Mum' (Chandler, 8 April 2007). The focus on Turney's return to her daughter communicates that Turney is finally back in her 'proper' element, that of being a mother, and that her temporary session as a soldier is over. Turney herself, however, was not keen on compromising her job in the Navy. Possibly as a result of the returning-mum narrative, a few days later an interview with Turney was titled 'Send me back' (Newton Dunn and Moult, *Sun*, 11 April 2007).

In these scenes and stories, the writing of Faye Turney as a heroic subject is conditioned by her identity as a mother. It is only if the tension between her dual identities of life-giving and life-taking could be overcome, that she is positioned as a heroic subject. In contrast to the writing of heroic subjects in *Female Agents*, where the tension between life-giving and life-taking can be permanently removed or overcome owing to the fact that it is a work of fiction, the writing of Turney as a heroic subject has temporal, and spatial, limitations. As a soldier, Turney has temporarily sacrificed her life-giving role; she is temporarily allowed agency; she is momentarily a masculinised subject. Still, the overall focus on her return to her daughter and to her proper role as a mother functions to reproduce and reinforce her life-giving identity at the expense of her life-taking identity. Motherhood is her first duty.

The point here is not to say that her role as a mother should not be her first duty, but to highlight that the way in which she was represented differs from the way in which her male colleagues, or indeed other male soldiers were/are treated, particularly when it comes to parenthood. This difference is political. In her exposure of how women murderesses are denied agency in media and legal discourses, Morrissey notes how certain narratives aim to recuperate female protagonists through returning them to a 'proper feminine place' (Morrissey 2003: 165). In a similar way, motherhood is signposted in these maternalist war stories as normative femininity. The focus on Faye Turney's maternal guilt or Jeanne's inability to give life are perhaps two of the most obvious examples.

Versions of motherhood

In this chapter, I have shown how female bodies are written as heroic subjects in representations of agency in political violence. These subjects are enabled agency through maternalist war stories that communicate *before, through* or *instead of* motherhood. The emphasis on being 'childless' or sacrificing motherhood in the writing of female heroic subjects throughout the empirical cases suggests that there is a particular body-politics involved in constructions of agency in political violence. My argument is that in order for female bodies to be written as heroic subjects the tension between life-giving and life-taking, which this book takes as its main focus, must be 'removed' or overcome, spatially and/or temporally. This is why Jeanne as a prostitute and the most obvious heroic subject in *Female Agents* 'cannot' have children, why Gudrun's maternal sacrifice is uncomplicated, why 'childless' is mentioned in the epilogue of *Female Agents*, why Karpinski's choice not to have children is relevant or newsworthy at all, and why the focus on Turney's maternal guilt is a way in which to discipline and return Turney to the realms of a normative femininity.

Crucially, I argue that no matter if the subjects are written through the narrative tropes of the *Vacant Womb*, the *Protective Mother* or the *Masculinised Subject*, the overall message in these maternalist war stories is a reinforcement of the foundation of sexual difference as maternal reproduction. Motherhood is, thus, by no means invisible in the construction of female heroic subjects with agency in political violence, but, importantly, is portrayed in very particular ways; according to a particular cultural grammar. The stories told in this chapter are, thus, told as versions of motherhood.

Notes

1 Interestingly, in stories of female heroines they are not necessarily part of the killing process. Although Joan of Arc was leading armies, she refused to kill personally (Goldstein 2001: 117). Similarly, Queen Elizabeth did not take an active part in the wars she led. Other examples of female heroines have been described in relation to sexual activities: Queen Zenobia and Matilda of Tuscany both led armies on the battlefield. Zenobia was 'incredibly beautiful [but] only had sex for purposes of procreation' and Matilda was described as 'largely chaste' (Goldstein 2001: 120).
2 Karpinski even dedicates her book *One Woman's Army* to 'Casey, my African Grey parrot'.

5   Monstrous abjects

For some reason the media chose to depict only photos of me. It didn't matter if there were worse things happening in some of the others. It had to be me for some reason. I have no idea why.

Lynndie England on BBC Radio 4, 30 May 2009

The mistreatment of Iraqi prisoners exposed in the Abu Ghraib scandal was shocking. The fact that women were involved in torture, including sexual/-ised torture, added yet another layer to the confused state of astonishment, simply because the story turned deeply held gendered presumptions upside down. Miranda Alison argues that the much greater public shock in reaction to a woman's involvement in the sexual torture of male prisoners at Abu Ghraib than to her male comrades' involvement indicates the continued naturalisation of men as perpetrators of sexual crimes and the naturalisation of women as non-aggressive, even when they are soldiers (Alison 2007: 76). Sjoberg and Gentry argue that the female soldiers in the Abu Ghraib scandal have committed a triple transgression: against the laws of war, against their femininity and against the military's prescribed roles for military women (Sjoberg and Gentry 2007: 23). In this chapter, I explore the second transgression and discuss what happens when female bodies do not conform to normative gender behaviour, when women act 'against their femininity'. I discuss how such bodies are considered a threat to hegemonic gender norms, more specifically, to what one might call heteropatriarchal conceptions of femininity (Morrissey 2003) where the foundation of sexual difference equals maternal reproduction. I start with Julia Kristeva's theory of social abjection but I also build on feminist and non-feminist applications of her ideas in relation to monsters as well as contributions to film- and legal theory on gender borders. In the first section, I discuss the process/practice of social abjection, the construction of subjects that cross 'the border' which, as a result, become abject subjects/ monsters/others. I theorise three main narrative tropes informing how female subjects become abject subjects; how female bodies are deemed monstrous: the *Monstrous-Feminine*, the *Deviant Womb* and the *Femme Castratrice*. In the second section, I show how these three themes influence the writing of monstrous abjects in the empirical cases. In the third section, I emphasise the politics of stories about monsters in greater detail. I show how monster stories are used in order to police the normative gender border by showing what happens when that border is crossed. In this process, not only is normative gender behaviour 'policed', but a naturalised femininity is also emphasised as that which the monstrous abject is not. This is how social abjection, the 'othering' of the monster, is intertwined with our understanding of ourselves. Thus, even though the subject itself might disrupt the foundation of sexual difference as maternal reproduction, overall, stories of monstrous abjects still function to reinforce heteronormative conceptions of femininity.

Abjection

According to the Oxford English Dictionary, abjection can mean a humiliated state or condition, but it can also, although apparently this is now rare, mean 'the action of casting out or away; rejection' (Oxford English Dictionary 2014). It is this latter meaning that is explored in this chapter. To Julia Kristeva, abjection is also about borders:

> [W]e may call it a border; abjection is above all ambiguity. Because, while releasing a hold, it does not radically cut off the subject from what threatens it – on the contrary, abjection acknowledges it to be in perpetual danger.
>
> (Kristeva 1982: 9)

Kristeva defines the abject as that which 'disturbs identity, system, order' and 'does not respect borders, positions, rules' (ibid.: 4). Ultimately, to Kristeva, the abject is part of ourselves. We reject it, identifying it as that which we are not. Because of this, the abject may reveal as much about ourselves as it does about external reality. The abject both fascinates and horrifies because it reveals our own conceptions of the world and our normative disposition. In this sense, as Imogen Tyler notes, to Kristeva subjectivity is always in revolt against itself; abjection is 'the border of my condition as a living being' (Tyler 2013: 28, 29). However, if one were to, as Tyler does, 'prise abjection out of the theoretical and political frames in which it is positioned in her [Kristeva's] work' (ibid.: 13), social abjection is suitable to also analyse practices of boundary-making, border-policing and construction of border agents much more broadly, beyond the parameters of psychoanalysis.

In *Revolting Subjects: Social Abjection and Resistance in Neoliberal Britain*, Imogen Tyler builds on Kristeva but also uses Butler's social theory of abjection wherein abjection is understood as a mechanism of governance through aversion. To Tyler, abjection is a theory of bordering which describes the labour of both subject formation and state formation. *Abjection is the bordering practices of the political present* (Tyler 2013: 37, 46, my emphasis). Crucially, this also means that abjection is *spatializing* in that these on-going bordering practices make and unmake the psychological and material boundaries of the subject: 'the abjecting subject attempts to generate a space, a distinction, a border, between herself and the polluting object, thing or person' (ibid.: 28). To Tyler it is important to examine the mechanisms through which norms of abjection are 'fabricated, operationalized and internalized' (37). It is only by critically engaging with abjection as *'contingent expressions of normativity'*, Tyler argues, that we might begin to disarticulate the effects of abjection as lived (ibid.: 38, my emphasis).

Whereas Tyler use Kristeva to theorise 'revolting subjects' opposing or challenging the British state, feminist film-theorist Barbara Creed and IR scholar Richard Devetak both build on Kristeva's theorising of the abject to discuss monsters and monstrosity. Devetak uses the concept in order to show how 'the other' is featured in thinking about international politics, in particular constructions of 'good' and 'evil' in the 'war on terror' (Devetak 2005). Monsters, Devetak argues, offer a negative definition of civility, virtue, and the good. In this way, monsters help to reinforce boundaries between self and other, civilisation and barbarism, good and evil (ibid.: 642). In addition, the designation of others as monsters always serves a moral function. It thrives on ambiguity and the transgression of taboos and boundaries. Monsters symbolise deviance, madness, depravity, brutality, violence, and are thought to threaten civilisation and social order (ibid.: 633).

Barbara Creed builds on Kristeva's idea about the abject in her account of how the horror film positions woman-as-monster. Monsters, Creed argues, are what crosses or threatens to cross the border, but what the border is bordering might differ. In some horror films the monstrous is produced at the border between human and inhuman; or human and the supernatural; or good and evil; or, Creed argues, the monstrous is produced at the border which separates those who take up their proper gender roles from those who do not; or between normal and abnormal sexual desire (Creed 1999: 253).

Creed argues that all human societies have a conception of *the Monstrous-Feminine*: 'of what it is about woman that is shocking, terrifying, horrific, abject' (Creed 1999: 251). Creed also makes the point that our attitude to the monster is frequently ambivalent: although society teaches us to be morally appalled by its terrible deeds, rarely is the monster presented as wholly unsympathetic. Indeed, part of us takes delight in its actions and identifies with them. The abject terrifies us but fascinates us all the same. According to Creed, horror films attest to the audience's desire to confront 'sickening, horrific images', to witness the taboo, that which provokes shock and terror; then, once we have taken our fill, 'to throw up, throw out, eject the abject' (Creed 2001: 10). Comments such as 'that made me feel sick' touch on this function of abjection in a literal sense. The depiction of the abject allows spectators to indulge in taboo forms of behaviour without having to act themselves, before order is finally restored. According to Creed, this is the horror film's central appeal.

In order to unpack such sickening feelings of revulsion further, it is useful to think about a politics of disgust. I return to Tyler's *Revolting Subjects*. First, building on Mary Douglas who, in 1966, suggested that disgust reactions are always anchored to wider social beliefs and structures of taboo (Douglas 1966), Tyler discusses 'disgust consensus':

> That which is experienced and/or imagined to be filthy corresponds with prevailing belief systems, and involves community-wide complicity. In this regard, disgust reactions are always contingent and relational, revealing less about the disgusted individual, or the thing deemed disgusting, than about *the culture* in which disgust is experienced and performed.
>
> (Tyler 2013: 23, my emphasis)

Thus, while disgust is a physically experienced 'urgent, guttural and aversive emotion, associated with sickening feelings of revulsion, loathing or nausea' (ibid.: 21), it is also socially performed and culturally negotiated. Tyler builds on Kolnai's differentiation between 'natural' (physiological) and 'moral' forms of disgust. In 'moral disgust', Kolnai suggests, and I am paraphrasing Tyler here, a physical experience of disgust slides into contempt and judgements or value. Yet, because disgust is an emotion associated with involuntary reaction, moral disgust is often experienced, or retroactively understood, as a *natural* response (ibid.: 22–3). Moreover, what Tyler is emphasising, and what I also find useful, is Kolnai's idea about disgust as a 'spatially' aversive emotion. In being disgusted, Kolnai writes, 'we perform a sort of "flight" from the "perceptual neighbourhood" of the revolting thing or person and from possible "intimate contact and union with it" (quoted in ibid.: 22). In other words, disgust creates (or attempts to create) boundaries and generates distance. As Tyler summarises: 'When we approach disgust as symptomatic of wider social relations of power, we can begin to ascertain why disgust might be attributed to particular bodies. Disgust is political' (ibid.: 24).

In order to understand social abjection, agency and the construction of monsters, legal theorist Belinda Morrissey's *When Women Kill* (2003) offers additional insight. Morrissey analyses media discourses and mainstream, as well as feminist, legal discourses narrating events about women who murder. Morrissey suggests that such story-telling to the public can be read as displaying evidence of trauma. Female killers gain humanity under only one circumstance – when they can be represented as politically neutered victims. If female killers do not correspond to the limitations of this stereotype, they are placed in the opposite and equally non-agentic category of the inhuman monster (Morrissey 2003: 17). This vilification of women who kill, Morrissey argues, operates to displace the offender from her society, to insist on her otherness, thereby avoiding the knowledge that she is produced *by* that society (ibid.: 24). Thus, by insisting upon the evil nature of the murderess, this process of vilification/monsterisation denies agency as well as humanity. She is transformed into a monster from outside society threatening the mainstream, rather than one of its members, produced, enabled by her social and cultural milieu. The murderess is considered to have acted, but not as a *human* woman (ibid.: 25).

Reactions to a cultural trauma result in discursive representations of women who kill as 'pure evil' and this ultimately denies them human agency. It is particularly traumatic when a woman kills her male partner as it threatens the social fabric of her culture. Such an act, Morrissey argues, disturbs, challenges and questions the modern Western incarnations of the ideologies of family, marriage and heterosexuality (Morrissey 2003: 97). This can of course be contrasted to the fact that when the situation is reversed, when a male kills his female partner, we often hardly notice; such acts are more common and, thus, in a sense 'normalised'. Morrissey adds that representations of trauma when women kill confirm that female aggression has no place in our culture (ibid.: 25).

To come back to the spatialising of social abjection, the politics of disgust enable the constitution of an identity through disidentification with another and it is this process that I think of as a form of interpellation. The following, in which Morrissey describes one of her cases, highlights the way I think about the politics of disgust's interpellating moment: 'Her monstrosity was insistently used to denote "our" normality, her evil to demonstrate "our" implied good, her supernatural inhumanity to indicate "our" humanity' (Morrissey 2003: 133).

In an article explaining how women's violence is portrayed through narratives of sexual deviance that reduces the actors involved to 'bad sex', Sjoberg and Gentry argue there are two main themes. Either the violence is explained as caused by a woman's sexual obsession and uncontrollable need to have sex with men, or, through the erotic dysfunction narrative which emphasises women's unwillingness or perceived inability to please men (Sjoberg and Gentry 2008: 13). The sexuality trope has been applied to women serving in militaries as a way to explain away their defiance of traditional gender roles (ibid.: 14). The very first paragraph in Kayla Williams's autobiography about her experiences as a young female soldier in the US Army is telling:

> Slut. The only other choice is bitch. If you're a woman and a soldier, those are the choices you get. I'm twenty-eight years old. Military Intelligence, five years, here and in Iraq. One of the 15 percent of the U.S. military that's female. And that whole 15 percent trying to get past an old joke. "What's the difference between a bitch and a slut? A slut will fuck anyone, a bitch will fuck anyone but you." So if she's nice or friendly, outgoing or chatty – she's a slut. If she's distant or reserved or professional – she's a bitch.
>
> (Williams 2006: 13)

In the erotic dysfunction narrative women's violence, or as I use it here, female bodies' capacity to kill, is blamed on, or justified by, irregularities in their sex lives. Because of their inability or unwillingness to please men sexually, women become emotionally disturbed and translate this emotional trouble into violence, so the story goes. The implication of the erotic dysfunction narrative is that women who commit violence do so because there is something wrong with them that stops them from fulfilling their (normal) biological destiny of becoming wives and mothers (Sjoberg and Gentry 2008: 10). This is because the association between femininity and sexual reproduction is one of the dominant notions of gender identity: maternity is usually recognised as 'natural', at the core of women's experience of themselves as gendered beings. Indeed, Myra Hird argues, the 'naturalness' of motherhood is so stubborn as to render women's actual experiences of childbirth and child-rearing often immaterial (Hird 2003: 6). Moreover, because gendered bodies tend to be homogenised, the link between femininity and sexual reproduction is 'natural' and childless women who deny their definitional gendered 'essence' are rendered deviant and/or denied adult status (ibid.: 8).

It is perhaps unsurprising therefore that, in the horror film, female monstrosity is almost always discussed in terms of the Freudian idea of woman as man's castrated other and nearly always depicted in relation to mothering and reproductive functions (Creed 2001). It is because the maternal body plays a key role in the construction of the abject that it has become the underlying image of all that is monstrous in the horror film, signifying that which threatens the stability of the 'Symbolic Order'. But, as Creed emphasises, 'woman is not, by her very nature, an abject being'. Rather, patriarchal ideology constructs her as such (ibid.: 83). Judith Butler argues that the foundation of sexual difference as maternal reproduction is no more than the truth effect of a 'tacit collective agreement to perform, produce, and sustain discrete and polar genders as cultural fictions (Butler 2006: 140). The maternal body is an effect of a discourse and performance that requires the 'female body … to assume maternity as the essence of its self and the law of its desire' (ibid.: 125).

These women and female subjects whose agency in political violence is explained through stories about erotic dysfunction have failed their gendered 'essence'. Because life-giving is intimately linked to normative femininity, these women are seen to have acted against their femininity and this, in turn, is what threatens the heteronormative way of life, or what some may call the stability of the Symbolic Order. I refer to this as the *Deviant Womb* narrative trope.

In addition, there is yet another aspect to the narrative trope of the *Deviant Womb*: monstrosity has also been discussed in relation to cyborgs, the boundary between what is considered human and what is considered non-human. In her 'Manifesto for Cyborgs', first published in the 1980s, Donna Haraway defines a cyborg as a 'cybernetic organism, a hybrid of machine and organism, a creature of social reality as well as a creature of fiction' (Haraway 2000: 50). Haraway argues that in the traditions of western science and politics, the relation between organism and machine has been a border war. The stakes in the border war have been the territories of production, reproduction and imagination (ibid.: 51). Moreover, according to Jennifer Gonzalez, the image of the cyborg body functions as a site of condensations and displacement: 'It contains on its surface and in its fundamental structure the multiple fears and desires of a culture caught in the process of transformation' (Gonzalez 2000: 58). Gonzalez makes a distinction between organic and mechanical cyborgs: an organic cyborg can be defined as a monster of multiple species, whereas a mechanical cyborg can be considered a techno-human mixture or fusion (Gonzalez 2000: 58):

> The body of the woman is not merely hidden inside the machine ... , nor is the organic body itself a mechanical replica, rather the body and the machine are a singular entity.
>
> (Ibid.: 59–60)

Anne Balsamo argues that cyborgs, as simultaneously human and mechanical, disrupt notions of otherness as the notion of the human relies upon an understanding of the non-human (Balsamo 2000: 150). In this sense, cyborgs function to challenge the stability of human identity. They fascinate us because they are not like us, and yet just like us. Formed through a radical disruption of otherness, Balsamo argues, cyborg identity foregrounds the constructedness of otherness. Cyborgs alert us to the ways culture and discourse depend upon notions of 'the other' that are arbitrary and binary, and also shifting and unstable. Who or what gets constructed as other becomes a site for the cultural contestation of meaning within feminist politics (ibid.: 155).

The metaphor of cyborgs is about transgressions of boundaries, including processes of abjection. The concept of the cyborg is therefore useful as the point of intersection, merger and boundary between human and machine in the narrative trope of the *Deviant Womb*. Thus, while there are many types of cyborgs I only use the idea of cyborgs as the (mechanical) cyborg body that can pass as human, more specifically, as a *Deviant Womb*. In contrast to how the narrative trope of the *Deviant Womb* informs the writing of subjects as empty wombs through stories about erotic dysfunction, the cyborg *Deviant Womb* is full/pregnant/meaningful/loaded/charged but its purpose is not to give life, but to take life.

Last, I borrow another concept from Creed, the *Femme Castratrice*, in order to conceptualise a particular type of monster in representations of female agency in political violence: a monster that enjoys and takes pleasure from participating in acts of political violence. Creed, writing from a psychoanalytic perspective, discusses, in addition to the idea of woman as man's castrated other, also the castrated woman's nemesis: the *Femme Castratrice*, the castrating woman. In films featuring the *Femme Castratrice*, it is the male body, not the female body, which bears the burden of castration. Here, the spectator is invited to identify with the avenging female castrator. It is the *Femme Castratrice* who controls the sadistic gaze and the male victim is her object (Creed 2001: 153). The castrating woman is not passive like the castrated woman. Instead, she represents an active monster. The *Femme Castratrice* is an all-powerful, all-destructive figure, who 'arouses a fear of castration and death while simultaneously playing on a masochistic desire for death, pleasure and oblivion [in men]' (ibid.: 130).

In her research about women murderesses, Morrissey found that those women murderesses who performed the roles of 'good', self-sacrificing wife and mother in the mainstream discourses, and of oppressed and angry victim in feminist legal discourse, were far more recuperable than women who enacted the roles of female sadist and dominatrix present in discourses like pornography. Morrissey argues that because female sadism is generally hidden, it is not supposed to exist, and remains deeply repressed within Western heteropatriarchy (Morrissey 2003: 171, 173).

Thus, female subjects produced through the *Femme Castratrice* narrative trope do not only challenge traditional views of women as passive victims associated with a naturalised, caring and nurturing femininity, but the fact that the female perpetrator of violence, whose victims are male, takes pleasure in such violence is particularly threatening. The *Femme Castratrice* is the subject and controls the gaze, whereas males are the objects of her violence. Furthermore, crucially, this discourse encompasses elements of sadomasochism and therefore gives the discourse sexual undertones of domination. Hence, it is through ideas about sex, power and domination that monstrosity is produced through the *Femme Castratrice*. Importantly, however, all subjects discussed in this chapter have transgressed the gender border by appearing threatening to the heteropatriarchal conception of femininity associated with maternal reproduction. Threatening, these maternalist war stories are told as perversions of motherhood.

Lynndie

The Monstrous-Feminine

> Because the photographs showing Private England were **especially shocking** and numerous, she became the face of the scandal, even more so than Private Graner, who was convicted in January of helping to orchestrate the abuse and who admitted during testimony in this case that he had struck a detainee.
>
> (Cloud, *New York Times*, 27 September 2005)

Here, I unpack and discuss two main ways in which the photos of England were 'especially shocking'. First, the fact that England was pregnant when the scandal broke meant that the tension between her identity as a [future] mother and her role as a soldier in the US army could not be ignored: 'Pictures of the **pregnant** 21-year-old US Army reservist in Iraq's notorious Abu Ghraib jail have **shocked** the world' (Chandler, *Daily Star*, 9 May 2004). In other words, England's pregnancy seemed to put even more emphasis on the fact that *women* were found participating in the scandalous activities depicted in the photos from Abu Ghraib:

> England remains a **mystery**. Is she a torturer? A pawn? Another victim of the Iraq war? While the world weighed in, England said very little.
>
> (McKelvey, *Marie Claire*, 2006)

The images were as notorious as they were **shocking**: the young woman grinning and giving a thumbs-up sign beside a naked Iraqi detainee and leading another around on a dog leash.

(Unattributed, *The Times*, 4 May 2005)

SMIRKING out of the vile photographs of the bludgeoned and humiliated Iraqi prisoners is Private Lynndie England. Her presence adds **a peculiar horror** to the scenes of suffering and inhumanity she helped to orchestrate at the notorious Abu Ghraib prison. Her wanton sadism denies the **natural virtues of womanhood:** compassion, gentleness and the capacity to conciliate. What then, in the theatre of conflict in Iraq, could have so corrupted a young American woman that she was willing to indulge in such savagery?

(James, *Daily Mail*, 7 May 2004)

In the last example, the author asks 'What turns a woman into a savage?' and tries to understand how a woman, who is 'naturally' peaceful, could participate in such torture. How can 'the brutality that Lynndie England seemed so eager to indulge in' be explained? The author suggests that:

To prove their worth, many female soldiers, police officers or prison warders too easily shed the distinctions of their sex in a drive to be tougher, more aggressive, less forgiving than any of their male colleagues. To do otherwise, they imagine, is to appear weak and inferior.

(James, *Daily Mail*, 7 May 2004)

As discussed in previous chapters in relation to Ulrike/Gudrun in *The Baader-Meinhof Complex* and Jeanne/Gaelle in *Female Agents*, fictional characters are often contrasted and positioned against each other. Although this might be easier to do with fictional characters, the case of Faye Turney illustrated that 'real' cases too are portrayed in similar ways. The composition of images and accompanying headings often gives us a clue. Hence, similarly to how Turney was presented as two, sometimes three, different subject positions, the headline 'The making of an **all-American monster**' is accompanied with an article and two photos of Lynndie England illustrating the tension between Lynndie – the woman and Lynndie – the monster (Knight, *Daily Mail*, 8 May 2004). Again, the confusion concerns how a woman like England could end up as a torturer:

The **enigma** is how a tomboyish, possibly stubborn, but by all accounts sweet-natured girl could have become involved in such atrocities?

(Knight, *Daily Mail*, 8 May 2004)

Similarly, a commentary in *The Times* asks:

What awful transgression has occurred to make a woman do this? In wars, as in civilian life, the overwhelming majority of sexual violence is committed by men against women. So that England, with her arm around her lover Charles Graner, thumbs up beside bodies kicked into obscene poses, is all the more **shocking**: a traitor, a collaborator, Rose West to his Fred. Just how culpable was England, a booking-in clerk with no reason to be there except to visit Graner? Was she participating in the fun and games to please him, a man violent enough to stalk his ex-wife?

(Turner, *The Times*, 8 May 2004)

Many other faces have emerged, but England's remains **iconic** – and tragically so, considering that a child is coming into Lynndie England's embattled world, and considering that the **new mother** could end up in jail in a case that has polarized the nation.

(Duke, *Washington Post*, 19 September 2004)

Once England had given birth to her son, the media representations changed. England was now simply reduced to 'the mum': 'Pictures of **the mum** and other troops posing with naked Iraqis sparked a storm in 2003' (Unattributed, *Sun*, 3 May 2005); 'But Private Charles Graner, the **22-year-old mum's** former boyfriend, said HE placed the dog leash around the prisoner's neck and asked England to lead him out of his cell' (Smith, *Sun*, 5 May 2005); '**The mother of one** was convicted by a military jury on six of seven charges, including committing an indecent act and maltreatment of prisoners at Baghdad's Abu Ghraib jail' (Thompson, *Sun*, 27 September 2005). The headline in the *Sun* regarding the fact that Lynndie England had given birth to her son was: '**Torturer's Baby**' (Unattributed, *Sun*, 14 October 2004). Then again, on 29 October, 2004, another article titled '**Torturer's tot**' was published both in the *Sun* and the *Daily Mirror* (Flynn, *Sun; Daily Mirror*, 29 October 2004).

According to Morrissey, when women murderesses are also mothers, their acts are often understood as particularly monstrous: 'Mothers who commit rapes and murders are seen to embody the "monstrous maternal" in all her fearsomeness' (Morrissey 2003: 154). It is possible therefore that England's identity as a mother was brought up to sensationalise the story about Abu Ghraib even more. In any case, the shock factor present in these stories of motherhood and torture highlight precisely the tension between capacities to give versus take life, and the cultural grammar with which such a tension is understood, that this book attempts to make sense of.

Second, as discussed above, characters are often written by being positioned in relation to an other, whether this other is a different person such as in Gudrun/Ulrike or another version of the self such as when Faye's identity splits into multiple ones (mother/soldier/pawn). In this sense, the monstrous abject is produced through what it is not. This was also the case with Lynndie England. England was written as a monstrous abject through a comparison of what she was not. As it happened, she was not Jessica Lynch (see also discussion about Lynch in Chapter 4).

> After all, the much-hailed Pfc. **Jessica Lynch**, that other iconic face from Iraq, also is from West Virginia, from a tiny place on the other side of the state called Palestine. But **one became a heroine; the other, a source of shame**, part of a crew of soldiers who somehow went over the edge and engaged in abuse like 'something out of sport,' as one witness described it during England's hearings.
>
> (Duke, *Washington Post*, 19 September 2004)

> It's almost too perfect. Two young working-class women from opposite ends of West Virginia go off to war. **One is blond and has aspirations to be a schoolteacher. The other is dark, a smoker, divorced and now carrying an out-of-wedlock baby.** One becomes the heroic poster child for Operation Iraqi Freedom, the subject of a hagiographic book and TV movie; the other becomes the hideous, leering face of American wartime criminality, Exhibit A in the indictment of our country's descent into the gulag. In the words of Time magazine, Pfc. Lynndie England is 'a **Jessica Lynch gone wrong**.'
>
> (Rich, *New York Times*, 16 May 2004)

> England's friends and family say she is similar to **Jessica Lynch**, another young woman from rural West Virginia who joined the military to broaden her horizons. When **Lynch**'s Army unit was attacked during the war's early days, England's family says, the military and the news media inaccurately **created a heroine**. In **England**'s case, they say, the same parties are creating **a villainess**.
>
> (Cauchon, Howlett and Hampson, *USA Today*, 7 May 2004)

In Chapter 4, I suggest that the writing of Lynch as a heroine is informed by the narrative trope of the *Vacant Womb*, which not only communicates *before* motherhood but can also signify before sexuality, i.e. virginity etc. Whereas Lynch's sexual life was less interesting/visible, England was labelled sexually deviant. England's (alleged) participation in prison abuse at Abu Ghraib, thereby, fits into the first of Sjoberg and Gentry's 'bad sex' explanations, that her participation at Abu Ghraib was caused by, or at least made sense due to, her 'sexual obsession and uncontrollable need to have sex with men' (Sjoberg and Gentry 2008: 13).

> We need to ask why, out of the thousands of photos that surfaced (and were made available to Congress), only the few highly sexualized photos were released to the public.
>
> (Marshall 2007: 52)

The initial reports usually mentioned that she was thought to be pregnant which reflected badly on her because in order to get pregnant England must have broken the rules:

> Getting pregnant in combat theater is forbidden; soldiers are not deployed to such areas if they are pregnant. 'That right there makes women look bad' Carney says of the pregnancy. 'Male soldiers do it, too, it's just that they don't get caught 'cause they don't get pregnant.'
>
> (Duke, *Washington Post*, 19 September 2004)

> DEPRAVED US soldier Lynndie England disobeyed orders to **sneak off for sex** with her lover at the Iraq jail where they tortured prisoners ... Private England, 21, was banned from leaving her quarters unescorted after being **caught in bed four times** with Specialist Charles Graner, 35 ... She is now seven months **pregnant** with his child.
>
> (Unattributed, *Sun*, 6 August 2004)

England was reprimanded three times for disobeying direct orders not to sleep with Graner, her boyfriend at the time (Zernike, *New York Times*, 27 May 2004). Thus, her alleged promiscuity, 'proven' by her pregnancy, was used to construct her as sexually deviant. Months later during her trials, England was heavily pregnant, which again functioned as yet another reminder of her indecent behaviour. The story of England as sexually deviant was also the military prosecutors' main strategy to show England's guilt in the prison abuse at Abu Ghraib. To this end, footage of England engaging in sexual acts was used. Importantly, the footage did not show her torturing prisoners:

> Private England, wearing a maternity version of military camouflage, appeared to suppress a smile as investigators described a **videotape that showed her having sex** with Cpl. Charles Graner, who prosecutors say was a ringleader of the abuse and Private England says is the father of the child she is carrying. Her mother sat stern-faced in the observation gallery, her eyes darting from the witness stand to her daughter as an investigator described photographs of Private England **topless and engaged in what he called oral sex.**
>
> (Zernike, *New York Times*, 4 August 2004)

> THE pregnant soldier accused of humiliating Iraqi prisoners was photographed performing **lewd acts** with fellow troops, a military hearing was told. Lynndie England was **pictured naked** by a pool, waving her breasts in front of a sleeping solider and **performing a sex act** with a colleague.
>
> (Gardner, *Daily Mail*, 5 August 2004)

However, Lynndie England's alleged promiscuity was not only portrayed as directed towards her then boyfriend:

> US senators who have viewed unpublished pictures from the prison say they show Lynndie England in **sex acts with numerous fellow soldiers**. 'Almost everybody was naked all the time,' a senator said.
>
> (Churcher, *Daily Mail*, 16 May 2004)

In the UK, headlines such as 'Baghdad jail **orgies**: Shamed GI **Lynndie had sex** in front of Iraqi prisoners', 'Lynndie's jail orgies' (Harwood, *Daily Mirror*, 14 May 2004) and 'Lynndie filmed a **sex orgy**' (Flynn, *Sun*, 14 May 2004) dominated the media coverage. England was portrayed as 'naked and **eagerly engaging in romps** with soldier pals' (Flynn, *Sun*, 14 May 2004) and a senator claimed that '**sex with numerous partners** seemed to be **consensual**' (Harwood, *Daily Mirror*, 14 May 2004). England's promiscuity was not even limited to fellow male soldiers; she was also represented as a beast preying on the prisoners in her care:

> Investigators are now probing claims that her unborn child was fathered when she **forced** an Iraqi **detainee** at Baghdad's notorious Abu Ghraib prison **into sex** … Insiders are now **doubting that Cpl Graner is the father** of her child … There were also questions of whether England was having sex with an Iraqi prisoner who could be the father of the child she's carrying. 'She definitely **had an eye for** some of the better-looking **guys being led around naked**.'
>
> (Nicks, *Daily Star*, 19 May 2004)

In the end, the charges of indecency bore a higher penalty than the charges for abuse (Zernike, *New York Times*, 07/08/2004). England's defence team argued that the charges regarding sexually explicit photographs were designed to distract attention from the real issue of widespread prisoner abuse by US forces in Iraq:

> 'They are intimate photographs of a young girl with her boyfriend at the time,' Mr Hernandez said. 'They are not something that had anything to do with prisoner abuse.'
>
> (Monaghan, *The Times*, 4 August 2004)

England and Graner had started their sexual relationship prior to their deployment to Iraq but it did not seem to matter that some of the photos depicting England in sexual acts, or implied sexual acts, were not even taken at Abu Ghraib. The mere existence of such photos made her easy to frame as a sexual predator and thereby sexually deviant to normative femininity. She was likened to a porn star:

In those pictures that have been printed, her facial expression is very often, as you might expect, a sneer, but the eyes are dark pools that don't even reflect the camera's flash. The eyes of Private England, **the woman tugging the leash around the neck of a naked Iraqi prisoner,** appear **empty of emotion**. The soldier smiles sadistically but her eyes, dark and devoid of empathy, emit as much emotion as a **hardened actress in a porn film**.

(Crichton, *Sunday Herald*, 9 May 2004)

In a similar way to how Kayla Williams explains the two 'labels' for women in armed forces, as sluts or bitches, and following Sjoberg and Gentry's (2008) argument about how women's agency in political violence is limited to narratives of 'bad sex', normative ideas about women's sexuality informed the writing of Lynndie England as a monstrous abject.

The Femme Castratrice

In addition, the writing of England as a sexually deviant monster was also informed by the narrative trope of the *Femme Castratrice*. When photos from the Abu Ghraib prison first became public, images of Lynndie England were prominent.[1] Among the first photos to be released was one in which England is pointing at the genitals of a naked Iraqi prisoner with a cigarette in her mouth. When more photos were released, it was one in which England is holding a leash attached to an Iraqi prisoner's neck while he is lying on the floor that dominated the media coverage (Marks, *Scotsman*, 7 May 2004). The 'leash-photo' made it onto newspapers' front pages with titles such as 'Treated like a dog' (Unattributed, *Daily Mail*, 7 May 2004) and '**Witch: Evil** soldier Lynndie in new torture photo' (Flynn, *Sun*, 7 May 2004). Moreover, it was the fact that England seemed to be smiling in the photos that created much fury:

[T]he same **smiling face** is splashed across newspapers and on television screens around the world and that patriotic scene at the family home in Fort Ashby, West Virginia, has been substituted by one of stunned shame… **one of the most reviled faces in recent history** … In one, sporting the same impish grin, she aims a make-believe rifle at the **genitals of naked and hooded** Iraqi detainees.

(Knight, *Daily Mail*, 8 May 2004)

In others, she **grinned** and gave a thumbs-up sign next to **humiliated naked** and hooded Iraqi **men**.

(Chandler, *Daily Star*, 9 May 2004)

Lynndie England, 'the grinning face in the graphic images of abuse from Abu Ghraib prison' (Goldenberg, *Guardian*, 3 May 2005), became a symbol of everything that was wrong with the war in Iraq. Her 'grin' became 'the symbol of sadistic practices at Abu Ghraib prison' (Goldenberg, *Guardian*, 8 May 2004). Morley Safer, correspondent for 60 Minutes said: 'We now have the new symbol of this war. It is no longer the picture of Saddam's statue tipping over – it's a girl with an Iraqi on a leash' (Horovitz, Grossman and Johnson, *USA Today*, 10 May 2004). She was 'A new **monster in chief**' and 'the latest **hate figure** to help obscure the bigger picture' (Riddell, *Observer*, 9 May 2004). According to BBC News, the photos of England were 'images that will haunt America's occupation of Iraq' and 'it is Lynndie **England's face most linked to the horror**' (Myrie, BBC news, 8 May 2004).

The initial representations of Lynndie England segmented and in the continuous coverage she was commonly referred to as 'the woman with the leash'; 'the pointer'; and 'the grinning-face' (Zernike, *New York Times*, 4 August 2004). She was also referred to as '**the** Iraq abuse girl' (Unattributed, *Daily Mirror*, 30 April 2005), even though there were more women involved, and 'Dog lead Lynndie' (Boffey, *Daily Mirror*, 3 May 2005). My argument here is that England was constructed as a monster through the *Femme Castratrice*; a sadist who takes pleasure in torturing her male victims. Because of the smiles, England was depicted as having an 'evident taste for cruelty' (Goldenberg, *Guardian*, 8 May 2004):

> It is England's **smile**, beaming as she holds a humiliated Iraqi prisoner on a leash or points an imaginary gun at the **genitals of naked detainees**, that has provided the **most shocking images** from the album of horrors at Abu Ghraib.
>
> (Watson and Farrell, *The Times*, 8 May 2004)

In *The Times*, one commentary reflected on what made Lynndie England participate, asking whether she was forced into it. The conclusion was that she was not: 'England's **face – enthusiastic, amused, triumphant** – does not, however, reflect someone dragged into **sadistic sex play**' (Turner, *The Times*, 8 May 2004).[2] England seemed to be participating freely. She is the *Femme Castratrice*. Later, when details of what England first told investigators were published, it was the fact that she 'was having fun' that was most upsetting:

> In a sworn statement to investigators, Pfc. Lynndie England explained the mystery of why soldiers at Abu Ghraib took pictures of detainees masturbating and piled naked with plastic sandbags over their heads by saying, 'We thought it **looked funny** so pictures were taken.'
>
> (Zernike, *New York Times*, 16 May 2004)

> Private Lynndie England told investigators that the pictures were taken 'while they were joking around, **having some fun**, working the nightshift.'
>
> (Unattributed, *Daily Mail*, 4 August 2004)

In the *Sun*, one headline read '**Torture fun**':

> **CRUEL** American soldier Lynndie England has told how Iraqi inmates were forced to wear women's panty pads and crawl through broken glass ... Pregnant England – sent home in disgrace after being pictured torturing Iraqis – also admitted the cruelty was **carried out for FUN**. Asked by army investigators in North Carolina who knew of the abuse, she said: 'Everyone in the company, from the commander down. We thought it **looked funny**, so pictures were taken.' She described the horrific abuse as 'basically us **fooling around**'.
>
> (Unattributed, *Sun*, 19 May 2004)

Most news coverage regarding Lynndie England's 'fun' at Abu Ghraib mentioned that she was smiling in the photos, that her victims were male, depicted naked and that she was pregnant with the child of the alleged ring-leader (Monaghan, *The Times*, 31 August 2004; Harwood, *Daily Mirror*, 7 May 2004). That England was torturing 'for fun' also formed part of the military prosecutors' main argument during her trials months later; the representation of England as the *Femme Castratrice*, enjoying, laughing and smiling while torturing her male victims, continued:

> They [the military prosecutors] argued that since England did not work at the cellblock where most of the prisoner abuse occurred and visited it despite orders to stay away, 'It's clear Pfc. England was not an MP. She was not recruited into a secret military mission as the defence would have you believe. She **was there to have some fun**.'
>
> (Parker, *USA Today*, 1 September 2004)

> 'The accused knew what she was doing,' said Capt. Chris Graveline, the lead prosecutor. 'She was **laughing and joking** ... She is **enjoying**, she is participating, all for her own sick humour.'
>
> (Unattributed, *USA Today*, 26 September 2005)

> A military prosecutor said England humiliated prisoners because she **enjoyed it** and had a sick sense of humour.
>
> (Thompson, *Sun*, 27 September 2005)

By focusing on her smile in the photos, the fact that her victims were naked males and the use of the leash, Lynndie England was constructed a monster through the trope of the *Femme Castratrice* both when the photos became public, during investigations and during her trials. Because of the smiles, England seemed to take pleasure in torture. The sexual sadomasochistic undertones of the discourse of the *Femme Castratrice* were, furthermore, made visible with references to the leash and the fact that her victims were naked males. Lynndie England became the 'sex sadist of Baghdad' (Brittain 2006: 86).

Nasima

The Deviant Womb

In *Britz*, Nasima is constructed as a monster through the narrative trope of the *Deviant Womb* as a cyborg body faking motherhood. Nasima is faking motherhood because the explosives that are strapped on her belly in the final scenes make her look pregnant. In addition, she wears a maternity suit that functions to hide the explosives. The suit not only covers the explosives on her belly but also her breasts; it makes them larger, more realistic of a pregnant woman. This gives Nasima a softer appearance, as human and womanly as possible. The maternity suit makes Nasima look heavily pregnant. It makes her look like an occupied womb symbolising life-giving. However, Nasima is deceptive. Her identity of life-giving is an illusion. Instead, her identity is one of life-taking. Nasima is using motherhood as a political strategy in order to achieve her political goal of life-taking.

Discussing 'Kiddy', a 1990s comic series character, Jennifer Gonzales suggests that she is an 'exotic' and vindicative cyborg who passes as simply human. It is when she removes her skin that she becomes the quintessential cyborg body. Her 'real' identity, Gonzales argues, lies beneath the camouflage of her dark skin-rather than on its surface (Gonzalez 2000: 70). Similarly, Nasima passes as 'simply human'. Instead, it is what is hidden beneath, not her skin in this case, but her clothing, that reveals her true identity as a cyborg, a monster, part human, part machine, a woman yet a bomb, a female suicide bomber.

While Nasima is constructed as a monster and a cyborg body, another maternalist narrative is subtly communicated in the scene where Nasima puts the bomb and the maternity suit on. From cinema studies we learn that how a shot is composed and framed is its mise-en-scène. How the shot is cut together into a sequence or scene is known as a montage (Rowley 2009: 316). As briefly discussed in Chapter 3, an object presented in a close-up inevitably draws attention to its perceptible qualities, to everything that makes it different. Mitry argues that the close-up appeals to the emotions but these can only be felt, experienced by seeing it. The close-up concentrates on the object, on its forms, and on all the 'recognitive and dynamogenic operations' relating to the knowledge we have of it. The close-up thereby presents a tactile, sensual impression of objects, importantly, before it makes any appeal to the intellect (Mitry 2000: 67). Because of these qualities, Mitry argues, of all shots the close-up is the most concrete, most objective through what it shows, the most abstract, most subjective through what it signifies (Mitry 2000: 68).

As Nasima straps the explosives on, there are many short close-ups of her belly. In these shots, Nasima's head is cut off. The close-ups on the bomb, therefore, denote depersonification. The bomb is the object that is magnified, appears relatively large and fills the entire frame to focus attention and emphasise its importance. The bomb is the main character, Nasima has transformed into the mechanical cyborg. As a cyborg, the body and the machine have become a singular entity.

Nasima touches her 'belly' as a pregnant woman would do and looks at herself in the mirror. She puts the maternity suit on and looks in the mirror again. In cinema studies, the affective relationships between audience and film have often been invoked by referring to Jacques Lacan and the 'mirror stage' (Mitry 2000: 193). To Lacan, the primary distinction between self and other is founded on identification with an image. According to Mitry, the mirror stage makes it easier to be conscious of the self, but it is not essential (Mitry 2000: 196). Thus, the portrayal of Nasima looking at herself in a mirror is a way of showing the audience that Nasima identifies with herself as a life-taker, she is conscious of the self she has become. However, the inclusion of the mirror also means that her feelings are reflected out to the audience. In cinema studies, mirrors can function to signify ambiguity or duplicity (Hayward 1996: 4). The inclusion of the mirror in the scene where Nasima is faking motherhood, therefore, emphasises the inherent ambiguity or tension in representations of female agency in political violence. It emphasises Nasima as both (seemingly) life-giving and life-taking and it illuminates the boundary of a normative femininity associated with motherhood. In this scene, the background music intensifies slightly when Nasima is looking at herself in the mirror, which enhances the emotional communication of the scene. The tension is also played out when Nasima is acting/faking motherhood during the walk towards the place for her attack. She is holding her hands on her 'pregnant' belly, appearing to be protecting life. Yet, as a cyborg body Nasima's motherhood performance is devious.

To sum up, the construction of Nasima as a monstrous abject is informed by the narrative trope of the *Deviant Womb* in two ways. On the one hand, Nasima's female body has failed to assume maternity as its gendered 'essence', and here both the mirror scene and the depiction of her maternal feelings as she hears about who/what her target is as mentioned in Chapter 3 communicates this 'problem'. However, because her intentions are secret, the most obvious maternalist story told in *Britz* is her being a deceitful cyborg *Deviant Womb*. This is how the subject becomes an abject subject and is, thus, written as monstrous. As a female suicide bomber, Nasima has become a non-agentic monstrous abject, an outcast alienated from society (see also Åhäll 2012c).

Faye

The Monstrous-Feminine

Three themes intersect when it comes to how Faye Turney was written as monstrous: first of all for having left her daughter behind, later for selling her story to the media and also by being ridiculed in comparison to the experience and sacrifice of 'true heroines'. First, the capture of Turney led to a debate in British media regarding whether or not mothers, or indeed women, should be allowed to serve in the military, particularly in 'combat roles'. *The Times* asked 'Should a mother join the Navy? Whatever your thoughts, post them below.' The article discussed a blog called 'Alpha Mummy': '"Alpha Mummy" is furious that the sailor has not put her child ahead of her own career and ambitions' (Unattributed, *The Times*, 29 March 2007). Simply by being a woman and a mother, Faye Turney was considered selfish:

> What in God's name was Faye Turney doing in those God-forsaken waters in the first place? Why was a 25-year-old mother with a three-year-old daughter putting her life and her freedom at risk? Was it in the name of equality? Because if it was, it's a pretty hollow cause when a child's future is at stake. Was she being **selfish** in doing a potentially dangerous job to satisfy her own personal needs? And if her career is so important, why have a baby at 22 when both she and husband, Adam, are both in the Navy. If, as some feminists have raged, it's because 21st Century woman has the right to do whatever job she chooses – then, I'm sorry, I disagree.
>
> (Malone, *Sunday Mirror*, 1 April 2007)

> I have to wonder what was she doing there, **risking** not just her own life but **the motherhood of an infant child**. Amid the relief that we will feel when she eventually returns, it still has to be asked why we are sending young mothers to a war zone of our own creation. Britain cannot be so short of military personnel that such women should be permitted – nay, encouraged – to go **gadding around** the world's most dangerous and volatile waterway. Call me old-fashioned but I think it is wholly wrong to separate a young mother from her child, put a gun in her hands and send her off to the Gulf ... The strain on this young woman must be intolerable. And she should not be under such strain, because she **should not have been there** in the first place. The person I feel sorry for in this appalling situation is little Molly, the wean that Mrs Turney **left behind** ... A diplomatic solution to this fiasco must swiftly be found. A solution to the moral issue of mother-and-child relationships in the armed services will take rather longer.
>
> (Routledge, *Daily Mirror*, 30 March 2007)

Similar arguments were printed in *The Times* ('A mother's place isn't in the war zone' by Jill Kirby, 1 April 2007) and in the *Daily Mail* ('Isn't a mother's first duty to her children?' by Jill Parkin). Parkin argues:

> No matter how we dress it up, men are always going to be better in battle and, if we're being honest, less vital to the children than mothers ... It may be politically incorrect to say so but for young children, the **loss of a mother** is likely to be **worse than the loss of a father**. In the end, that's what we're thinking about when we look at those pictures of Faye Turney at home before her capture, cuddling her baby. We're talking about the possibility of a **motherless child**. All this in the name of what is called 'equality' but which is actually a misguided belief that men and women are the same. But we are not.
>
> (Parkin, *Daily Mail*, 30 March 2007)

Routledge writes that 'the strain on this woman must be intolerable' implying that Faye Turney, because she is a mother, is more deeply affected than men in a similar situation (Routledge, *Daily Mirror*, 30 March 2007). Captain Anthea Burdus responded that women join the armed forces with their eyes open and that being a mother makes no difference. Burdus said: 'People always ask the same question "How do you cope?" And I think "Do you ask the men?" I have seen a lot of men away from their children for the first time who find it terribly, terribly hard' (Judd, *Independent*, 1 April 2007). Similarly, Sue Carroll called on those who questioned how Turney could contemplate serving on the front line with a three-year-old daughter at home to ask the same of her male colleagues, many of them married with children (Carroll, *Daily Mirror*, 4 April 2007). Interviewed in the *Daily Mirror*, Britain's first female fighter pilot Jo Salter tried to explain why women want to be on the front line, even if they are mothers:

> If there was ever a national emergency, and all the reserves were called up to fight, I wouldn't hesitate to sign up again even though it would mean leaving my children behind. Serving your country is more than a job – it's a life, a belief system of honour and loyalty.
>
> (McCaffrey, *Daily Mirror*, 7 April 2007)

What is interesting about the fact that the capture of Faye Turney ignited a debate whether or not women should be allowed in combat roles is how quickly the debate turned from a mother's role to a woman's role. Although temporarily, Turney had given up her role as a mother in order to serve as a soldier. She was represented as having left her daughter behind as this caption to an image of Faye and her daughter shows:

Left behind: Faye Turney in 2003 with daughter Molly, who is at home with Faye's husband Adam.

(Salkeld, *Daily Mail*, 28 March 2007)

Faye Turney was also compared to a British climber who died scaling K2:

Faye Turney risks being put in the same category as Alison Hargreaves, the British climber. Accused of selfishly putting her career before her family, Hargreaves died scaling K2 and left behind two young children.

(Thomson, *Daily Telegraph*, 29 March 2007)

Being a mother, Turney was portrayed as selfish for wanting a career, for risking her own life and careless for risking her daughter becoming motherless. Turney had seemingly transgressed a gender boundary and thus disrupted heteropatriarchal ideas of normative femininity linked to motherhood.

In addition, Faye Turney was also compared to other female British soldiers. At the time of the hostages' release, two British female soldiers were killed in Basra, Iraq. Having paid the ultimate price, being killed, the two women were portrayed as 'HEROINES' as a front page of the *Daily Mail* picturing the two women read (Seamark and English, *Daily Mail*, 7 April 2007). Turney's experience and heroism paled in comparison. In addition, in a rare attempt to control the media, the Ministry of Defence allowed the sailors and marines involved in the hostage taking to sell their stories to the news media. Turney was offered close to £100,000 to talk about 'her ordeal' in the *Sun* and in a television interview with ITV's Trevor McDonald. However, as she accepted the deal, she was turned into a monster of a different kind, a greedy monster:

The two sailors [Turney and Barchelor], pawns in a military, political and media game, were vilified for dishonouring their uniforms. The welcome home had suddenly turned nasty.

(Judd, *Independent*, 14 April 2007)

In comparison to what other soldiers were going through, Faye Turney's experience was ridiculed as she had been treated fairly well (the captives even received 'goody bags' from the Iranians). One commentary in the *Daily Telegraph* was titled: 'Faye a heroine? That's an insult to our dead soldiers' (Moir, *Daily Telegraph*, 11 April 2007). In addition, families of soldiers who had died in Iraq expressed that their sons or daughters were the true heroes and heroines; they were true patriots serving their country who never would have accepted any money for their story (Chapman, Greenhill and Koster, *Daily Mail*, 10 April 2007).

Ulrike/Gudrun

The Monstrous-Feminine

In *The Baader-Meinhof Complex* it is the transformation of Ulrike Meinhof, from someone who is publically advocating non-violence to someone who actually joins the armed resistance movement herself, that is most clearly told through a maternalist story. As mentioned in Chapter 3, the film starts by showing Ulrike on the beach with her children, but there are also other scenes in which motherhood is communicated as the border between non-violent respective violent means. In a couple of scenes in particular, the border is communicated and embodied by a character called Peter. First, when Peter, a fellow activist, hears about Ulrike's plan to take part in the freeing of Baader he protests: 'This is crazy!' he cries, whereupon Ulrike says: 'I have to do it'. At this stage the plan is only for Ulrike to set up the meeting in order for the RAF members to free Baader, not to actually join in the armed struggle, thus, Peter's disapproval concerns the association, whether public or not, with a group that is promoting violence. By expressing his disapproval, Peter represents the 'old Ulrike' who believed in non-violent means for political change. Ulrike, of course, does not listen to Peter's concerns. Not only does she agree to host the opportunity for the RAF members to free Baader, but as fighting erupts between the armed RAF members and Baader's guards, one of whom is shot, Ulrike decides to follow the RAF members by jumping out of a window. In this scene, the music is fast, powerful and intense and increases both in volume and in keys leading to a climax when Ulrike too jumps out of the window.

Where Peter's concerns might have voiced, and signposted, the border between non-violent and violent means, the window *visually* signifies Ulrike actually transgressing the border; the window is the signified physical border between non-violence and violence. The very next scene shows Ulrike's role on the other side of the border, as the writer of the RAF's political statements. In the first political statement for the RAF, published in *Der Spiegel*, she motivates the use of force:

> We say, the man in uniform is a pig, not a human being. That's how we have to deal with him. This means we don't talk to him and it's wrong to talk to these people at all. And **of course it's ok to shoot**. What we're doing, and what we want to show is that armed struggle is possible, and it is possible to take action and win, and the other side does not win. So it's important that they do not catch us. That is essential to our success.

Ulrike has transgressed the border; she has chosen violence as means for her political struggle. In another statement, Ulrike writes:

We demand a stop of the bombing in Vietnam. We demand the withdrawal of American troops from Indochina. We demand the lifting of the mine blockade against North Vietnam.

Images of bombings at US military headquarters and police departments are shown as the statement is read out. Ulrike's voice continues:

We will continue to **carry out bombings** against judges and prosecutors until they cease violating the rights of political prisoners. Our demands on the justice system are not unreasonable. We have no other means to force them to comply.

Another scene in which Ulrike's transformation and crossing of the border is communicated, not only through Peter but through motherhood, is during the RAF members training camp (with the PLO) in Jordan. When the RAF members arrive, Ulrike is sitting next to Peter on the back of a truck. Soon afterwards, a fight between Andreas Baader and Peter erupts and it seems that Ulrike must make a choice between which 'camp' to belong to, Andreas' or Peter's. In this scene, in a similar way to how Louise in *Female Agents* was used as a passive tool of communication between her brother Pierre and Heindrich, the Nazi Officer, as discussed in Chapter 3, Ulrike's choice here is one between which of the [fighting] men to follow. Ulrike remains passively quiet when the two men fight; they are the subjects in this scene, she is but an object. In a later scene showing a conversation between Ulrike and Peter at the training camp in Jordan, Ulrike's choice is confirmed:

ULRIKE: You want to go back [to West Germany], don't you?
PETER: (nods.)
ULRIKE: So you're giving up?
PETER: These people are at war. What's that got to do with our situation in West Germany? You think you can start a revolution in Germany with a Kalashnikov?
ULRIKE: West Germany is just one front. We fight oppression and injustice with our comrades around the world. I thought you knew that.
PETER: Then **why not start with your kids?** You've gone underground. **What is to become of them?**
ULRIKE: (silence.)

Peter offers to take care of the children when he returns to Germany but Ulrike thinks it 'sounds a lot like betrayal'. Ulrike stands up and says: 'Take care of yourself' and walks off. In this scene, Ulrike's transformation is complete. The rejection of Peter is at the same time a rejection of her old self, the one who believed in non-violent solutions. Interestingly, this transformation is again communicated through Ulrike's role as a mother. As mentioned above, in the beginning of the film, Ulrike tells Gudrun that she could never leave her children, however, at this stage Ulrike has changed, not just in the sense that she now supports violence but her role as a mother is also as a result compromised. To the audience, this means that motherhood in these scenes functions as the boundary between violence and non-violence; agency in political violence seems associated with the sacrifice of parenthood. Thus, what is communicated is that choosing violence, ultimately means giving up on motherhood. The identities of life-giving and life-taking cannot co-exist. In this sense, motherhood functions as the gender border agent.

Janis

The Monstrous-Feminine

When the images of the Abu Ghraib prison scandal became public, Janis Karpinski was the only higher ranking officer to be named and pictured, whereas other higher ranking officials were anonymous:

> The military is considering action against Brig. Gen. **Janis Karpinski**, the senior officer at the prison when the abuse occurred against 20 detainees in November and December. **Pentagon officials** said Friday that no final action had been determined. **General Karpinski and other officers** who are the subjects of the inquiry are now in a stage of the military legal process where they are allowed to write responses to the investigators' findings.
> (Shanker and Steinberg, *New York Times*, 1 May 2004)

> The highest-ranking officer to be suspended was Army Reserve Brig. Gen. Janis L. Karpinski, commander of the 800th Military Police Brigade.
> (Chan and Spinner, *Washington Post*, 30 April 2004)

> Karpinski was in charge of all U.S. military prisons in Iraq last October when prison guards began abusing Iraqi prisoners at Abu Ghraib prison near Baghdad. **Top Army officials** have criticized Karpinski's performance in the wake of a scandal that has resulted in criminal charges against seven guards, one of whom has pleaded guilty. Seven more soldiers have received career-threatening reprimands.
> (Moniz and Morrison, *USA Today*, 25 May 2004)

The article in *USA Today* is also accompanied with a photo of Karpinski with the caption: 'Under scrutiny: Brig. Gen. Janis Karpinski commanded the 800th Military Police Brigade in Iraq until Monday'. Again, Karpinski is named whereas 'Top Army officials' are not (Moniz and Morrison, *USA Today*, 25 May 2004). The *Daily Mail* reported on the 'Torture jail General' who 'may be kicked out of the Army':

THE U.S. general at the centre of the Iraqi PoW torture scandal faces being thrown out of the army in disgrace. General Karpinski, who was the only U.S. female commander in Iraq, has denied knowing anything about the torture and claims she is being made a scapegoat to cover up for intelligence chiefs who ordered soldiers to 'soften up' the Iraqis prior to interrogation.

(Shears, *Daily Mail*, 4 May 2004)

This article is accompanied with a photo of Karpinski and the caption: 'Carpeted: General Janis Karpinski says the US commander in Iraq should also bear responsibility' (Shears, *Daily Mail*, 4 May 2004). In an interview with *The Times*, Karpinski describes the moment news about the images was released:

There were the photographs and there, too, was footage of herself. A general was saying: 'This is Janis Karpinski the commander, and these are her soldiers.'

(de Bertodano, *The Times*, 13 August 2004)

The media subsequently reported on her failure as a leader as outlined in the Taguba report:

Maj. Gen. Antonio Taguba, author of the internal Pentagon report on prisoner abuse at Abu Ghraib prison by Army Reserve military police, said it was a 'failure in leadership' from Brig. Gen. Janis Karpinski on down. He said there was 'no training, no supervision.'

(Moniz, *USA Today*, 12 May 2004)

In this way, as soon as the scandal broke, it was Karpinski's name and also identity as female that immediately became associated with the images of abuse. Other officials in the chain of command, the majority of which were men, remained anonymous and, thereby, at least initially, avoided responsibility. The fact that a woman was in charge of those soldiers pictured in photos of sexual abuse added to the shock factor of the Abu Ghraib scandal, but this also made it easier to label the scandal a leadership failure. Despite the fact that most others involved were men, and despite that Karpinski was not in charge of interrogations at Abu Ghraib, but quite the contrary, prisoner care across all detainment centres in Iraq, the failure in leadership got a female face. The Monstrous-Feminine at Abu Ghraib had yet another face.

Lynndie

The Monstrous-Feminine

Stories of monsters are ambiguous, thus, every monster story also includes a counter narrative, an attempt at rescue, to put things right. In her research on media portrayals of women murderesses, Morrissey found that certain narratives aim to recuperate female protagonists by returning them to a 'proper feminine place' (Morrissey 2003: 165). In Chapter 4 I built on this notion to contextualise the temporal and spatial limitations to Faye Turney as a heroic subject soldier. The emphasis on maternal guilt there was an attempt at disciplining the subject, to police the gender border and make sure that the subject remain on the right side of the border. Here, I return to the case of Lynndie England and guilt to show how attempts to rescue the monstrous abject risk failing. This is because stories with monstrous abjects ultimately serve a purpose that has more to do with 'us' than the protagonist herself. And, this is why we tend to become obsessed with monster stories. I start with how her defence team attempted to rescue the monstrous abject.

> **Appealing** to the jury **as a mother**, Private England described her fear after the photos of the mistreatment became public. She said she was scared she would be sent to prison, separated from her young son, whose father is Private Graner. 'I was **scared I'd have to leave him** and he wouldn't know me when I returned, and he **wouldn't view me as his mother**, he'd view me as a stranger,' she said.
>
> (Cloud, *New York Times*, 28 September 2005)

> England, a reservist in the US Army, talked at length about how the child, who bears a striking resemblance to Graner, **had changed her life**.
>
> (Unattributed, *The Times*, 28 September 2005)

In this sense, Lynndie England's experience of becoming a mother has not only changed her life but in effect rescued her from monstrosity. England is no longer a monster capable of torture and abuse. Instead, through her 'natural' maternal insights she has realised her 'first duty', which of course is as a mother. The maternal insights are also prominent in the *Vanity Fair* article: 'Lynndie England: a Soldier, a Mother – and a Court-Martial'. The subheading reads: 'With a 7-month-old boy to care for, the Abu Ghraib Private **admits her guilt**' (Rockey Fleming, *People*, 16 May 2005). The article seems to suggest that it is *because of* England's motherhood that she supposedly realises and admits her guilt in the Abu Ghraib prison scandal. The association of a mother's feeling guilt communicates that even for England, the monstrous abject, there is an opportunity for forgiveness.

What I would like to draw attention to here is not necessarily England's alleged guilt but what the writing of England's guilt actually *does*. As mentioned above, Morrissey discusses one of her cases as 'Her monstrosity was insistently used to denote "our" normality, her evil to demonstrate "our" implied good, her supernatural inhumanity to indicate "our" humanity' (Morrissey 2003: 133). In a similar way, it seems that the representation of England as 'bad sex', as an Other, as a monster, as guilty of abuse at Abu

Ghraib, has served a purpose: even though Lynndie England finished serving her punishment years ago, it seems we are still obsessed to hear her story. In 2009, five years after the images became public, the BBC radio conducted two separate lengthy interviews with her and an interview in the *Guardian* was introduced as:

> In 2004, photographs of abuses at Abu Ghraib shocked the world. Seven people were charged, but the **face of the scandal will always be Lynndie England,** the 21-year-old private **grinning** at the camera.
>
> (Brockes, *Guardian*, 3 January 2009)

Despite the fact that investigations and documentaries such as *Standard Operating Procedure* (2008), have shown that England's role in the abuse was minor in comparison to what actually took place during interrogations which was not captured on camera, and that blame should have been shared amongst a larger group of people, higher ranking officers as well as military intelligence officers, we are still obsessed with Lynndie England. In particular, we are still obsessed with her smile as this remark in an interview with BBC radio 4 highlights: 'You **look happy** in the photographs ...', the reporter asks. England replies: 'It is just like smile for the camera, it is for the person holding the camera' (BBC Radio 4, 30 May 2009). The obsession with England also concerns the emotions of guilt and regret:

> In her first interview in three years Lynndie England talks about Abu Ghraib, about Charles Graner, about **guilt,** her current life – and the role of the Bush administration.
>
> (Unattributed, *Stern*, 19 March 2008)

> Mrs. England, we've listened to you for hours. And the whole time we've been asking ourselves: **Where is your feeling of regret?**
>
> (Ibid.)

In a radio interview for a Special edition of Outlook with the BBC World Service, Lynndie England is asked: 'Do you **feel sorry** for the prisoners?' England does not want to answer the question. The journalist continues: 'But you do have **regrets?**' England responds: 'I can't change what happened. I believe everything happens for a reason. To me the reason that I was there with Graner was that I would have my son' (BBC Outlook, 4 Febuary 2009). In yet another radio interview with the BBC during 2009, England is asked: 'Do you accept that what you did was **wrong?**' England replies:

> Still, five years later, I believe that we were told to do this. Yes, the acts themselves were wrong, but in the military you do what you are being told to do. Yes, we could have said something. Graner actually told both

his Platoon Sergeant and Platoon Leader, but they said, just do whatever they say.

(BBC Radio 4, 30 May 2009)

After the interview, the radio hostess and the studio guest discussed what Lynndie England had said. The hostess found 'the complete lack of remorse' the most disturbing whereas the guest highlighted that England did not see the prisoners as individuals.

Feinman argues that 'when we only ask questions about women, when we are only appalled and confused by women soldiers' acts of brutality, we continue to cast women as victims and men as brutes' (Feinman 2007: 66). While this is certainly the case, the writing of monstrous abjects also seems to have the function of allowing a space for reflection on who we are. Because the 'othering' of the monster is deeply intertwined with our understanding of ourselves, as the monster shows us what we are not, stories about monsters are used as a way of identifying what we, as a larger collective, are not. As mentioned in Chapter 2, interpellation is a process by which ideological systems 'hail' social subjects and tell them their place in the system. Building on Kristeva's idea of abjection, albeit 'unfaithfully', I suggest that the obsession with the monstrous abject, here exemplified with England, can be read as [unconscious] ideologies calling upon 'us' not to identify with the monstrous abject. Through a politics of disgust, this process of interpellation is emotional. At the same time, we need the monster to exist because it is intimately linked with what we are. The monster shows us what we are not and where the boundary of normative gender behaviour is drawn. This is how, on a meta-level, normative femininity is emphasised by our obsession with monstrous abjects. In other words, the obsession with monsters serves a purpose. This purpose is political. By emphasising a transgression of the border, the monster story functions to police and to guard the border of normative femininity.

Perversions of motherhood

In this chapter I have explored what happens when female bodies are seen to act 'against their femininity'. I have shown how subjects become abject subjects through social abjection which means that they become social outlaws and as such are deprived of human agency. More specifically, a politics of disgust is important in order to understand how this process of social abjection is linked to cultural norms, morality and normative gender behaviour. In an essay from 1955 called 'Striptease', Barthes offers an interesting way of thinking about the purpose of what Morrissey calls 'monsterizing manoeuvres' (Morrissey 2003: 173):

French striptease seems to stem from what I have earlier called "Operation Margarine," a mystifying device which consists in inoculating the public with a touch of evil, the better to plunge it afterward into a permanently immune Moral Good: a few particles of eroticism, highlighted by the very situation on which the show is based, are in fact absorbed in a reassuring ritual which negates the flesh as surely as the vaccine or the taboo circumscribe and control the illness or the crime.

(Barthes 2000b: 85–86)

In this sense, the monster story functions as a form of vaccine; an injection of evil that ultimately functions to reassure 'consumer others'. The taboo depicted by the monstrous abject is a way in which others are allowed, as Creed mentions in relation to the appeal of the horror film, to indulge in taboo forms of behaviour without having to act themselves, before order is finally restored. To return to the politics of disgust, the idea of disgust as a spatialising emotion means that disgust creates boundaries and generates a distance between the monstrous abject and oneself. The implication of such a politics of disgust and process of social abjection, therefore, is a bordering practice. This bordering practice relies on essentialist understandings of gender that reinforce a heteropatriarchal understanding of femininity where the foundation of sexual difference is maternal reproduction.

Thinking about social abjection as a 'bordering practice of the political present' (Tyler 2013: 46) has facilitated a focus on how maternalist war stories are told as perversions of motherhood. The three narrative tropes writing female bodies as monstrous abjects, the *Monstrous-Feminine*, the *Deviant Womb* and the *Femme Castratrice*, all include distancing monsterising manoeuvres that are informed by ideas about sexual difference as maternal reproduction. This is how motherhood is policing the gender border in stories of monstrous abjects.

Notes

1 According to the *Sunday Herald*, Lynndie England was depicted in five of fourteen initial images. The title of the article discussing Lynndie England's visibility is 'the picture that lost the war' (Mackay, *Sunday Herald*, 2 May 2004).
2 The author also reflected over whether or not it was England's underwear that was draped over an Iraqi's face in another photo.

Conclusion

Making feminist sense of maternalist war stories

Mythology ... proves nothing: it is a work of art in which a great deal of faith circulates; a fine fiction in which one agrees to believe because it explains life (it affords the image of an ideal; every mythology is a dream).

(Roland Barthes 2000a: 13)

The regulatory norms of 'sex' work in a performative fashion to constitute the materiality of bodies and, more specifically, to materialize the body's sex, to materialize sexual difference in the service of the consolidation of the heterosexual imperative.

(Judith Butler 2011: xii)

In the previous chapters I have discussed three different types of stories told in representations of female agency in political violence: victimised objects, heroic subjects and monstrous abjects. I have demonstrated how in all three types of stories 'motherhood' is, in one way or another, communicated as a negotiation over female bodies capacities to give life versus their capacities to take life. These stories are *maternalist* as they keep naturalising female bodies' association with motherhood. In this concluding chapter, I unpack what is going on in these representations further. In my quest to make feminist sense of the maternalist war stories told in this book, to re-politicise the way in which female bodies are understood – through *common sense* – in relation to agency in political violence, I first return to Roland Barthes's writings on myth and, indirectly, ideology, as well as to Judith Butler's writings on gender and the materialisation of sex. Drawing on their insights, I theorise the Myth of Motherhood as a cultural grammar, a value that informs stories about women's political violence. The theorisation of the Myth of Motherhood is the first step in which I make feminist sense of maternalist war stories. I argue that representations of female agency in political violence told as maternalist war stories, as inversions, versions and perversions of motherhood, are based in the *value* of a Myth of Motherhood. The content of the myth is that, overall, these maternalist war stories naturalise female bodies' association with life-giving, irrespectively of what individual women (objects, subjects or abjects) are saying or doing. Maternalist war stories told about female agency in political violence are therefore one way in which bodies are materialised and 'sexed'. However, maternalist war stories do not only function to 'sex' the subject/object/abject involved but ideas about war and bodies more broadly. This is how stories of female agency in war form part of writings of 'sex' as a cultural norm and one way in which the heterosexism of culture is preserved.

Importantly, the value of the Myth of Motherhood also functions to 'police', used in its broadest sense, what one might call the 'gender border' through its interpellating disciplining – of any potential resistance or abject subjects as seen in Chapter 5 but also 'the ideal viewer' or consensual community more generally. The maternalist war stories told in this book are, thus, ultimately stories about borders and, crucially, it is motherhood that is acting as the border agent at the border crossing. Maternalist war stories are both sexing war and policing gender borders. Thus, while the first section focuses on *what* the Myth of Motherhood *is* and *does*, the second section in this chapter shifts the focus onto *how* the Myth of Motherhood disciplines and police gender borders. To this end, I argue that a politics of emotions is at work.

I end the book by discussing its broader implications. There are two aspects to this. First of all, through its focus on how maternalist war stories function to 'make sense' of the confusion that is often communicated in representations of female agency in political violence, this book offers some ideas for how to study the politics of emotions through the idea of interpellation. The topic of emotions and emotionality remains understudied in IR/security studies, especially methodologically – *how to* study emotions and affective practices – thus, with this book I call on further studies on the political *how* of emotions.[1] The other aspect is that the study of world politics will benefit from more attempts, as Barthes says, to reintroduce society into it, and that, to this end, a study of the hidden politics of the everyday, of popular culture and the seemingly apolitical fictional, offers an alternative opening into broader dynamics and deeper logics related to world politics.

Theorising the Myth of Motherhood

To conceptualise motherhood as myth I first draw on Barthes' ideas on myth in the essay collection *Mythologies*, originally published in 1957 (with the caveat mentioned in Chapter 2 in mind, that I am using a 'postmodernised' Barthes), and then on Butler's thinking about the reiteration of sex. To start with, Barthes thinks of myth as a type of speech, a system of communication, a message. But it is also *a value*, a language which does not want to die (Barthes 1993: 110, 120). The essential function of myth as a language, moreover, is the *naturalisation of the concept* (ibid.: 118). In this sense, myth transforms what is particular, cultural and ideological into what appears to be universal, natural and purely empirical. Myth naturalises meanings, makes them into *common sense*, when they are really products of cultural practices. In other words, myth makes 'facts' out of interpretations; something we tend not to question. This is why Barthes refers to myth as depoliticised, innocent, speech:

> Myth is constituted by the loss of the historical quality of things: in it, things lose the memory that they once were made ... A conjuring trick has taken place; it has turned reality inside out, it has emptied it of history and has filled it with Nature ... The function of myth is to empty reality: it is, literally, a ceaseless flowing out, a haemorrhage, or perhaps an evaporation, in short, a perceptible absence.
>
> (Barthes 1993: 131)

Yet, mythical language is of course not at all apolitical but in fact a highly political practice that depends on formations of power. Myth does not deny things. On the contrary, its function is to talk about them. Simply, it purifies them, it makes them innocent. It gives them a natural and eternal justification. Myth gives things a clarity which is not that of an explanation but that of a statement of fact. Myth is fabricated and this is why Barthes suggests one must understand *political* in its deeper meaning, 'as describing the whole of human relations in their real, social structure, in their power of making the world' (Barthes 2000b: 131). Essentially, it is because myth constructions form part of our cultural grammar that it is important to look beyond obvious 'political settings', to actually study that which is seen as apolitical.

For the purpose of my argument in this book, myth's relationship to ideology is crucial. In the essay 'Myth Today' Barthes suggests that mythology is a part both of semiology and ideology as it studies ideas-in-form; politics is already a representation, a fragment of ideology (Barthes 1993: 115, 127). Cynthia Weber discusses the concept of 'unconscious' ideology as part of her reading of Barthes (see also discussion in Chapter 2). Unconscious ideology is ideology that is not formally named and that is therefore difficult to identify. It is the common sense foundation of our world-views that is beyond debate (Weber 2005: 5). Weber argues that we use unconscious ideologies to help make sense of our worlds, very often without realising it. And because we do not realise we hold unconscious ideologies or use them to make sense of our worlds, we very rarely interrogate them. We rarely ask difficult questions about them that might upset them as common sense (Weber 2005: 5). In this way, the reason we tend not to notice the ideological construction of our world is because ideology denies itself as an ideology. Ideology appears to be reality because it conceals its own construction (Lacey 1998: 101). What is important here is that, in a general sense, power works through myths by *appearing to take the political out of the ideological*. This is because something that appears to be *natural* and unalterable also appears to be apolitical (Weber 2005: 7). To sum up, key words in my reading of Barthes' work are myth as *apolitical*, as *unconscious ideology*, as *common sense* but also that such mythical construction is the result of a *naturalisation* of the concept. And, of course, that the process of naturalisation of the concept is a political process.

The second pillar in my theorising of motherhood as myth is founded in Judith Butler's influential work that critiques the naturalness of the gender/sex relation as a simple conception where gender gains its specificity through its opposition to sex, conceived as a biological fact. In the preface to *Bodies That Matter*, first published in 1993, Butler asks what the constraints by which bodies are materialised as 'sexed' are, and how we are to understand the 'matter' of sex, and of bodies more generally, as 'the repeated and violent circumscription of cultural intelligibility? Which bodies come to matter – and why?' (Butler 2011: x). Butler recognises how gender and biological sex, in order to acquire their oppositional value, relied on each other for existence. This means that the understanding of 'sex' is no longer a bodily given on which the construct of gender is artificially imposed. Instead, Butler argues 'sex' is *a cultural norm* that governs the materialisation of bodies (ibid.: xii).

The point is not to deny physical differences between men and women as biological animals. Butler does not dispute the materiality of the body as 'the body is not simply linguistic stuff or that it has no bearing on language: it bears on language all the time' (Butler 1993: 68). On the contrary, Butler shows the normative conditions under which the materiality of the body is framed and formed: Sexual difference, despite often being invoked as an issue of material differences, is never simply a function of material differences which are not in some way both marked and formed by discursive practices (ibid.: 1). In her own account, Butler '[t]races materiality as the site at which a certain *drama of sexual difference* plays itself out' (Butler 2011: 22, my emphasis). To me, the topic of female agency in political violence is another such site at which a drama of sexual difference plays itself out.

What Butler suggests, then, is that sex is as culturally constructed as gender and, therefore, sex is itself a 'gendered category' (Butler 2006: 5). As a gendered category that is produced through repetition, moreover, sex is not a simple fact or static condition of a body, but a *process* whereby regulatory *norms* materialise sex and achieve this materialisation through a forcible *reiteration* of those norms (Butler 1993: 1, my emphasis). Sexing the subject is a gendering process about the embodying of norms and this is a repeated process (Butler 2011: 176).

In my reading, Butler's understanding of 'sex' as an ideal construct, continuously repeated, performed and reinforced as cultural intelligibility, resonates with Barthes's thinking on (unconscious) ideology and myth. Thus, in combination, these insights offer a critical engagement with the subject positions that are enabled but also closed off by particular discourses of gender, agency and political violence. It also facilitates a critique of gender roles as *common sense*, as 'natural', which effectively means that sex as a cultural norm can be exposed and the naturalisation of women's association with life-giving re-politicised. The awareness that gender identities are cultural and naturalised fictions rather than natural entities means that gender can be decoupled from sex and that there is no necessary link between women and femininity, or women and motherhood. For my argument in this book the most important aspect of Butler's theorising about gender and sex is the insight that *the sexing of bodies is a culturally negotiated discursive performative production of the reiteration of cultural norms*. It is also Butler's

understanding of power: '[that] there is no power that acts, but only a reiterated acting that is power in its persistence and instability' (Butler 2011: xviii);
and, more specifically, the power invested in constructions of sex as *natural*
that is most useful. This concerns the power of the reiteration of sex.

This book is about the *idea of motherhood*, rather than actual experiences
of motherhood and mothering. Thus, by motherhood I mean ideas about
women's *capacity to give life*. Informed by Barthes' ideas on myth, and
Cynthia Weber's use of 'unconscious' ideologies in her reading of Barthes, I
suggest that a myth of motherhood *naturalises* the association of female
bodies with motherhood. Women's capacity to give life is thereby *assumed* to
be *natural*; that motherhood as *naturally* linked to female bodies becomes
part of *common sense*, something we do not question. However, through
Butler's theorisation of the cultural construction of sex and ensuing pro-
blematisation of heternormativity, it becomes clear how the naturalness of
women's capacity to give life, motherhood, is but a social and cultural construction. Crucially, however, what is important for the purpose of this book
is not so much women's 'natural' association with motherhood but in effect its
opposite: the implications, expressions, and, ultimately, the politics that
becomes apparent in the context of women's [political] violence. My argument
is that a Myth of Motherhood materialises as a tension between a female
body's [assumed] natural *capacity* to give life and [assumed] incapacity to take
life. In other words, the tension seems to indicate that because of women's
assumed capacity to give life, they cannot 'naturally' take life. Seemingly, for
female bodies the capacity for motherhood is naturalised whereas capacity for
taking life is 'unnaturalised'; made alien. Motherhood and killing are juxtaposed; a capacity to kill is the most 'unnatural' feminine trait. What is more,
as an idea motherhood also forms a part of the 'heterosexual matrix as a
permanent and incontestable structure of culture' (Butler 2011: xxviii).
Motherhood as *an idea* is thereby also *sexing* representations of female
agency in political violence; motherhood is sexing ideas about war. At this
point it is useful to return to the table outlining the structure of my argument
as presented in the introductory chapter.

To reiterate, the way in which motherhood is sexing war contextualises
differently in the three different types of maternalist war stories. In Chapter 3,
covering scenes in which female bodies are written as Victimised Objects,
the 'default position' of *passivity*; the 'motherhood performance' of
'*womenandchildren*' and the 'disciplining move' through *emotionality* all
function to deny female bodies agency in political violence. I conclude the
chapter by arguing that in this type of story motherhood is communicated as
'inversions of motherhood' and that the subject positions in such stories are
not seen as threatening or challenging the Myth of Motherhood. In Chapter 4,
which cover stories about female bodies written as Heroic Subjects, the
'default position' of the *Vacant Womb*, the 'motherhood performance' of the
Protective Mother and the 'disciplining move' through the idea of the *Masculinised Subject* all function to write female bodies with agency in political

violence. In this chapter the type of story told is 'versions of motherhood' and similarly to the stories in Chapter 3 the subject positions covered are not seen as threatening to the Myth of Motherhood. In contrast, in Chapter 5, all stories involve female bodies seen to 'act against their femininity'. The 'default position' of the *Monstrous-Feminine*; the 'motherhood performance' of the *Deviant Womb* and the 'disciplining move' through the notion of the *Femme Castratrice* all include a tension in how gender/sex is culturally understood and this tension, moreover, is often communicated through emotions. In this chapter the subject positions discussed do challenge the Myth of Motherhood. However, here I also build on discussions on the politics of disgust and interpellation in order to argue that there is a spatialising distancing process involved in the writing of monstrous abjects. This means that the writing of monstrous abjects has more to do with 'us' than the monster itself. I conclude by arguing that in this type of story motherhood is communicated as perversion but also that despite that the subject in these stories itself threaten the Myth of Motherhood, overall, *the story* of the monstrous abject function to reinvigorate the Myth of Motherhood.

It is in relation to this latter argument, about that which 'escapes or exceeds the norm'; that which cannot be 'wholly defined or fixed by the repetitive labor of the norm' (Butler 2011: xix), that there is a gap or crack that open up the constitutive instabilities in such constructions. It is this instability, or crisis, that forms part of the second part of my concluding argument on how I make feminist sense of maternalist war stories: There is a politics of emotions involved in the way in which women's political violence is communicated.

Women's political violence: an emotional border politics

In order to understand what the myth *does*, how it functions to police gender more broadly, we need to think about borders, boundaries and above all the encounters with such borders in more depth. We need to return to the idea of interpellation. First, however, I emphasise the emotional aspects of an instability/crisis or border practice by focusing on the confusion or shock often expressed in relation to women's agency in political violence, mentioned in Chapter 1 but also illuminated throughout the three empirical chapters in this book, particularly in relation to discussions about social abjection in Chapter 5. For example, the confusion, incomprehension to accept, and later obsession with the fact that *women* were involved in various ways in the Abu Ghraib scandal is one example of when the instability of the reiteration of sex leads to a crisis. Discussing the Abu Ghraib scandal, Davies notes that the representation of women soldiers provided the most powerful evidence of what the most interesting feminist analyses have tried to explain: 'that there is a difference between the body gendered as female and the set of discourses and ideologies that inform the sex/gender system' (Davies 2007: 25). This book is about discourses and ideologies that inform the binary sex/gender system, but, is also about *how* such processes take place in mass media and popular culture. Thus, the 'crisis' of Abu Ghraib showed the instability of sex; the shock and confusion expressed in relation to Lynndie England and Janis Karpinski (as well as other females involved) communicated a disruption to the cultural grammar with which 'the consensual community' understand gender and sex to begin with. With Butler's terminology we can think about this as the destabilisation of gender itself, a destabilisation that is *denaturalising* and that 'calls into question the claims of normativity and originality by which gender and sexual oppression sometimes operate' (Butler 2011: 87). While such processes of destabilisation on the one hand offers an opening for the questioning of norms and values, they also, I suggest, constitute a threat to the Myth of Motherhood. The emotional communication of confusion or shock involved in representations of female agency in political violence is thereby a testament to the fact that we have reached some form of societal border-crossing as *common sense is no longer making sense*.

In a discussion of 'the traumatic press photograph' Barthes suggests that such photographs are indicated via a rhetorical code that *distances, sublimates* and *pacifies* them (Barthes 2000b: 209). Furthermore, in her research about women murderesses, Morrissey shows how murders committed by women are narrated repeatedly as traumatic events. The trauma, Morrissey argues, resides in the *structure of the experience* of the event, rather than in the event itself. This experience, moreover, causes an inability to assimilate or understand the event, yet the traumatised society condemns by repeating it over and over via narrative representation (Morrissey 2003: 10). It seems, then, that the repetition of the traumatic event means something. It seems to fulfil a particular function for society. Morrissey argues that the use of what she calls 'conventional stock stories' across a range of empirical cases points to the influence of an imaginary realm, an unconscious aspect structuring the development of narratives and discourses. These stories, Morrissey argues, present stereotypical or mythic characters who embody traits evaluated as either ideal or condemnable, positive or negative. Such stories are usually familiar to those receiving them as they are culturally based, and are therefore vital to understanding because they provide easily identifiable and acceptable evaluations of both character and behaviour. In essence, they represent the *cultural capital* on which discourses rely for community acceptance and comprehension. These stock stories may be specific to a particular discourse, but most frequently 'they *exist transdiscursively*, extant within the *cultural unconscious*' (ibid.: 9, my emphasis).

In the essay 'The Third Meaning' written in 1970 (published in the collection *Image-Music Text*) Barthes addresses what he calls 'the obtuse meaning'. The obtuse meaning is different from the 'obvious' meaning. The obtuse meaning is about disguise, and, more importantly for the purpose of my argument, the obtuse meaning is about emotions. Caught up in the disguise, Barthes argues, such emotion is never sticky, it is an emotion that simply designates 'what one loves, what one wants to defend'. The obtuse meaning is about 'an *emotion value*, an evaluation' (Barthes 2000b: 324). Discussing crime reporting, Morrissey argues that one of the most common stock narratives used is the morality play that places the forces of good on one side and the forces of evil on the other. And, as the object of morality plays is for good to overcome evil, the resolution of the tale is usually a given (Morrissey 2003: 15). In this sense, morality functions to bind a community together through emotional values of goodness. The obtuse, disguised meaning involved in such representation shows what one loves and wants to defend, but it is also about where the boundary is drawn and who is excluded; it is about the preservation of 'the outside.' This is important because the outside is where discourse meets its limits. In Butler's words:

> [W]here the opacity of what is not included in a given regime of truth acts as a disruptive site of linguistic impropriety and unrepresentability, illuminating the violent and contingent boundaries of that normative regime precisely through the inability of that regime to represent that which might pose a fundamental threat to its continuity.
>
> (Butler 2011: 25)

Butler refers to such notions of foreclosure as a *policing of the borders of intelligibility* (Butler 2011: 154). Similarly, even though he does not call it 'policing', Barthes too, in his discussion of the traumatic press photograph talks about 'the forms our society uses to ensure its peace of mind' (Barthes 2000: 210). Moreover, in relation to how the policing of borders constitutes [emotional] cultural grammar, we need to return to the idea of interpellation and social abjection. Here, I draw on the ideas about borders of 'intelligibility', of 'consensual community', and a society's 'peace of mind' to make sense of interpellation as emotional communication in the form of a response to the potential trauma felt by women's agency in political violence, indicated in representations of confusion or shock. I suggest that the emotional communication of interpellation is in this way linked to a *value* one wants to defend. In this book, this value is the Myth of Motherhood. When the value of the Myth of Motherhood is threatened, as in Chapter 5 in particular, 'the ideal viewer' is emotionally, as well as verbally and visually, interpellated to abject those Others (monstrous abjects) that have transgressed the gender border. The reactions to the border crossings are, thus, emotional/emotive. The purpose of interpellation as emotional communication, thus, is its function 'to integrate man, to reassure him' (Barthes 2000b: 210). Through interpellation, the simple logic that we are not monsters – monsters are evil – thus, we are good, 'we' are reassured. In this way, interpellation can be thought of as a series of 'normativizing injunctions that secure the borders of sex through the threat of psychosis, abjection, psychic unlivability' (Butler 2011: xxiii). What I am trying to get at here is that the sexing of war and the policing of gender norms in representations of female agency in political violence taps into the Myth of Motherhood for its cultural intelligibility. The result is the telling of maternalist war stories as described in Chapters 3, 4 and 5. In these stories, it is the reiteration of 'sex' that is powerfully policing gender in representations of female agency in political violence. Motherhood acts as the border agent.

More specifically, the stories told of victimised objects, heroic subjects and monstrous abjects all make the potential societal border crossing visible, or perhaps more accurately put, *felt*. However, the policing of the gender border works in different ways depending on what type of maternalist story is told; the value of motherhood is policed in different ways. In stories of victimised objects female bodies, despite their roles as potential perpetrators of political violence, are ultimately not threatening to the Myth of Motherhood. Instead, the subjects in these stories become objects through the default position of being passive and by being infantilised. But, the value of motherhood is also protected through emotional disciplining. In stories of victimised objects female bodies are often written as 'being emotional'. Here, the disproportional focus on Faye Turney's *fear* of being raped, for example, functions to write her, in comparison to her male colleagues, as a *particularly* vulnerable victim in need of protection; as an alien body that thereby risks endangering war's missions, irrespective of her individual capabilities and experience as a naval officer. Similarly, the value of motherhood is also protected in the emphasis on both Nasima's and Ulrike's hesitation about their acts of political violence. The emotional disciplining move here is not only communicated through narratives of parenthood and children, but, the emphasis on these two terrorists' personal motivations throughout suggests that these actors' politics is ignored. In stories of heroic subjects the value of motherhood is, for example, protected through the emphasis on Faye Turney's maternal guilt once back in safety in the UK; by making Jeanne – the prostitute capable of killing – 'unable' or unsuited to have children; through the valuing of both Turney and Karpinski as members of the armed forces in maternal language; how Gudrun's maternal sacrifice is uncomplicated; why Karpinski's choice not to have children is relevant or newsworthy at all; and why 'childless' is mentioned in the epilogue of *Female Agents*. In these stories, the value of motherhood is protected because the tension between life-giving and life-taking is 'removed' or overcome, spatially and/or temporally.

The societal gender border is most visibly and emotionally communicated in stories of monstrous abjects. This is because the abjected subject not only signposts the gender border but actually transgresses it. Importantly, however, through a politics of emotions, namely of disgust, the subject is abjected, othered, which means that while the Myth of Motherhood is threatened by the monstrous abject who crosses the gender border, its value is ultimately not challenged. Here, the politics of disgust is *spatialising*, it creates boundaries and generates a distance between the monstrous abject and oneself. The implication of such a politics of disgust and process of social abjection, therefore, is a bordering practice. Thinking about the portrayal of Lynndie England as the 'all-American monster' or 'the sex sadist of Baghdad', of the confusion expressed about the fact that she was seen smiling in the photos, as well as the following obsession with her in particular (rather than others involved), ultimately serves a political purpose: The monster story functions as a form of vaccine; an injection of evil that ultimately function to reassure 'consumer others'. This is how the value of motherhood is protected through a politics of disgust and practice of othering.

Sexing war/Policing gender: some concluding thoughts

With this book, I set out to make sense of the confusion with which women's political violence is often communicated. I wanted to trace the politics of the female body, as negotiated in representations of women's political violence. I wanted to understand the 'what-goes-without-saying', the ideological abuse hidden in such representations. For the purpose of this book, the meaning of 'what-goes-without-saying', moreover, is twofold. What Barthes is hinting at in the quote at the very beginning of this book is of course the assumed apolitical nature of a particular reality, the construction of myth, but here I have also tried to make sense of communication beyond the limitations of speech and written text simply because the topic of my investigation, representations of female agency in political violence, seemed to communicate more than words. More than words, moreover, turns out to mean a politics of emotions.

What this book demonstrates is that while the increased visibility of female perpetrators of political violence might give the impression of an increased space for gender flexibility, what actually is going on in the representations of such events, acts and stories, at least the ones I am discussing in this book, is that boundaries and limits to such flexibility are emphasised and reinforced. As I have shown throughout this book, contemporary examples of female agency in political violence are still communicated, and made sense of, through *ideas* of motherhood; they form part of maternalist war stories. I argue in this book that such maternalist war stories are informed by a value, a cultural grammar that structures the way we think, breathe and feel stories of war. I call this value the Myth of Motherhood.

I started this concluding chapter with a quote by Barthes in which he talks about myth as faith, fiction, belief, ideal and as a dream. With this book I hope to have shown how when it comes to representations of female agency in political violence, we are talking about a particular, heteropatriarchal, dream that is valuing female subjects through ideas about motherhood. Through interpellating moments founded in the Myth of Motherhood, not only is the threat of the destabilisation of gender itself managed but *the foundation of sexual difference as maternal reproduction is also reinforced.* This is problematic because it strengthens the naturalness, the uncontested status of sex within what Butler calls the 'heterosexual matrix', which secures the workings of certain symbolic orders (Butler 2011: xxiv). Last, as these and other symbolic orders is politics as its most effective, precisely because it barely registers as politics at all, I suggest that a critique of what is considered apolitical, common sense and simply 'normal' is probably the most political of all. As I have discovered, there is a politics of emotions involved in the working of symbolic orders. Thinking about interpellation and abjection merely offers a beginning to understand the politics of emotional processes, thus, with this book I would like to call on further studies on how politics is emotional but above all how emotions are political. In addition, world politics is, and should be, intimately related to the everyday. The everyday is not isolated from the global. It is here the focus on popular culture comes in. Often reaching a much wider audience than typical policy documents, political speeches, events etc., popular culture artefacts can discuss 'politics' in a seemingly apolitical context. Even if a film or television series is 'inspired by real life events', it is still considered 'just entertainment'. As I have tried to show in this book, moreover, the potential politics involved in a particular film goes beyond whatever story the director or producer might have wanted to tell. If we think the purpose for studies of world politics is, as Barthes puts it, to reintroduce society into it, then a study of the hidden politics of the everyday, of popular culture and the seemingly apolitical fictional, is perhaps not only the most political site of all but able to offer an alternative opening into broader dynamics and deeper logics of world politics.

Note

1 See Åhäll and Gregory (eds) 2013; 2015 for a range of recent contributions to the study of emotions, politics, security and war.

Bibliography

Abu-Lughod, L. (2013) *Do Muslim Women Need Saving?* Boston, MA: Harvard University Press.

Åhäll, L. (2012a) 'The writing of heroines: Motherhood and female agency in political violence', *Security Dialogue*, 43(4): 287–303.

Åhäll, L. (2012b) 'Confusion, fear, disgust: Emotional communication in representations of female agency in political violence'. In *Gender, Agency and Political Violence*, edited by L. Åhäll and L. J. Shepherd. Basingstoke: Palgrave Macmillan, 169–183.

Åhäll, L. (2012c) 'Motherhood, Myth and Gendered Agency in Political Violence'. In *Intenational feminist journal of Politics*, 14(1): 103–120.

Åhäll, L. (2013) 'The fear of the unknown: women, agency and legitimate violence in war', paper presented at the International Studies Association conference in San Francisco 2013.

Åhäll, L. and Borg, S. (2012) 'Predication, presupposition and subject-positioning'. In *Critical Approaches to Security*, edited by L. J. Shepherd. London and New York: Routledge, 196–207.

Åhäll, L. and Gregory, T. A. (eds) (2013) 'Security, emotions, affect', *Critical Studies on Security*, 1(1): 117–141.

Åhäll, L. and Gregory, T. A. (eds) (2015) *Emotions, Politics and War.* London and New York: Routledge.

Alison, M. (2007) 'Wartime sexual violence: Women's human rights and questions of masculinity', *Review of International Studies*, 33: 75–90.

Alison, M. (2004) 'Women as agents of political violence: Gendering security', *Security Dialogue*, 35(4): 447–463.

Ashley, R. K. (1989) 'Living on border lines: Man, post-structuralism, and war'. In *International/Intertextual Relations: Postmodern Readings of World Politics*, edited by J. Der Derian and M. Shapiro. New York: Lexington Books, 259–321.

Aust, S. (2008) *The Baader-Meinhof Complex.* London: The Bodley Head.

The Baader-Meinhof Complex (2008). Dir. Uli Edel. DVD.

Ballinger, L. 'I was stripped and feared I'd be raped, says Faye', *Daily Mail*, 9 April 2007.

Balsamo, A. (2000) 'Reading cyborgs writing feminism'. In *The Gendered Cyborg: A Reader*, edited by G. Kirkup, L. Janes, K. Woodward and F. Hovenden. London: Routledge, 148–158.

Barthes, R. (1993) 'Myth today'. In *A Roland Barthes Reader*, edited by S. Sontag. London: Vintage, 93–149.

Barthes, R. (2000a) *Mythologies*. London: Vintage.

Barthes, R. (2000b) *A Roland Barthes Reader*, edited by S. Sontag. London: Vintage.

Basham, V. (2009) 'Effecting discrimination operational effectiveness and harassment in the British armed forces', *Armed Forces & Society*, 35(4): 728–744.

Basham, V. M. (2013) *War, Identity and the Liberal State: Everyday Experiences of the Geopolitical in the Armed Forces*. London and New York: Routledge.

Basu, S. (2013) 'Emancipatory potential in feminist security studies', *International Studies Perspectives*, 14(4): 455–458.

Baxter, J. (2003) *Positioning Gender in Discourse: A Feminist Methodology*. New York: Palgrave.

Bayard de Volo, L. (2004) 'Mobilizing mothers for war: Cross-national framing strategies in Nicaragua's Contra war', *Gender and Society*, 18(6): 715–734.

BBC Radio 4, 30 May 2009.

BBC Outlook, 4 February 2009.

Beeston, R. And Kennedy, D. 'Family of woman sailor abducted by Iranians speak of their distress', *The Times*, 27 March 2007.

de Bertodano, H. 'My army life: Lonely, restless and afraid', *The Times*, 13 August 2004.

Bleiker, R. (2001) 'The aesthetic turn in International Political Theory', *Millennium: Journal of International Studies*, 30(3): 509–533.

Bleiker, R. (2003) 'Learning from art: A reply to Holden's "World literature and world politics"', *Global Society*, 17(4): 415–428.

Bleiker, R. (2009) *Aesthetics and World Politics: Rethinking Peace and Conflict Studies*. Basingstoke: Palgrave Macmillan.

Bloom, M. (2007) *Dying to Kill: The Allure of Suicide Terror*. New York: Colombia University Press.

Bloom, M. (2011) *Bombshell: The Many Faces of Women Terrorists*. London: Hurst.

Blumenthal, R. 'Sentencing hearing starts for G.I. featured in Abu Ghraib pic', *New York Times*, 4 May 2005.

Blumenthal, R. 'Judge rejects abuse plea after ringleader testifies', *New York Times*, 5 May 2005.

Boffey, D. 'Dog lead Lynndie jail deal', *Daily Mirror*, 3 May 2005.

Borger, J. and Wintour, P. 'Fury as Iran shows footage of captured sailors on television', *The Guardian*, 29 March 2007.

Borger, J. and Wintour, P. 'Tehran raises the stakes in hostage crisis', *The Guardian*, 30 March 2007.

Bourke, J. (1999) *An Intimate History of Killing*. London: Granta Publications.

Bracewell, W. (1996) 'Women, motherhood, and contemporary Serbian nationalism', *Women's Studies International Forum*, 19: 25–33.

Brittain, M. (2006) 'Benevolent invaders, heroic victims and depraved villains: White femininity in media coverage of the invasion of Iraq'. In *(En)gendering the War on Terror*, edited by K. Hunt and K. Rygiel, 73–96. Aldershot: Ashgate.

Britz (2007) Dir. Peter Kosminksy. DVD. Shown on Channel 4, 4–5 November.

Brockes, E. '"What happens in war happens"', *The Guardian*, 3 January 2009.

Brunner, C. (2005) 'Female suicide bombers – male suicide bombing? Looking for gender in reporting the suicide bombings of the Israeli-Palestinian conflict', *Global Society*, 19(1): 29–48.

Brunner, C. (2012) 'Assassins, virgins, scholars: Epistemologies and geopolitics in scholarly knowledge on suicide bombing'. In *Gender, Agency and Political Violence*, edited by L. Åhäll and L. J. Shepherd. Basingstoke: Palgrave Macmillan, 132–147.

Bundtzen, L. (2000) 'Monstrous mothers: Medusa, Grendel, and now Alien'. In *The Gendered Cyborg: A Reader*, edited by G. Kirkup, L. Janes, K. Woodward and F. Hovenden. London: Routledge, 101–109.

Burchell, I. 'Mum paraded on telly by Iran: She's forced to confess and wear Muslim head-dress', *Daily Star*, 29 March 2007.

Butler, J. (1992) 'Contingent foundations: Feminism and the question of "post-modernism"'. In *Feminists Theorize the Political*, edited by J. Butler and J. Scott. London: Routledge, 3–21.

Butler, J. (1993) *Bodies That Matter: On the Discursive Limits of "Sex"*. London: Routledge.

Butler, J. (1995) 'For a careful reading'. In Benhabib, S., Butler, J., Cornell, D. and Fraser, N. (1995) *Feminist Contentions: A Philosophical Exchange*. New York: Routledge, 127–144.

Butler, J. (2004) *Undoing Gender*. New York and London: Routledge.

Butler, J. (2006 [1990]) *Gender Trouble*. London: Routledge.

Butler, J. (2011 [1993]) *Bodies That Matter: On the Discursive Limits of "Sex"*. London: Routledge.

Buus, S. (2009) 'Hell on earth: Threats, citizens and the state from Buffy to Beck', *Cooperation and Conflict*, 44(4): 400–419.

Carroll, S. 'Respect for fighter Faye', *Daily Mirror*, 4 April 2007.

Carver, T. (2007) '*GI Jane*: What are the "manners" that "maketh a man"?', *British Journal of Politics and International Relations*, 9: 313–317.

Cauchon, D., Howlett, D. and Hampson, R. 'Abuse scandal meets in disbelief in hometown', *USA Today*, 7 May 2004.

Chan, S. and Spinner, J. 'Allegations of abuse lead to shakeup at Iraqi prison', *Washington Post*, 30 April 2004.

Chandler, N. 'Faye: I'm back to being mum', *Sunday Star*, 8 April 2007.

Chandler, N. 'Dog-lead girl GI on rap', *Daily Star*, 9 May 2004.

Chapman, J. Greenhill, S. and Koster, O. (2007) 'Condemnation grows over Faye's £100,000 payday', *Daily Mail*, 10 April.

Chodorow, N. (1978) *The Reproduction of Mothering: Psychoanalysis and the Sociology of Gender*. Berkeley: University of California Press.

Churcher, S. and Graham, C. 'Here if you're a different race, you're sub-human', *Mail on Sunday*, 2 May 2004

Churcher, S. 'US troops had orgy room in torture prison', *Daily Mail*, 16 May 2004.

Cloud, D. 'G.I.'s role in detainee abuse is starkly contrasted at retrial', *New York Times*, 22 September 2005.

Cloud, D. 'Private found guilty in Abu Ghraib abuse', *New York Times*, 27 September 2005.

Cloud, D. 'Private gets 3 years for Iraq prison abuse', *New York Times*, 28 September 2005.

CNN 'MP Commander: "No knowledge" of alleged abuse', 4 May 2004.

Cohen, R. 'The missing apology', *Washington Post*, 1 October 2005.

Cohn, C. (1987) 'Sex and death in the rational world of defense intellectuals', *Signs: Journal of Women in Culture and Society*, 12(4): 687–718.

Cohn, C. (2011) '"Feminist Security Studies": Toward a reflexive practice', *Politics and Gender*, 7(4): 581–586.

Coles, J. 'Hero Mum', *Sun*, 28 March 2007.

Colvin, S. (2009) *Ulrike Meinhof and West German Terrorism: Language, Violence and Identity*. New York: Camden House.

Cooke, M. (1996) *Women and the War Story*. Berkeley: University of California Press.

Copeland, L. 'Prison revolt: Brig. Gen. Janis Karpinski says the Abu Ghraib investigation is about scapegoating, but she's having none of it', *Washington Post*, 10 May 2004.

Coulter, C. (2008) 'Female fighters in the Sierra Leone war: Challenging the assumptions?', *Feminist Review*, 88: 54–73.

Cragin, K. R. and Daly, S. A. (2009) *Women as terrorists: Mothers, recruiters and martyrs*. Praeger Security International.

Creed, B. (1999) 'Horror and the Monstrous-Feminine: An imaginary abjection'. In *Feminist Film Theory: A Reader*, edited by S. Thornham. Edinburgh: Edinburgh University Press, 251–266.

Creed, B. (2001) [1993] *The Monstrous-Feminine: Film, Feminism and Psychoanalysis*. London: Routledge.

Crichton, T. 'Lynndie England has come to symbolise America's degradation of Iraqi prisoners ... but is she a sadist or a scapegoat?', *Sunday Herald*, 9 May 2004.

Davies, A. (2007) 'Sexual coercion, prisons, and female responses'. In *One of the Guys: Women as Aggressors and Torturers*, edited by T. McKelvey. Emeryville, CA: Seal Press, 23–28.

Der Derian, J. and Shapiro, M. J. (eds.) (1989) *International/Intertextual Relations: Postmodern Readings of World Politics*. New York: Lexington Books.

Devetak, R. (2005) 'The gothic scene of international relations: ghosts, monsters, terror and the sublime after September 11', *Review of International Studies*, 31: 621–643.

Dietz, M. G. (1985) 'Citizenship with a feminst face: The problem with Maternal Thinking', *Political Theory*, 13(1): 19–37.

Dietz, M. G. (2003) 'Current controversies in feminist theory', *The Annual Review of Political Science*, 6: 399–431.

Doty, R. L. (1993) 'Foreign policy as social construction: A post-positivist analysis of U.S. counterinsurgency policy in the Philippines', *International Studies Quarterly*, 37 (3): 297–320.

Douglas, M. (1966) *Purity and Danger: An Analysis of Concepts of Pollution and Taboo*. London: Routledge and Kegan Paul.

Duke, L. 'A woman apart', *Washington Post*, 19 September 2004.

Duncanson, C. (2009) 'Forces for good?: Narratives of military masculinity in peacekeeping operations', *International Feminist journal of Politics*, 11(1): 63–80.

Eager, P. W. (2008) *From Freedom Fighters to Terrorists: Women and Political Violence*. Aldershot: Ashgate.

Edkins, J. and Vaughan-Williams, N. (eds) (2009) *Critical Theorists and International Relations*. London and New York: Routledge.

Elshtain, J. B. (1995 [1987]) *Women and War*. New York: Basics Books.

Enloe, C. (2000a) *Maneuvers: The International Politics of Militarizing Women's Lives*. Berkeley: University of California Press.

Enloe, C. (2000b [1989]) *Bananas, Beaches and Bases: Making Feminist Sense of International Politics*. Berkeley: University of California Press.

Enloe, C. (2004) *The Curious Feminist: Searching for Women in a New Age of Empire*. Berkeley: University of California Press.

Enloe, C. (2007) *Globalization and Militarism: Feminists Make the Link*. Lanham: Rowman & Littlefield Publishers.

Enloe, C. (2010) 'Foreword'. In *Gender, War, and Militarism: Feminist Perspectives*, edited by L. Sjoberg and S. Via. Santa Barbara, CA: Praeger Publishers, xi–xv.

Feinman, I. (2007) 'Shock and awe: Abu Ghraib, women soldiers, and racially gendered torture'. In *One of the Guys: Women as Aggressors and Torturers*, edited by T. McKelvey. Emeryville, CA: Seal Press, 56–80.

Female Agents (2008). Dir. Jean-Paul Saromé. DVD.

Ferguson, M. L. (2005) '"W" stands for women: Feminism and security rhetoric in the post-9/11 Bush administration', *Politics and Gender*, 1: 9–38.

Flynn, B. 'Witch: Evil soldier Lynndie in new torture photo', *Sun*, 7 May 2004.

Flynn, B. 'Lynndie filmed a sex orgy', *Sun*, 14 May 2004.

Flynn, B. 'Torturer's tot', *Sun*, 29 October 2004.

Flynn, B. 'Torturer's tot', *Daily Mirror*, 29 October 2004.

Fortin, A. J. (1989) 'Notes on a terrorist text: A critical use of Roland Barthes' textual analysis in the interpretation of political meaning'. In *International/Intertextual Relations: Postmodern Readings of World Politics*, edited by J. Der Derian and M. Shapiro. New York: Lexington Books, 189–206.

Foucault, M. (1972) *The Archaeology of Knowledge*. London: Tavistock.

Gardner, D. 'Sex shame of abuse-case soldier', *Daily Mail*, 5 August 2004.

Gentry, C. (2009) 'Twisted maternalism', *International Feminist Journal of Politics*, 11 (2): 235–252.

G.I. Jane (1997) Directed by Ridley Scott. DVD.

Gilligan, C. (1982) *In a Different Voice: Psychological Theory and Women's Development*. London: Harvard University Press.

Goldenberg, S. 'From heroine to humiliator: Lynndie England', *The Guardian*, 8 May 2004.

Goldenberg, S. 'Abu Ghraib soldier admits indecent act', *Guardian*, 3 May 2005.

Goldstein, J. S. (2001) *War and Gender*. Cambridge: Cambridge University Press.

Gonzalez, J. (2000) 'Envisioning cyborg bodies: Notes from current research'. In *The Gendered Cyborg: A Reader*, edited by G. Kirkup, L. Janes, K. Woodward and F. Hovenden. London: Routledge, 58–73.

Grayson, K. (2012) 'The ambivalence of assassination: Biopolitics, culture and political violence', *Security Dialogue*, 43(1): 25–41.

Grayson, K., Davies, M., Philpott, S. (2009) 'Pop goes IR? Researching the Popular Culture-World Politics Continuum', *Politics*, 29(3): 155–163.

Gutierrez, T. 'Lynndie England convicted in Abu Ghraib trial', *USA Today*, 26 September 2005.

Hall, S. (1985) 'Signification, representation, ideology: Althusser and the post-structuralist debates', *Critical Studies in Mass Communication*, 2(2): 91–114.

Hall, S. (ed.) (1997a) *Representation: Cultural Representations and Signifying Practices*. London: Sage.

Hall, S. (1997b) 'Introduction'. In *Representation: Cultural Representations and Signifying Practices*, edited by S. Hall, 1–12. London: Sage.

Hall, S. (1997c) 'The work of representation'. In *Representation: Cultural Representations and Signifying Practices*, edited by S. Hall. London: Sage, 13–74.

Hansen, L. (2006) *Security as Practice: Discourse Analysis and the Bosnian War*. London: Routledge.

Hansen, L. (2011) 'Theorizing the image for security studies', *European Journal of International Relations*, 7(1): 51–74.

Haraway, D. J. (2000) 'A manifesto for cyborgs: Science, technology, and socialist feminism in the 1980s'. In *The Gendered Cyborg: A Reader*, edited by G. Kirkup, L. Janes, K. Woodward and F. Hovenden. London: Routledge, 101–109.

Harwood, A. 'Pvt Lynndie England, the trailer-park girl in the eye of the storm', *Daily Mirror*, 7 May 2004.

Harwood, A. 'Lynndie's jail orgies', *Daily Mirror*, 14 May 2004.

Hasso, F. S. (2005) 'Discursive and political deployments by/of the 2002 Palestinian women suicide bombers/martyrs', *Feminist Review*, 81: 23–51.

Hayward, S. (1996) *Key Concepts in Cinema Studies*. London: Routledge.

Heffer, S. 'Faye should not be in the front line', *Daily Telegraph*, 31 March 2007.

Herbst, C. (2004) 'Lara's lethal and loaded mission: Transposing reproduction and destruction'. In *Action Chicks: New Images of Tough Women in Popular Culture*, edited by S. Inness. New York: Palgrave Macmillan, 21–45.

Hersh, S. 'Torture at Abu Ghraib: American soldiers brutalized Iraqis. How far up does the responsibility go?', *New Yorker*, 10 May 2004.

Hickley, M. 'Frontline women: the great debate', *Daily Mail*, 30 March 2007.

Hicks Stiehm, J. (2001) 'Women, peacekeeping and peace making: Gender balance and mainstreaming', *International Peacekeeping*, 8(2): 39–48.

Higham, S., Stephens, J. and White, J. 'Prison visits by General reported in hearing; alleged presence of Sanchez cited by lawyer', *Washington Post*, 23 May 2004.

Hird, M. J. (2003) 'Vacant wombs: Feminist challenges to psychoanalytic theories of childless women', *Feminist Review*, 75, 5–19.

Hodgson, M. 'Iran captives disagree over cashing in on their stories', *The Guardian*, 9 April 2007.

Horovitz, B., Grossman, C. L. and Johnson, P. 'Photos bring our agony into focus', *USA Today*, 10 May 2004.

Howarth, D. and Stavrakakis, Y. (2000) 'Introducing discourse theory and political analysis'. In *Discourse Theory and Political Analysis: Identities, Hegemonies and Social Change*, edited by D. Howarth, A. Norval and Y. Stravrakakis. Manchester: Manchester University Press, 1–23.

Hudson, V. (2011) 'But now can see: One academic's journey to Feminist Security Studies', *Politics and Gender*, 7(4): 586–590.

Hughes, C. 'Family's fears for Iran mum hostage', *Daily Mirror*, 27 March 2007.

Hughes, C. and Stansfield, R. 'Brave colleague got me through my kidnap horror', *Daily Mirror*, 9 April 2007.

Hughes, C. and Prince, R. 'A sick charade: Fury as Iran forces sailor Faye to "confess" on TV', *Daily Mirror*, 29 March 2007.

Hunt, K. and Rygiel, K. (eds) (2006) (*En*)*gendering the War on Terror*. Aldershot: Ashgate.

Ingham, J. and Flanagan, P. 'Fears growing for "Topsy", the mum who went to war', *Express*, 28 March 2007.

Inness, S. A. (1999) *Tough Girls: Women Warriors and Wonder Women in Popular Culture*. Philadelphia: University of Pennsylvania Press.

Inness, S. A. (ed.) (2004) *Action Chicks: New Images of Tough Women in Popular Culture*. New York: Palgrave Macmillan.

ITV (2007) 'A Tonight Special: Captured, paraded and exploited: the inside story of Leading Seaman Faye Turney's ordeal'. Interview with Trevor McDonald. Aired 8 April. Available at www.youtube.com/watch?v=BQ1b3dNKkCo and http://www.youtube.com/watch?v=PnBykQEK1zY&feature=related. Retrieved 16 January 2008.

James, L. 'What turns a woman into savage?', *Daily Mail*, 7 May 2004.

Jones, D. E. (2005) *Women Warriors: A History.* Washington DC: Potomac Books.

Judd, T. 'My little girl is growing up every day. I'm missing that', *Independent*, 28 March 2007.

Judd, T. 'Women at war; equality under fire', *Independent*, 1 April 2007.

Judd, T. 'How losers in the bidding war turned on minister', *Independent*, 14 April 2007.

Kampfner, J. 'The truth about Jessica', *Guardian*, 15 May 2003: A1.

Karpinski, J. 'SCV Newsmaker of the week: Brig. Gen. Janis Karpinski', *Signal City*, 4 July 2004. Radio interview. Transcript available at www.scvhistory.com/scvhistory/signal/iraq/sg070404.htm. Retrieved 5 February 2009.

Karpinski, J. 'SCV Newmaker of the week: Janis Karpinski, former commander, Abu Ghraib prison, Iraq', *Signal City*, 13 November 2005. Radio interview. Transcript available at www.scvhistory.com/scvhistory/signal/iraq/sg111305-nm.htm. Retrieved 5 February 2009.

Karpinski, J. with Strassner, S. (2005) *One Woman's Army: The Commanding General of Abu Ghraib Tells Her Story.* New York: Miramax Books.

Kelly, T. 'Smiles that say Mummy's home', *Daily Mail*, 6 April 2007.

Kennedy, D. 'I knew the risks, said woman boat driver held by Iranians', *The Times*, 28 March 2007.

Kennedy, D. Webster, P. and Sanderson, D. 'A mother on parade in Iran's propaganda war', *The Times*, 29 March 2007.

Kirby, J. 'A mother's place isn't in the war zone', *The Times*, 1 April 2007.

Khalili, L. (2011) 'Gendered practices of counterinsurgency', *Review of International Studies*, 37(4): 1471–1491

Knight, K. 'The making of an all-American monster', *Daily Mail*, 8 May 2004.

Kristeva, J. (1982) *Powers of Horror: An Essay on Abjection.* New York: Colombia University Press.

Kronsell, A. and Svedberg, E. (eds) (2012) *Making Gender, Making War: Violence, Military and Peacekeeping Practices.* London and New York: Routledge.

Kumar, D. (2004) 'War propaganda and the (ab)uses of women: Media constructions of the Jessica Lynch story', *Feminist Media Studies*, 4(3): 297–313.

Lacey, N. (1998) *Image and Representation: Key Concepts in Media Studies.* New York: Palgrave.

Lawson, D. 'New Labour has sacrificed principle for the sake of waging a propaganda war', *The Independent*, 10 April 2007.

Lawton, J. 'I sold my story for Molly', *Daily Star*, 9 April 2007.

Levy, N. 'Private England pleads guilty to abuses', *New York Times*, 3 May 2005.

Linge, N. 'First pics of mum held by mad mullahs', *Daily Star*, 28 March 2007.

Lloyd, M. (2005) *Beyond Identity Politics: Feminism, Power & Politics.* London: Sage Publications.

Lobasz, J. K. and Sjoberg, L. (2011) 'The state of feminist security studies: Introduction', *Politics and Gender*, 7(4): 573–576.

Lyons, J. 'Faye knew the risks when she left Molly to serve in Iraq: courage of sailor held captive in Iran', *Daily Record*, 28 March 2007.

Mackay, N. 'The picture that lost the war', *Sunday Herald*, 2 May 2004.

MacKenzie, M. (2009) 'Securitization and desecuritization: Female soldiers and the reconstruction of women in post-conflict Sierra Leone', *Security Studies*, 18(2): 241–261.

Malone, C. 'Don't put mums in the firing line', *Sunday Mirror*, 1 April 2007.

Managhan, T. (2012) *Gender, Agency and War: The Maternalized Body in US Foreign Policy.* London and New York: Routledge.

Marks, C. 'Images that shook the US and the wider world', *Scotsman*, 7 May 2004.

Marks, L. U. (1991) 'Tie a yellow ribbon around me: Masochism, militarism and the Gulf War on TV', *Camera Obscura*, 27: 55–75.

Marshall, L. (2007) 'The misogynist implications of Abu Ghraib'. In *One of the Guys: Women as Aggressors and Torturers*, edited by T. McKelvey. Emeryville, CA: Seal Press, 51–56.

Marway, H. (2011) 'Scandalous subwomen and sublime superwomen: Exploring portrayals of female suicidebombers' agency', *Journal of Global Ethics*, 7(3): 221–240.

McCaffrey, J. 'Why women must go to war', *Daily Mirror*, 7 April 2007.

McKelvey, T. (ed.) (2007) *One of the Guys: Women as Aggressors and Torturers*. Emeryville, CA: Seal Press.

McKelvey, T. 'A soldier's tale: Lynndie England', *Marie Claire*, 2006. Available at www.marieclaire.com/print-this/world/news/lynndie-england-1. Retrieved 7 January 2009.

Milliken, J. (1999) 'The study of discourse in International Relations: A critique of research and methods', *European Journal of International Relations*, 5(2): 225–254.

Mitry, J. (2000) *Semiotics and the Analysis of Film*. London: The Athlone Press.

MOD (Ministry of Defence) (2002) *Women in the Armed Forces: A Report by the Employment of Women in the Armed Forces Steering Group*. London: Ministry of Defence.

Moir, J. 'Faye a heroine? That's an insult to our dead soldiers', *Daily Telegraph*, 11 April 2007.

Monaghan, E. '"Scapegoat" to answer Abu Ghraib accusations', *The Times*, 4 August 2004.

Monaghan, E. 'Lynndie England "had fun" at Abu Ghraib', *The Times*, 31 August 2004.

Moniz, D. 'Army will demote general in Abu Ghraib scandal to colonel', *USA Today*, 6 May 2005.

Moniz, D. 'Highlights', *USA Today*, 12 May 2004.

Moniz, D. and Morrison, B. 'General's duties shift after flap', *USA Today*, 25 May 2004.

Morris, E. (2008) *Standard Operating Procedure*. DVD

Morrissey, B. (2003) *When Women Kill: Questions of Agency and Subjectivity*. London and New York: Routledge.

Moser, C. and Clark, F. (eds) (2001) *Victims, Perpetrators or Actors? Gender, Armed Conflict and Political Violence*. London: Zed Books.

Moult, J. and Newton Dunn, T. 'MUMMY MUMMY: Tears as Faye holds little Molly again', *Sun*, 10 April 2007a.

Moult, J. and Newton Dunn, T. 'I burst into tears and told family I'M SORRY', *Sun*, 10 April 2007b.

Moult, J., Newton Dunn, T. and Lazzeri, A. 'We were blindfolded and lined up … then we heard guns cock', *Sun*, 7 April 2007.

Muller, B. J. (2008) 'Securing the political imagination: Popular culture, the security dispositive and the biometric state', *Security Dialogue*, 39(2–3): 199–220.

Myrie, C. 'Hometown shocked by scandal', *BBC news*, 8 May 2004.

Nacos, B. L. (2005) 'The portrayal of female terrorists in the media: Similar framing patterns in the news coverage of women in politics and in terrorism', *Studies in Conflict & Terrorism*, 28: 435–451.

Narozhna, T. (2012) 'Power and gendered rationality in Western epistemic constructions of female suicide bombings'. In *Gender, Agency and Political Violence*, edited
by L. Åhäll and L. J. Shepherd. Basingstoke: Palgrave Macmillan, 79–95.

Neumann, I. B. and Nexon, D. H. (eds) (2006) *Harry Potter and International Relations*. Lanham: Rowman and Littlefield.

Newton Dunn, T. 'Q: How is your daughter? A: I don't know, I haven't seen her for 13
days', *Sun*, 10 April 2007.

Newton Dunn, T. and Moult, J. 'Hello Molly!', *Sun*, 6 April 2007.

Newton Dunn, T. and Moult, J. 'I heard saws and hammers. Then a woman measured
me. I feared it was for my coffin', *Sun*, 9 April 2007a.

Newton Dunn, T. and Moult, J. 'Terror as boat raider pointed RPG at my head', *Sun*,
9 April 2007b.

Newton Dunn, T. and Moult, J. 'Send me back', *Sun*, 11 April 2007.

Newton Dunn, T. and Parker, A. 'Let Mummy Go!', *Sun*, 27 March 2007.

Nicks, G. 'Jail torture yank to have baby... and Iraqi prisoner is the dad!', *Daily Star*,
19 May 2004.

Oxford English Dictionary (2014). Available at http://www.oed.com. Retrieved 16
January 2014.

Pankhurst, D. (2004) 'The "sex war" and other wars: Towards a feminist approach to
peacebuilding'. In *Development, Women and War: Feminist Perspectives*, edited by
H. Afshar and D. Eade, 8–42. Oxford: Oxfam.

Parashar, S. (2009) 'Feminist international relations and women militants: case studies
from Sri Lanka and Kashmir', *Cambridge Review of International Affairs*, 22(2):
235–256.

Parashar, S. (2013) 'Feminist (in)securities and camp politics', *International Studies
Perspectives*, 14(4): 440–443.

Parker, L. 'England may face more charges', *USA Today*, 1 September 2004.

Parkin, J. 'Isn't a mother's first duty to her children?', *Daily Mail*, 30 March 2007.

Pascoe-Watson, G. 'How Dare They?', *Sun*, 29 April 2007.

Payne, S. and Britten, N. 'Mother set her heart on life in the Royal Navy', *Daily Telegraph*, 28 March 2007.

Peterson, V. S. (1992) *Gendered States: Feminist (Re)visions of International Relations
Theory*. Boulder, CO: Lynne Rienner.

Pettman, J. J. (2004) 'Feminist international relations after 9/11', *The Brown Journal of
World Affairs*, X(2): 85–96.

Pin-Fat, V. and Stern, M. (2005) 'The scripting of Private Jessica Lynch: Biopolitics,
gender, and the "feminization" of the US military', *Alternatives*, 30: 25–53.

Platell, A. 'It's Faye's little girl we should be thinking of', *Daily Mail*, 31 March 2007.

Priest, D., Booth, W. and Schmidt, S. 'A broken body, a broken story, pieced together',
Washington Post, 17 June 2003.

Prividera, L. C. and Howard III, J. W. (2006) 'Masculinity, whiteness, and the warrior
hero: Perpetuating the strategic rhetoric of U.S. nationalism and the marginalization
of women', *Women and Language*, 29(2): 29–37.

Rich, F. 'Saving Private England', *New York Times*, 16 May 2004.

Richter-Monpetit, M. (2007) 'Empire, desire and violence: A queer transnational
feminist reading of the prisoner "abuse" in Abu Ghraib and the question of "gender
equality"', *International Feminist Journal of Politics*, 9(1): 38–59.

Riddell, M. 'A new monster in chief: Lynndie England's snapshots have provided the
latest hate figure to help obscure the bigger picture', *Observer*, 9 May 2004.

Robinson, F. and Confortini, C. (2014) 'Symposium: Maternal thinking for international relations? Papers in honor of Sara Ruddick', *Journal of International Political Theory*, 10(38).

Rockey Fleming, A. 'Lynndie England: a soldier, a mother – and a court-martial', *People*, 16 May 2005.

Rose, G. (2001) *Visual Methodologies: An Introduction to the Interpretation of Visual Materials*. London: Sage Publications.

Routledge, P. 'No to mums with babes...and arms', *Daily Mirror*, 30 March 2007.

Rowley, C. (2009) 'Popular culture and the politics of the visual'. In *Gender Matters in Global Politics: A Feminist Introduction to International Relations*, edited by L. J. Shepherd, 309–325. London: Routledge.

Rowley, C. and Weldes, J. (2012) 'The evolution of international security studies and the everyday: Suggestions from the Buffyverse', *Security Dialogue*, 43(6): 513–530.

Ruddick, S. (2002 [1989]) *Maternal Thinking: Towards a Politics of Peace*. Boston: Beacon Press.

Said, E. (1997) *Covering Islam*. London: Vintage.

Salkeld, L. 'A dedicated sailor and a loving mother', *Daily Mail*, 28 March 2007.

Saper, C. J. (1997) *Artificial Mythologies: A Guide to Cultural Invention*. London: University of Minnesota Press.

Seamark, M. 'Another turn of the screw', *Daily Mail*, 30 March 2007.

Seamark, M. and English, R. 'Heroines', *Daily Mail*, 7 April 2007.

Seamark, M. and Chapman, J. 'D-day for the Navy hostages', *Daily Mail*, 4 April 2007.

Segal, L. (2008) 'Gender, war and militarism: Making and questioning the links', *Feminist Review*, 88: 21–35.

Sengupta, K. 'Should women in the armed forces be allowed to serve on the front line?', *Independent*, 30 March 2007.

Shanker, T. and Steinberg, J. 'Bush voices "disgust" at abuse of Iraqi prisoners', *New York Times*, 1 May 2004.

Shapiro, M. J. (2009) *Cinematic Geopolitics*. London and New York: Routledge.

Shapiro, M. J. (2013) *Studies in Trans-Disciplinary Method: After the Aesthetic Turn*. London and New York: Routledge.

Sharp, R. and Judd, T. 'Supporters rally round Faye Turney', *Independent*, 15 April 2007.

Shears, R. 'Torture jail general may be kicked out of the army', *Daily Mail*, 4 May 2004.

Shenon, P. 'Officer suggests Iraqi jail abuse was encouraged', *New York Times*, 2 May 2004.

Shepherd, L. (2006) 'Veiled references: Constructions of gender in the Bush administration discourse on the attacks on Afghanistan post-9/11', *International Feminist Journal of Politics*, 8(1): 19–41.

Shepherd, L. J. (2008a) *Gender, Violence and Security: Discourse as Practice*. London: Zed Books Ltd.

Shepherd, L. J. (2008b) 'Visualising violence: Legitimacy and authority in the "war on terror"', *Critical Studies on Terrorism*, 1(2): 213–226.

Shepherd, L. J. (2009) 'Morality, legality and gender violence in Angel', *Journal of Gender Studies*, 18(3): 245–259.

Shepherd, L. J. (2010) 'Sex or Gender? Bodies in world politics and why gender matters'. In *Gender Matters in Global Politics: A Feminist Introduction to International Relations*. London and New York: Routledge, 3–16.

Shepherd, L. J. (ed.) (2012a) *Critical Approaches to Security: An Introduction to Theories and Methods.* London and New York: Routledge.

Shepherd, L. J. (2012b) 'Introduction'. In *Critical Approaches to Security*, edited by L. J. Shepherd. London and New York: Routledge.

Shepherd, L. J. (2012c) *Gender, Violence and Popular Culture: Telling Stories.* London: Routledge.

Sjoberg, L. (2007) 'Agency, militarized femininity and enemy others: Observations from the war in Iraq', *International Feminist Journal of Politics*, 9(1): 82–101.

Sjoberg, L. (2011) 'Looking forward, conceptualizing Feminist Security Studies', *Politics and Gender*, 7(4): 600–604.

Sjoberg, L. and Gentry, J. (2007) *Mothers, Monsters, Whores: Women's Violence in Global Politics.* London: Zed Books Ltd.

Sjoberg, L. and Gentry, C. E. (2008) 'Reduced to bad sex: Narratives of violent women from the bible to the war on terror', *International Relations*, 22(1): 5–23.

Sjolander, C. T. and Trevenen, K. (2010) 'One of the boys?', *International Feminist Journal of Politics*, 12(2): 158–176.

Skjelsbæk, I. (2001) 'Sexual violence and war: Mapping out a complex relationship', *European Journal of International Relations*, 7(2): 211–237.

Smith, E. 'Judge kicks out troop's abuse case', *Sun*, 5 May 2005.

Smith, J. 'Soldiers vented frustration, doctor says', *Washington Post*, 24 May 2004.

Smith, R. and Jackson, K. 'Women at war in numbers', *Daily Mirror*, 3 April 2007.

Spivak, G. C. (1999) *A Critique of Postcolonial Reason: Toward a History of the Vanishing Present.* Boston, MA: Harvard University Press.

Stachowitsch, S. (2012) 'Military gender integration and foreign policy in the united states: A feminist international relations perspective', *Security Dialogue*, 43(4): 305–321.

Stansfield, R. and Hughes, C. 'Faye feared they'd rape and kill her … they called me Mr Bean', *Daily Mirror*, 9 April 2007.

Steans, J. (2006) *Gender and International Relations.* Cambridge: Polity Press.

Steans, J. (2008) 'Telling stories about women and gender in the war on terror', *Global Society*, 22(1); 159–176.

Storey, J. (1993) *An Introduction to Cultural Theory and Popular Culture.* London: Prentice Hall/Harvester Wheatsheaf.

Strassner, S. (ed.) (2004) *The Abu Ghraib Investigations: The Official Reports of the Independent Panel and the Pentagon on the shocking prisoner abuse in Iraq.* New York: Public Affairs.

Sturken, M. and Cartwright, L. (2001) *Practices of Looking: An Introduction to Visual Culture.* Oxford: Oxford University Press.

Sylvester, C. (2002) *Feminist International Relations.* Cambridge: Cambridge University Press.

Sylvester, C. (2012) 'Preface: Those difficult war questions in feminism', in *Making Peace, Making War*, edited by Annica Kronsell and Erika Svedberg. London: Routledge, ix–xi.

Sylvester, C. (2013) 'Passing American security', *International Studies Perspectives*, 14(4): 444–446.

Taguba, A. (2004) 'Article 15–16 investigation of the 800th Military Police Brigade'. U.S. Army. Available at www.npr.org/iraq/2004/prison_abuse_report.pdf. Retrieved 12 December 2008.

Tasker, Y. (1998) *Working Girls: Gender and Sexuality in Popular Cinema.* London: Routledge.

Taylor Martin, S. 'Her job: Lock up Iraq's bad guys', *St. Petersburg Times*, 14 December 2003.

Thompson, P. 'Iraqi jail abuser guilty', *Sun*, 27 September 2005.

Thomson, A. 'A mother's place is in the Navy', *Daily Telegraph*, 29 March 2007.

Tickner, J. A. (1992) *Gender in International Relations: Feminist Perspectives on Achieving Global Security*. New York: Colombia University Press.

Tickner, J. A. (1997) 'You just don't understand: Troubled engagements between feminists and IR theorists', *International Studies Quarterly*, 41(2): 611–632.

Tickner, J. A. (2002) 'Feminist perspectives on 9/11', *International Studies Perspective*, 3: 333–350.

Toles Parkin, T. (2004) 'Explosive baggage: Female Palestinian suicide bombers and the rhetoric of emotion', *Women and Language*, 27(2): 79–88.

True, J. (2012) 'Securitizing feminism or feminist security studies?', *International Studies Review*, 14(1): 193–195.

Turner, J. 'If equality looks like Lynndie, why would we want it?', *The Times*, 8 May 2004.

Tyler, I. (2013) *Revolting Subjects: Social Abjection and Resistance in Neoliberal Britain*. London: Zed Books.

Unattributed, 'They love it here said General Janis', *Daily Mail*, 30 April 2004.

Unattributed, 'Jail boss in denial', *Sun*, 4 May 2004.

Unattributed, 'Findings on Abu Ghraib prison: Sadism, "deviant behaviour" and a failure of leadership', *New York Times*, 25 August 2004.

Unattributed, 'Treated like a dog', *Daily Mail*, 7 May 2004.

Unattributed, 'Lynndie told to pose', *Daily Star*, 13 May 2004.

Unattributed, 'Torture "fun"', *Sun*, 19 May 2004.

Unattributed, 'It was just for fun', *Daily Mail*, 4 August 2004.

Unattributed, 'Lynndie's Iraq sex trysts', *Sun*, 6 August 2004.

Unattributed, 'Torturer's baby', *Sun*, 14 October 2004.

Unattributed, 'Iraq abuse girl jail deal', *Daily Mirror*, 30 April 2005.

Unattributed, 'Iraqi jail girl guilty', *Sun*, 3 May 2005.

Unattributed, 'After Abu Ghraib', *The Times*, 4 May 2005.

Unattributed, 'Lynndie England convicted in Abu Ghraib trial, *USA Today*, 26 September 2005.

Unattributed, '3 years for Abu Ghraib abuser', *The Times*, 28 September 2005.

Unattributed, 'The mother held captive in Teheran', *The Times*, 28 March 2007.

Unattributed, 'Should a mother join the Navy?', *The Times*, 29 March 2007.

Unattributed, 'Woman at war in numbers', *Daily Mirror*, 3 April 2007.

Unattributed, 'Should women serve on the front line?', *Daily Mail*, 4 April 2007.

Unattributed, 'Military views on the captives and frontline mums', *Daily Mail*, 6 April 2007.

Unattributed, 'HOSTAGES: Faye: I feared they'd rape and kill me', *Daily Mirror*, 9 April 2007.

Unattributed, 'Hostage Faye has quit sea', *Sunday Mirror*, 3 February 2008.

Unattributed, '"Rumsfeld knew"', *Stern*, 19 March 2008.

Varzi, R. (2008) 'Iran's pieta: Motherhood, sacrifice and film in the aftermath of the Iran-Iraq war', *Feminist Review*, 88: 86–98.

Victor, B. (2004) *Army of Roses: Inside the World of Palestinian Women Suicide Bombers*. London: Constable and Robinson.

Watson, R. and Farrell, S. 'Private Jessica helped America to win the war', *The Times*, 8 May 2004.

Webb, J. 'No place for us women', *Daily Mail*, 7 April 2007.

Weber, C. (2002) 'Flying planes can be dangerous', *Millennium: Journal of International Studies*, 31(1): 129–147.

Weber, C. (2005) *International Relations Theory: A Critical Introduction*. London: Routledge.

Weber, C. (2008) 'Popular visual language as global communication: the remediation of United Airlines Flight 93', *Review of International Studies*, 34(1): 137–153.

Weldes, J. (1999) 'Going cultural: Star Trek, state action and popular culture', *Millennium: Journal of International Politics*, 28(1): 117–134.

Weldes, J. (2003a) 'Popular culture, science fiction, and world politics: Exploring intertextual relations'. In *To Seek Out New Worlds: Exploring Links between Science Fiction and World Politics*, edited by J. Weldes. New York: Palgrave, 1–27.

Weldes, J. (ed.) (2003b) *To Seek Out New Worlds: Exploring Links between Science Fiction and World Politics*. New York: Palgrave.

West, J. (2004) 'Feminist IR and the case of "Black Widows": Reproducing gendered divisions', *Innovations: A Journal of Politics*, 5: 1–16.

White, J. 'General demoted, but cleared in abuse probe', *Washington Post*, 6 May 2005.

White, R. (2007) *Violent Femmes: Women as Spies in Popular Culture*. New York: Routledge.

Wibben, A. (2011a) *Feminist Security Studies: A Narrative Approach*. London and New York: Routledge.

Wibben, A. (2011b) 'Feminist politics in feminist security studies', *Politics and Gender*, 7(4): 590–595.

Wibben, A. and McBride, K. (2012) 'Counterinsurgency and gender: The case of the female engagement teams', *e-ir*. Available at www.e-ir.info/2012/07/17/counterinsurgency-and-gender-the-case-of-the-female-engagement-teams/. Accessed 5 October 2012.

Wilcox, L. (2011) 'Beyond sex/gender: The feminist body of security', *Politics and Gender*, 7(4): 595–600.

Williams, K. (2006) *Love My Rifle More Than You: Young and Female in the US Army*. London: Orion Books.

Williams, M. C. (2003) 'Images, words, enemies: Securitization and international politics', *International Studies Quarterly*, 47(4): 511–531.

Woodward, R. and Winter, P. (2006) 'Gender and the limits to diversity in the contemporary British army', *Gender, Work and Organization*, 13(1): 45–67.

Woodward, R. and Winter, T. (2007) *Sexing the Soldier: The Politics of Gender and the Contemporary British Army*. London: Routledge.

Young, I. M. (2003) 'The logic of masculinist protection: Reflections on the current security state', *Signs: Journal of Women in Culture and Society*, 29(1): 1–25.

Younge, G. 'What about Private Lori?', *The Guardian*, 10 April 2003.

Yuval-Davies, N. (1997) *Gender and Nation*. London: Routledge.

Zalewski, M. (1995) 'Well, what is the feminist perspective on Bosnia?', *International Affairs*, 71(2): 339–356.

Zalewski, M. (2000) *Feminism after Postmodernism: Theorising through Practice*. London: Routledge.

Zalewski, M. (2007) 'Do we understand each other yet? Troubling feminist encounters with(in) International Relations', *British Journal of Politics and International Relations*, 9: 302–312.

Zalewski, M. (2010) 'Feminist international relations: Making sense ...'. In *Gender Matters in Global Politics: A Feminist Introduction to International Relations*, edited by L. J. Shepherd. London: Routledge, 28–43.

Zalewski, M. (2013) *Feminist International Relations: Exquisite Corpse*. London: Routledge.

Zernike, K. 'Prison guard calls abuse routine and sometimes amusing', *New York Times*, 16 May 2004.

Zernike, K. 'Three accused soldiers had records of unruliness that went unpunished', *New York Times*, 27 May 2004.

Zernike, K. 'The woman with the leash appears in court on Abu Ghraib abuse charges', *New York Times*, 4 August 2004.

Zernike, K. 'At abuse hearing, no testimony that G.I.'s acted on orders', *New York Times*, 7 August 2004.

Index

abjection 14, 41, 107, 108, 109, 134; the abject/myth relationship 45; definition 44, 108; emotionality 44, 45, 146; social abjection 44, 108, 111, 134, 141, 144 (a bordering practice 134–35, 144; 'othering' of the monster 108, 109, 110, 133, 143); subject position 44; *see also* monstrous abject

Abu Ghraib scandal 141–42; prisoner abuse at 2, 47, 107, 141; triple transgression 107; women acting 'against their femininity' 107; *see also* England, Lynndie; Karpinski, Janis

Afghanistan 51–52, 57

agency 1, 10, 26, 39; agency as an effect of the power of discourse 26; 'ethnographic' approach to 10, 40; 'grammatical' approach to 10, 13, 16, 18, 26, 39–45; subject position 39, 42; *see also* denied agency; female agency in political violence; motherhood, agency in war

Aliens 85–86

Alison, Miranda 9, 17, 25, 107

Althusser, Louis 43, 44

The Baader-Meinhof Complex 11, 48; Aust, Stefan 12; Baader, Andreas 48, 49; *see also* Ulrike Meinhof/Gudrun Ensslin

Balsamo, Anne 113

Barthes, Roland 1, 2, 13, 134, 142, 145, 146; discourse analysis 28, 32–39; *Image-Music-Text* 32, 43, 142; myth 28, 34–38, 40, 136, 137–38, 140, 145; *Mythologies* 1, 28, 34–35, 38, 137; obtuse meaning 43, 142

Basu, Soumita 6, 7

Batchelor, Arthur 49, 58, 87–88

Beamer, Lisa 22

Beamer, Todd 22

Bhutto, Benazir 23

Black Widows 25

Bleiker, Roland 10, 28, 33

Bloom, Mia 17–18, 24

body politics 1, 8, 32, 145; cultural grammar of body politics 45; policing of gender norms and borders 2, 15, 27, 103; Turney, Faye 57; writing 'sex' 2, 15, 27; *see also* female agency in political violence; female body; motherhood, ideas about; Myth of Motherhood

Boudicca 85

Bourke, Joanna 2, 9, 24, 85

Brittain, Melisa 59, 84

Britz 11; 2005 London bombings 12, 48; Kosminsky, Peter 12; *see also* Nasima

Brunner, Claudia 25–26, 52

Bush, George W. 11, 22, 45, 51, 59

Bush, Laura 51–52

Butler, Judith 10, 33, 108, 112, 143, 145; agency 26, 39; destabilisation of gender 142; discourse 30; feminism 30–31; materialisation of sex 136; reiteration of sex 137, 138–40; social abjection 44

Carver, Terrell 86

cases 13; gender, agency and political violence 12, 13; motherhood, ideas about 11; popular culture 11–12; real/fictional empirical cases 11; representation 11, 12, 13; 'war on terror' context 11, 12, 45; *see also* England, Lynndie; *Female Agents*; Karpinski, Janis; methodology;

concept 37, 43, 137, 138; unconscious ideologies 43, 138, 140; *see also* Myth of Motherhood; Myth of Protection

Myth of Motherhood 10, 13–15, 27; common sense 140; a cultural grammar 136; female agency in political violence 15, 136–37, 140, 145; heroic subject 14, 141, 144; inversions of motherhood 13, 14, 68, 80–81, 136, 140; life-giving/life-taking tension 2, 14, 80, 136, 140; maternal-ist war stories 136–37; methodologi-cal approach 28; monstrous abject as threat to Myth of Motherhood 14, 141, 142, 143, 144; naturalising female body's association with motherhood 136–37, 140; perversion of motherhood 13, 14, 114, 134–35, 136, 141; policing of gender norms and borders 137, 141, 143–44, 145–46; reinforced by disgust and inter-pellation 134, 143, 145; sexing war 137, 140, 143, 145–46; theorisation of 137–41 (myth 137–38; gender/sex relation 138–40); versions of mother-hood 13, 14, 106, 136, 141; victimised object 13, 14, 144; writing 'sex' 137; *see also* life-giving/ life-taking tension; motherhood, ideas about; myth

Myth of Protection 13, 50–53, 80, 140; emotionality 50, 52–53; *Female Agents* 71; passivity 50–51; Turney, Faye 57; *womenandchildren* 50, 51–52; *see also* victimised object

Nasima 11, 48; denied agency 79; deviant womb 123–24 (cyborg 123–24); doubts and maternal insights 78, 79–80, 144; emotionality 78–80; fake pregnancy 123–24; female terrorist 12, 48; life-giving/life-taking tension 123, 124; Sabia 78–79; suicide bomber 11, 48, 78, 123–24 (emo-tional/personal motivations 78–79, 144; political motivation 48, 79); victimised object 78–80, 144; *see also Britz*; suicide bomber; terrorism

nationalism 22–23, 26

passivity 13, 14, 50–51, 140, 144; England, Lynndie 67–68, 91; *Female Agents* 69–71; Myth of Protection 50–51; passive maternalism 23, 26;

Turney, Faye 55–57; Ulrike Meinhof/ Gudrun Ensslin 61, 63–65, 129; *see also* denied agency; victimised object

patriarchy 44; female combat roles 4, 9; heteropatriarchal conception of femininity 32, 107, 112, 114, 127, 135, 145; militarization 4, 21; motherhood 17, 24

peace/pacifism 12; female identity as life-giving being 16, 18; maternal peace thinking 12, 18–20 (active maternalism 18, 26); motherhood, agency and peace 19; peace activism 16–17; peace/femininity link 17, 20, 50; women's politics of resistance 19

Peterson, Spike 3

Pettman, Jindy 51

Piestewa, Lori Ann 59, 83, 84

Pin-Fat, Veronique 97

policing of gender norms and borders: body politics 2, 15, 27, 103; maternalist war stories 137, 144; monstrous abject 108, 134; mother-hood, ideas about 2, 14–15, 107, 135; Myth of Motherhood 137, 141, 143–44, 145–46; *see also* gender

politics: the apolitical 36, 37, 138, 145–46; and culture 2, 45; politics of emotions 137, 141–45; *see also* body politics

popular culture 141–42, 146; combat roles 24, 27; female agency in political violence 2, 28; fictional cases 11–12; heroic subject 83, 85; *see also* TV and films

poststructuralism 2, 10, 29; feminism/ post-structuralist analysis tensions 13, 30–31; gender 45; poststructuralist feminism 29, 30–32; tension between Barthes' early work and post-structuralist discourse analysis 28, 35–39

pregnancy 95; England, Lynndie 47, 68, 114, 116, 118, 122; *Female Agents* 69, 94–95; suicide bomber and fake pregnancy 17–18, 26, 123–24

prostitution 86, 98, 111; *Female Agents* 96, 97–99, 106; 'whore narrative' of female violence 9, 10

protective mother 14, 83, 85–86, 140; Karpinski, Janis 89–2, 144; life-giving/ life-taking tension 85; Turney, Faye 87–89, 144; *see also* heroic subject